KRÁSNÁ AMERIKA:
A Study of the Texas Czechs, 1851-1939

by

Clinton Machann
and
James W. Mendl

EAKIN PRESS
Austin, Texas

FIRST EDITION
Second Printing

Published in the United States of America
By Eakin Press, P.O. Box 23066, Austin, Texas 78735

ISBN 1-57168-565-0

Věnováno panu profesoru V. Hunáčkovi

Krásná Amerika

Krásná, krásná,
Krásná Amerika.
V Americe tam je blaze,
Tam teče pivo po podlaze,
Krásná Amerika.

Beautiful America

Beautiful, beautiful,
Beautiful America.
It's crazy there in America;
Beer flows on the floor there,
Beautiful America.

— from a trad. Czech waltz

ACKNOWLEDGMENTS

We wish to thank, first, our parents, who helped to instill in us an appreciation for our cultural heritage, and our wives and children, who patiently endured the many months when we must have seemed almost obsessed with the preparation of this book.

We deeply appreciate the bibliographical and editorial assistance of Joseph G. Svoboda, Curator of the University of Nebraska Libraries at Lincoln, and the cooperation of Otto Hanuś, Curator of the Library and Archives Division of the Supreme Lodge of the SPJST in Temple, Texas. Also very helpful was the encouragement of Texas Czechs such as Albert Blaha, Calvin Chervenka, John Karas, Joseph J. Skrivanek, and many others who work tirelessly and unselfishly to preserve a sense of historical and cultural identity among the Czechs in this state.

In addition to the libraries mentioned above, the Barker Collection at the University of Texas at Austin provided indispensable sources for our study, and many more were obtained through the Interlibrary Loan services at Texas A&M University.

We also wish to thank other individuals who took the time to read our manuscript and make helpful comments: William Owens, Sylvia Grider, David H. Stewart, Katharine H. Newman, and Marta Bobková. Finally, we are grateful to the family of the late Henry R. Maresh, as well as Roger Kolar, and the staff of the Institute of Texan Cultures in San Antonio, for making available many of the photographs used in this book.

Grants from the College of Liberal Arts at Texas A&M University and the Czech Ex-Students Association of Texas helped make time for crucial research available during the summer of 1980. Portions of the discussion of Czech-American literature in Chapter 6 originally appeared in *MELUS*, vi (1979), 32-40.

C.M.
J.W.M.

TABLE OF CONTENTS

ILLUSTRATIONS

INTRODUCTION

It has been estimated that at least five percent of the Texas population, or over 750,000 individuals, are of Czech or Slovak extraction.[1] The fact that Texas has the largest Czech-American population in the South is reflected in various ways. Although the exact number of speakers is not known, Czech may be the third-most-spoken language in the state, after English and Spanish. Texas still supports four important Czech-language periodicals. An estimated 30 to 40 Czech-American polka dances are held in Texas each week, and about 15 Texas radio stations regularly broadcast programs that feature music with Czech lyrics. Twenty-one major Czech-American festivals or celebrations are held in the state annually.

Czech Texans, in short, constitute an important ethnic group, one which has maintained a distinctive identity up to the present day. Like Czech-Americans in general, however, Texas Czechs have not received a great deal of attention from historians, sociologists, or other scholars. The standard book-length study of Czechs in America was written in the twenties, and the last major book about the Czechs in Texas appeared in the thirties. Studies originating from the Czech-American community have tended to reflect familial, religious, or organizational biases, although the many family and community histories, most of them privately printed, are a valuable source for any study of this ethnic group.

The present volume cannot hope to be exhaustive. Almost any chapter of this book could itself be expanded to book length by a scholar with the resources and interest to do the job. *Krásná Amerika* is intended to provide the general reader with a historical survey of the

[1] This estimate is based on Václav Huňáček, *Czechoslovakia: Information Minimum* (Austin, 1970), 19. Estelle Hudson and Henry R. Maresh estimated the total to be between 350,000 and 500,000 in 1934. *Czech Pioneers of the Southwest*, (Dallas, 1934), xi. A low recent estimate is that of Jan L. Perkowski, who cited the figure of 500,000 in "A Survey of the West Slavic Immigrant Languages in Texas," *Texas Studies in Bilingualism*, ed. Glenn G. Gilbert, (Berlin: 1970), 163-69.

Texas Czech population and a general examination of its culture. We hope that it will inspire others to do much more.

As the subtitle indicates, this study is primarily concerned with historical developments from the 1850s to the late 1930s. The first major group of Czech immigrants arrived in 1851. 1939 marks the beginnings of World War II in Europe and a turning point in the development of Czech-American culture in Texas. That year as a "cut-off" point is distant enough in the past to permit a degree of perspective and, we hope, objectivity, but it is not an arbitrary choice. A series of cataclysmic events were about to permanently alter the nature of the young Czechoslovak state in Europe. Meanwhile, the Czech population of Texas was poised on the verge of a war which, with its attendant disruption of community life, urbanization, increased industrialization, and technological advances, would not only end the Great Depression but signal the end of a stable, coherent Czech ethnic community in Texas. In retrospect, the late thirties seem to be the end of an era.

The 1910 Census of the United States shows a foreign-born Czech population of over 15,000 in Texas,[2] making Czechs the second-most-numerous European ethnic minority in the state (after the Germans). During the first three decades of the twentieth century, the Czech population in Texas was large enough to sustain a coherent Czech-American culture. And it did: by the early 1900s, more than 250 communities had distinctively Czech identities. Some of these were originally settled by Czechs; others had a majority of Czech citizens. Thousands of Texas Czechs were tied together by a common language and culture, religious and fraternal loyalties, and kinship ties, to an extent that seems incredible in our more mobile modern society.

The history of the Texas Czechs, the development of their tightly knit society, and the ways in which they both retained their Czech identity and were influenced by the American society in which they thrived are the subjects of this book. The first two chapters will provide a historical survey which describes social and economic conditions in the nineteenth-century Czech homeland, traces the immigration of the Czechs to Texas, and outlines the evolution of the Czech ethnic community of Texas during the first one hundred years. The purpose is to help the reader grasp the overall pattern of development and provide him with a general chronological sequence of significant historical

---

[2] United States Department of Commerce, Bureau of the Census, *Thirteenth Census of the United States: 1910*, Volume I, General Report and Analysis, Table 15, 981.

events. The narrative survey of the first two chapters prepares the way for a more in-depth, critical analysis of the ethnic community. As Katharine Neils Conzen has pointed out, "in the country as in the city, the presence or absence of an ethnic community was crucial for the endurance of ethnically distinctive traits" and, in the country, "clustered settlement was essential for community formation."[3] Chapters 1 and 2 map the chain migration and pattern of clustered settlements that allowed for the formation and growth of an ethnic community. Chapters 3-6 examine various social and religious institutions, folklore, literature, and other expressions of that distinctive Texas Czech community. The concluding chapter is more comprehensive, drawing on the material presented in earlier chapters in order to show how various aspects of that community fit into an overall pattern of ethnic identity, and it considers the crucial issue of the assimilation of the Czechs into mainstream Texan society and culture. A short "Afterword" briefly examines the present condition of this ethnic group in Texas.

A central dilemma plagued the composition of this book from beginning to end. On the one hand, we felt an obligation to make available to our readers the greatest possible amount of information that our research had uncovered: names of people and places, dates, and all sorts of other facts and figures that would be of interest to many. On the other hand, our manuscript, in its early versions, sometimes bore a closer resemblance to an encyclopedia or catalog rather than a book that could be easily read from cover to cover. Our solution was to excise some of the data but to consign much of them to notes and appendices, while retaining a fair number of what we considered significant and illustrative details within the text. No doubt all readers will not be completely satisfied with the final result, but we hope that all will appreciate the problem and find our response reasonable.

Nearly all significant studies of the Czechs in Texas have been written by Czech-Americans. The present volume is no exception. This tie to the community has given some of the previous works pungency and vitality; they are often authentic ethnic expressions. Their implicit associations, however, often led to a narrowness of perspective and special pleading. The period of time covered by our study ends approximately a decade before our births; we hope this fact helps to

---

[3] Kathleen Neils Conzen, "Historical Approaches to the Study of Rural Ethnic Communities" in *Ethnicity on the Great Plains*, ed. Frederick C. Luebke (Lincoln, Neb., 1980), 5.

give us a perspective consistent with our scholarly goals. This book was not written to promote or celebrate any particular religious, fraternal, political, or familial allegiance within the Czech ethnic community of Texas.

Nonetheless, we have lived most of our lives within that community. We have a deep love and respect for our heritage which, in all honesty, provided the principal motivation for writing the book. It was a labor of love, but our goal was to examine our subject as analytically and as thoroughly as was possible within our limitations. Our lives within the Texas Czech community have provided us with innumerable personal, "naive" sources of information. Although we attempt to document all our sources, to do so thoroughly would be impossible. Our personal backgrounds also lead us to understand the extent of our ignorance and to mourn the unexplored wealth of information — and cultural heritage — that continues to fade away with the death of each senior citizen of Czech ancestry. The authors of *Czech Pioneers of the Southwest*, in 1934, yearned to "tune in" to the life of the Czech settlers in Texas as it existed "fifty to one hundred years ago."[4] Today, from a greater distance, that yearning would be even more appropriate. We hope, however, that the increased span of time will help us form a better understanding of our subject's significance.

HISTORICAL BACKGROUND

The Czechs and Slovaks originate in Slavic tribes which, prior to about 500 A.D., formed a relatively cohesive group sharing a common culture. As they extended their territory towards Western Europe, however, their unity began to dissolve. Today the Czechs, Slovaks, Poles and Wends (Sorbs) are known as the West Slavs. The South Slavs are the Slovenes, Croats, Serbs, Bulgarians and Macedonians, and the East Slavs are the Russians, White Russians and Ukrainians. The total Slavic population today is about 250 million.

The Czechs came to inhabit their present-day locale sometime after 500 A.D. According to ancient legends, they were led to Bohemia by a chieftain named Čech, for whom the land, people, and language were named. Those Czechs who settled to the east, in an area which is today in the central portion of Czechoslovakia, were called the Moravians. Just to the east of the Moravians are the Slovaks. These three groups comprise the majority of the population of modern

---

[4] Hudson and Maresh, 2.

Czechoslovakia. (See Map 1.) Another area settled by Czechs is called Silesia, which lies north of Eastern Bohemia and Moravia, and part of which is today Poland. Many Czechs lived in this area and some came to Texas.

The Moravians were the first to develop a state, the Great Moravian Empire of the 9th Century. In 863 Prince Rostislav, fearing German domination of his fragile empire, devised a plan to avoid their interference in his affairs. He asked the Pope to send missionaries, knowing that the Pope had no teachers who were capable of explaining Christianity to the people in their own language. After giving the Pope his chance, Rostislav then turned to the other capital of Christendom, Constantinople. Since the Byzantine Empire had already proselytized Slavic tribes in the Balkans and Southern Russia, missionaries who could speak a Slavic language which the Moravians could understand were soon supplied. In 863, two Slavic-speaking Greeks from Salonika arrived in Moravia. Cyril and Methodius created an alphabet for the Moravians and began their work. Christianity was soon established in Moravia and Bohemia by these two saints. Rostislav had gained politically by adopting Christianity, for now the Germans could not use his paganism as an excuse to invade and conquer. Also, he could now expand his empire under the guise of Christianity. The prince's ambitions were short-lived however, because he became the victim of a plot hatched by his nephew Svatopluk. The effect of the work done by Cyril and Methodius, on the other hand, lives on today, though the Church in Czech lands soon adopted the Latin rite. Even in Texas several Czech Catholic churches are named for the two missionaries who gave the Slavs Christianity and an alphabet, and, therefore, access to the civilized world.

After the fall of the Great Moravian Empire late in the 9th century, the city of Prague in Bohemia became the center of political power for both Bohemia and Moravia. Since that time the political fortunes of the two regions and the two peoples have been intertwined.

The native dynasty of Bohemia came from the house of Přemyslide. It was able to keep Bohemia relatively independent of control by its powerful neighbor in the west, the Holy Roman Empire, until 1306, when the dynasty died out. One of the best known of the Přemyslides was Saint Václav, Good King Wenceslaus of the English carol.

After the time of the Přemyslides, a closer relationship with the Empire was established. The greatest Czech ruler of this age was Charles IV, who was not only the King of Bohemia but also the Emperor of the Holy Roman Empire. In 1348 he established the first university in Central Europe, Charles University in Prague.

After Charles' death in 1378, a period of political uncertainty ensued, ending with the Hussite Wars. After an uneasy compact with the Catholic emperor, and a short rule by Czech kings, the Hapsburgs became the royal family in 1526. From then on Bohemia and Moravia were drawn ever more tightly into the Austrian Empire, and Austrian rule became especially oppressive after 1620. The final dissolution of the Empire, along with the fall of the Hapsburgs and the rise of the first Czechoslovak Republic, came in 1918 as a result of World War I.

NAMES AND TERMS

The terms "Czech," "Bohemian," "Moravian," "Slovak"; and "Czechoslovakia," "Bohemia," "Čechy," "Moravia," and "Slovakia" are confusing to most Americans, including many Czech-and Slovak-Americans. For example, it is common for a Czech-American today to assert that his great-grandparents emigrated from "Czechoslovakia" in the nineteenth century, although the nation of Czechoslovakia was not created until 1918, and, up until World War I, Bohemia (along with Moravia) and Slovakia were ruled by quite separate governments within the Austro-Hungarian Empire. In order to avoid confusion as far as possible, the following distinctions will be made in this volume.

The term "Czech" will be used to refer to a native of the traditional Czech regions or homelands: Bohemia, Moravia, and portions of Czech- speaking Silesia. Although Čechy, the Czech name for Bohemia, is in many ways preferable to the latinate word, it does not provide a suitable distinguishing adjectival form in English, so we have reluctantly used "Bohemia." In general, the term "Czech" can be taken to refer to Slovaks, also, particularly since the proportion of Slovaks in the Texas Czech population is very small.[5] It must be remembered, however, that in spite of the great similarity between the Czech and Slovak languages and the (sometimes uneasy) political union of the two groups in Czechoslovakia, the Slovaks have a somewhat different culture and, for the most part, consider themselves a separate ethnic group. The term "Czechoslovak," naturally, is a general one which refers to either a Czech or a Slovak. The term "Bohemian" will be used only to distinguish between Bohemian and Moravian Czechs. Many Czech-Americans living in the Midwest and Eastern United States still refer to themselves by this term, which originated in the Latin name for the Celtic Boii tribe inhabiting the area which later became Bohemia before the arrival of the Slavs. It was generally used for all Czechs in the United States prior to the First World War. Nevertheless, "Bohemian" has negative connotations for many Texas Czechs, most of whom, in any case, are of Moravian stock.[6] For the sake of convenience, the term "Czech" will often be used to describe Czech-Americans, that is, American citizens of Czech descent, when the context makes the meaning obvious.

The political and cultural history of the Czech homelands is complex, and this volume cannot serve as an adequate introduction to this subject.[7] Background information will be given in the text where it is

[5] Finally, the term "Czech" might also be applied to natives of Ruthenia, a tiny province which lies just to the east of Slovakia. Ruthenia is now part of the Soviet Union.

[6] The term "Bohemian" is thus technically incorrect when used to designate Texas Czechs of Moravian origin. In addition, the secondary meanings of "Bohemian" associated with wanderers, vagabonds, and shiftless French artists, are widely resented. (Sir Walter Scott, in the novel *Quentin Durwood,* identifies Bohemians with Gypsies.) This secondary meaning of the word derives from a tragic historical development. After the Protestant Czechs were defeated at the Battle of White Mountain in 1620 by the Catholic Hapsburgs, they were forced to either reconvert to Catholicism or leave their country. Hundreds of thousands of homeless Czechs streamed across Western Europe as a result. Many were poor peasants with few belongings. A few individuals may have come to America. See Tomáš Čapek, *The Čechs (Bohemians) in America* (Boston, 1920), 1-18.

[7] No very good English-language history for the general reader has been published in America, but several British works are available. They include J.F.N. Bradleys *Czechoslovakia: A Short History* (Edinburg, 1971); A.H.

essential to understanding developments in America.

Because the Czech language may not be familiar to the general reader and because morphological changes in Czech surnames in America sometimes lead to confusion, it is necessary to explain a few basic conventions to be followed in this book.

The feminine form of Czech surnames usually ends in "-ová." By the second or third generation, Texas Czechs normally shifted to the short (masculine) form for both men and women. "Paní Nováková" becomes "Mrs. Novak." The traditional long form of a particular woman's name will be used consistently throughout this book if that form is found in a major source. It would be as improper to refer to the Texas Czech poet Marie Nováková as "Marie Novak" as it would be to refer to the present-day tennis star Martina Navrátilová as "Martina Navratil." Therefore, the reader should be aware that "Novák" and "Nováková," for example, are different forms of the same surname. Other surnames in Texas may exist in the Czech form as well as a Germanized or Americanized form. The written form of "Červenka" becomes "Chervenka," for example, as part of the process of assimilation. More confusingly, Šilar, Šiller, Schiller, and Shiller are all variants of the same family name. The form used in the most authoritative source will be used consistently throughout this book for each individual. In uncertain cases, the traditional Czech form will be preferred.

Similarly, each individual's given name will be used consistently throughout the book. For example, if the name František Lidiak is recorded in a Czech-language source but appears elsewhere as "Frank Lidiak," the former will be used consistently in this book.

Standardization of capitalization regarding Czech names of organizations and titles of books, articles, newspapers, and so forth also presents a problem. Although Czech-American sources are inconsistent, the standard Czech form will be used throughout. That is, such titles and names will be capitalized in the initial letter of the initial word only: thus *Naše dějiny* instead of *Naše Dějiny*. These practices will not eliminate confusion, but should minimize it.

One final note: Those readers familiar with the Czech language may notice a few apparently nonstandard usages in Czech quotations, names of organizations, etc. These will usually be attributable to dialectical variations. (See the discussion of Texas Czech dialects in Chapter 6.)

Herrmann, *A History of the Czechs* (London, 1975); and William V. Wallace, *Czechoslovakia* (London, 1976).

CHAPTER 1

Emigration From Europe
And Early History In Texas

Moc lidi, ne zemi.
(Too many people, not enough land.)
— Czech immigrant

BACKGROUND IN EUROPE

The phenomenon of emigration/immigration may be seen as the result of a set of circumstances affecting great masses of people or of one overpowering circumstance in the life of a particular individual. Various contributing causes can usually be found in the home country as well as in the welcoming foreign one. The Czech emigration to Texas is no exception: conditions in the nineteenth-century Austrian Empire stimulated many Czechs to leave their native land, and the reports they received concerning conditions in America encouraged them to settle there. Although each individual's reason for emigration was probably a variable combination of many reasons, several factors were dominant.

Before considering the reasons for Czech emigration, however, it is important to grasp the magnitude of not only the Czech but of all Austrian emigration to the United States during the period 1850-1914. As Table 1 reveals, over 100,000 Czechs had come to the United States by the early date of 1880, and the stream of emigrants continued right up to the eve of World War I, when virtually all emigration ceased. In the decade 1901-1910 alone, the United States received almost 95,000 Czechs. The Czechs began to emigrate in large numbers relatively early, and their emigration levels were relatively consistent throughout the period. Until the 1880s, however, they accounted for well over half of the Austrian total, but at the highwater mark of their emigration, in the years 1901-1910, they accounted for only 4.3% of the Austrian total.

TABLE 1

Emigration to the USA From the Czech Lands 1850-1914*

	Total Number of Emigrants	Yearly Number of Emigrants		Czech Emigration As percent of Austrian Emigration	Yearly percentage of Czech Emigration Compared to Austrian Emigration	
		Lowest	Highest		Lowest	Highest
1850-1860	23,009	179 (1850)	6,426 (1854)	73.8%	35.3% (1850)	90% (1854)
1861-1870	33,123	1,176 (1863)	7,801 (1867)	82.8%	77.8% (1863)	87.3% (1870)
1871-1880	52,079	2,261 (1878)	11,858 (1880)	50.6%	37.4% (1877)	76.5% (1871)
1881-1890	62,050	3,085 (1889)	12,189 (1881)	18.9%	7.1% (1890)	43.1% (1881)
1891-1900	42,079	1,607 (1895)	11,758 (1891)	7.3%	2.8% (1900)	16.6% (1891)
1901-1910	94,603	3,766 (1901)	13,554 (1907)	4.3%	2.8% (1901)	7.2% (1904)
1911-1914	38,681	8,439 (1912)	11,091 (1913)	4.5%	3.1% (1914)	5.8% (1911)

*Based on Josef Polišenský, *Začiatky českej a slovenskej emigrácie do USA*. (Bratislava, 1970), p. 48.

The Czech emigration was thus only part of a tremendous exodus from the Austrian Empire. Total Austrian emigration from 1850 to 1914 was well over 3.5 million.[1] Large numbers of Austrian emigrants headed for Canada, South America, Africa, Australia, and Asia. Most of them were bound for the United States, however, and Austria's

[1] John Chmelar, "The Austrian Emigration, 1900-1914," trans. Thomas C. Childers, in *Perspectives in American History, Vol. III* (Cambridge, Mass., 1973), 282-83. The lands composing the Austrian or Austro-Hungarian Empire, with their respective areas in geographical square miles, were Lower Austria (360.03), Upper Austria (348.91), Styria (407.79), Carinthia and Carniola (369.79), Tyrol (532.61), Bohemia (943.72), Moravia-Silesia (497.19), Galicia (1593.11), Littoral (127.99), Dalmatia (232.33), Hungary (4160.68), Transylvania (997.82), Military Frontier (742.84), and Lombardy and Venetia (825.62). Slovakia was part of Hungary.

proportion of the United States total immigration increased steadily in the years preceding World War I. From 1821 to 1890, emigration from Austria accounted for only 2.9% of all U.S. immigration, but from 1891 to 1900, it made up 15.5%, and it continued to grow until the war. Over one million Austrian immigrants came during the short period 1909-1913.

The remarkable size of the Austrian emigration is a measure of the widespread discontent within the Empire. It would be impractical here to thoroughly discuss the complex political, economic, and social problems which caused this discontent, but the general situation in the Czech lands of Bohemia and Moravia can be described. Before the revolutionary year of 1848, Austria was in some ways a century behind Western Europe in political development. In an age when democratic ideas were influencing the development of societies in Western Europe, Czech peasants were still performing feudal obligations and paying manorial dues to the nobility, the state, and the church. These dues and obligations, which had evolved through ten centuries, kept the peasant in almost total economic bondage. By the eighteenth century the church, the state, and the nobility taxed away about 70% of all the peasant earned, raised or grew.[2]

Ostensibly these taxes were paid by the peasant in reward for services performed for his benefit, especially by the lord: for the rights to farm on the manor of the lord, rely on a local judicial system, and appeal for personal protection. Ironically, the peasant sometimes literally needed protection from his "protector."[3] Beating a peasant with a cane for failure to meet his duties to the lord was legally permitted until 1848. In 1793 a decree had been issued requiring permission from a regional government official to inflict this punishment; however, the majority of government officials were biased on the side of the nobility, and the lord still ruled almost as he wished, with little concern about government interference.

The most despised obligation the peasant owed the lord was *robota*. This bound the peasant to work free for the lord a specified number of days a year. Of course, these days were taken during the most important periods of the year—during planting and harvesting. Obviously, this situation would lead to resentment on the part of the

[2] Jerome Blum, *Noble Landowners and Agriculture in Austria, 1815-1848* (Baltimore, 1948), 68.
[3] Stanley Z. Pech, *The Czech Revolution of 1848* (Chapel Hill, N.C., 1969), 15.

peasant, for every day spent working for the lord was a day less he could work for his own gain. Although by 1848 *robota* had been commuted to a monetary payment in much of Bohemia and Moravia, it was by no means extinct. It is significant that the term "robot" was chosen by Karel Čapek in his 1920 play *RUR* to mean a machine that performs human labor, but without desire or will.

While the economic and political power of nobles over peasants was oppressive, the social obligations were degrading. The peasant was supposed to take off his hat when he was within three hundred steps of the manor house.[4] Also, he was obligated to address all officials as *jemnost pane* ("gracious lord").[5]

These conditions were part of the dynamics of Austrian life which benefitted those on top and kept those on the bottom in their place. But the ideas of Locke, Rousseau and the American Revolution spread even into reactionary Austria. In 1848, peasants, workers, students and liberals combined forces, and it seemed as though the old order would be swept away. Serfdom was abolished. The peasant was legally freed from control by the lord. *Robota,* the most despised obligation of all, was canceled. The state, instead of the lord, took over control of the judicial system and both lord and peasant were bound by the laws decreed by the state. However, some of the peasants did not gain as much from these reforms as others.

The term "peasantry" can refer to most rural inhabitants of Austria at this time, but within this class there were three distinct subclasses. The *sedláci (rolnici)* or farmers were the most prosperous. They owned anywhere from twenty to one hundred acres and a house. Because they were now free from the political, economic and social control of those above them, the farmers profitted from the reforms even though they had to compensate the lords for their losses. The *chalupníci* or cottagers, and *nádeníci* or day laborers, however, felt left out of the reforms. The cottager owned a house and, sometimes, a very small plot of land. The laborer owned nothing but his labor. These two sub-classes were now better off in the sense that they were emancipated but felt cheated by the reforms because they did not have the economic means to improve their standards of living. Moreover, there was virtually no political or economic improvement for these two groups until the "Gotterdamerung" of 1918. The cottagers could sell

    [4] Ernest Knapton and Thomas Derry, *Europe 1815-1914* (New York, 1965), 92.
    [5] Pech, 16.

their homes, land, and whatever meager possessions they had for enough money to pay for a passage to America, with, in some cases, a sum left over to buy land in the new country. The opportunity seemed all the more attractive when the cottagers, restless for democratic reforms, began to lose strength in the Moravian Diet (Parliament) which had been created after the revolution in 1848, and the Austrian government took no steps to solve their economic and political problems.

Conditions were especially favorable, then, for the emigration of this cottager class, and, in fact, cottagers made up the majority of the Czech immigrants in Texas. The economic and political background of these people helps to explain distinctive features of the society which they developed in Texas. These features, in particular their attitude toward the land, will be discussed in Chapter 3.

The holders of small plots of land saw their economic situation grow progressively worse. The larger land owners, most of them nobles, could afford to apply the latest scientific agricultural methods. The small land holders found it more and more difficult to compete in agricultural markets. By 1900, less than one tenth of one percent of the population of Bohemia owned the land.[6] This situation created an ever greater problem for the sons of small and even middle-sized land holders. How could the father divide his small holdings among his heirs? It was traditional for the father to provide a farm for each of his sons as he reached the age of twenty. When the land was divided, each strip was partitioned lengthwise, resulting in a series of ever-narrower, long strips.

The situation was even worse for day laborers, who found it difficult or impossible to raise sufficient funds to pay for their passage to America. They usually lived in the homes of cottagers and farmers and helped with the work in season. In the winter they helped the host family in weaving cloth, the principal cottage industry of Bohemia and Moravia. By the 1850s however, the further industrialization of Bohemia was driving many home weavers out of business. They could not successfully compete with mechanized production. The story of František Branecký is typical.

> I was born on December 1, 1821, in Lišná, Moravia. My father was a farmer but when I was twenty-one they drafted me. I served in the first infantry regiment of the Austrian army in 1848 and '49. Luckily I lived through the war with Marshall Radetzky. I was in the army nine years, after which I went on leave. What was I going to do? I

[6] Chmelar, 342-43.

was a weaver by trade but couldn't find work. I knew farming, having learned it from a farmer (my parents died when I was 13), but there were six of us kids, so for me, by inheritance, there was very little. I got eighty *zlatý* for all of my share. I was tired of the service so a desire to go to America began to stir in me. In 1855 several families were getting ready to go to America so I prepared to go with them.[7]

Branecký did come to America, settling finally in Praha, Texas, where he became a successful farmer.

Along with economic difficulties came increasingly overcrowded living conditions. An example can be seen in a description of Čermna, Bohemia in 1850. (See Map 2.) The example is particularly appropriate since Čermna produced the first major group of Czechs to emigrate to Texas. Cottages were very small, sometimes consisting of only one room; the average number of people per house was ten. In house Number 109 the owner lived with four children, four orphaned children (from a relative) and a laborer and his four children, making a total of sixteen people. In Number 143 lived the Jan Marek family, totaling eleven members; all of them later came to Texas. In Number 141 lived the Josef Hejl family, which included nine children. Hejl's son Josef later came to Texas. Together in house Number 149 were Josef Šilar, his wife and five children, a pensioner named Josef Šilar

Selected Villages of Origin of early Czech Immigrants to Texas.

[7] *Amerikán narodní kalendář*, 1886, 189. (Authors' trans.)

(probably the grandfather), a widow with four children, a laborer named Jan Chaloupka, his wife and son, another laborer, a retired soldier, and another widow: a total of nineteen people.[8] Certainly the reason for emigration given by an elderly widow some seventy years after coming to Texas applies to many who came to America: *"Moc lidi, ne zemi"* ("Too many people, not enough land.")[9]

Letters and personal accounts collected from immigrants who settled in Snook, Texas, also describe a depressed environment. Here is an excerpt from one:

> My mother and father had ten children, and they owned a little farm. We poorer people had to farm the hills and had to do all the work by hand. We raised Irish potatoes and stuff to eat. Our biggest tool was a hoe. Some of the bigger farmers had mules, but these were very few. Everywhere the Germans wanted to teach school in German and to populate the area. We couldn't live on the farm produce, so we had to go to work. When I was 13 years old, I went to work in a furniture factory for 23 cents a day and had to board myself. My older brother had gone to Texas and he wrote to have the family come to America, as things were better here. He sent us the money for the trip. We thought he must have been awfully rich to send that much money.[10]

There is little doubt that the experience of economic hardship — and the hope of an improved standard of living — were the chief motivating factors for the emigration of Bohemians and Moravians. Other factors, such as Czech nationalism, compulsory military service, and religious persecution were also significant, although their relative importance is difficult to evaluate.

The pressure of Germanization had been so great in the period stretching from the early seventeenth to the beginning of the nineteenth century that the Czech language had almost become extinct, at least in the towns and cities. At one point it was spoken only by the peasants in the countryside, and even this Czech was heavily influenced by German. However, beginning in the early 1800s, a renascence of Czech nationalism brought about a resurgence of the people's

[8] František Šilar, "The First Nepomuky and Cermna Emigrants in Texas," trans. Calvin C. Chervenka. Unpublished manuscript, 2.

[9] Interview with Francis Mendl, August 20, 1971.

[10] Quoted in Robert L. Skrabanek, *Social Organization and Change in a Czech American Rural Community: A Sociological Study of Snook, Texas.* Ph.D. Dissertation, Louisiana State University, (1950), 57.

language and culture. Linguists such as Jungmann, Dobrovský, and their students studied the dying Czech language, often with the thought of reviving it. Scholars such as František Palacký rediscovered the history of the Czechs and made the people aware of it. Gradually, the work of these reformers bore fruit, and Czech language and culture began to revive. However, this rebirth of nationalism met only resistance from the ruling class. The Hapsburgs and the German elite saw it as divisive and ultimately destructive for the Empire. Of course, they were being realistic. As many of the reformers such as Palacký were being forced into exile after 1848, many other Czechs and Moravians were deciding to emigrate for political reasons.

The immigrants were enthusiastic about the relative political freedom they found in America. Although prejudice and political oppression existed, they were not supported by a continual, historical policy on the part of the national government. The attitude of many Czechs was summed up by the father of Augustin Haidušek, one of the most influential leaders of the Czech community in Texas at the turn of the century. When asked by an old friend who had just arrived in America why he had come to Texas when he "had a better pig sty at home," Haidušek answered, "I would rather live in this cabin as a free citizen than live in a palace and be subject to the ruler of Austria."[11]

Another Austrian policy which influenced immigration was a three-year compulsory military service for males, with few exceptions. Obviously, an ethnic group which considered itself suppressed by its government did not relish dangerous military service in that government's army. In 1847, thirty-nine men of the 35th Pilsen Regiment escaped from Austria and made their way to America. When a military accountant named Toužimský fled with the regimental funds, the action was hailed as a patriotic act.[12] F. J. Pešek, who came to Texas in 1868, was one of many who emigrated to avoid military service. He settled in Praha, Texas, and became a teacher. Some Czech families came to America so their sons would not have to fight. Some young men came individually, before draft age, and others deserted the army in order to emigrate.

Religion was a significant factor in the early emigration of Czech Protestants. Many Czech Protestants, as well as anti-clerical "free-

[11] Estelle Hudson and Henry R. Maresh, *Czech Pioneers of the Southwest* (Dallas, 1934), 86.

[12] Vera Laska, *The Czechs in America, 1633-1977: A Chronology and Fact Book* (New York, 1977), 8.

thinkers," closely associated Hapsburg oppression with the state-supported Catholic Church. Followers of the Hussite tradition (which antedates Lutheranism by a century) were particularly unhappy because they had not been allowed to organize their own congregations in the Czech lands, whereas other Protestants had. Although some of them attended the churches organized by Lutherans and other Protestant groups, the desire to follow their own religious tradition was strong. The search for religious freedom in America, then, was a prime motivating factor for this group. In fact, the "father of Czech immigration into Texas," Rev. Josef Arnošt Bergman, was at least partially motivated to emigrate by a dream of building a religious community modeled after that of the old Czech Unity of the Brethren.[13] Although his personal dream was not realized, many Czech Protestants followed him, and eventually, a distinctively Czech Protestant denomination evolved in Texas. The remarkable rebirth of the Unity of the Brethren in Texas will be described in Chapter 4.

Social and economic pressures for emigration were allowed to work upon the restless Austrian population, unchecked by any effective laws prohibiting it. In fact, the Constitution of 1867 guaranteed the principle of free emigration.[14] Certain groups with vested interests were careful to support this principle, also. The state-subsidized railroads and the shipping lines wanted to insure higher profits by carrying ever larger numbers of emigrants through and away from Austria. The Austrian Ministry of Trade, as well as other governmental agencies, believed that the increased flow of emigrants was not only good for business but also served as a relief valve for the revolutionary pressure created by unfavorable social, economic, and political conditions.

On the other hand, the large landowners, industrialists, and military leaders constantly agitated for restriction of emigration: the first two because they needed a large pool of cheap, exploitable labor, and the last because they needed new recruits and also because they were afraid of providing recruits for some other country's army. Ironically, many Czech nationalists agreed with the generals, landowners, and capitalists on this issue. The patriots were afraid that their awakening

---

[13] See Josef Arnošt Bergman, *Letopisy pamatných událostí evang. Křestanské obce v Strouzným* (Brno, 1930), 57. At this point Bergman did not have in mind an organized denomination, as such, but rather a congregation in the tradition of the Czech and Moravian Brethren. See Chapter 4 for a discussion of this tradition.

[14] Chmelar, 276.

nation could not achieve success if more and more of its people left for distant lands.

In stark contrast to the conditions in Austria at this time were the political, social, and economic conditions prevalent in America. To the Czech peasant, America was a place to make a new start, where he would not be a prisoner of history. The perception of America as the fabled "land of milk and honey" made his situation in Europe seem all the more bleak, and America seem to be utopia. A broadside ditty often sung in Bohemia and Moravia went, *"v Americe tam je blaze, teče pivo po podlaze."* "It's crazy there in America, beer flows on the floor." The following account illustrates a typical attitude:

I was born in Hranice, Moravia in 1877. My father was a "chalupník" (cottager) who raised a large family, and we never were well off.

We were compelled to serve three years under the Hapsburgs in the army. Two of my brothers were compelled to serve before me, and neither of them liked it. When I became of age, according to law, I had to serve in the army too.

In the army we were treated very badly — for instance, our pay was six cents a day for foot soldiers and eight cents a day for those who rode horses [cavalrymen]. We were expected to keep our beards waxed and our boots shined, so that took all the money we made in the army. After buying the wax and shoe polish, we didn't have money left to buy cigarettes. If we wanted to smoke, our folks had to send us money from home to buy tobacco with. Since my father was rather poor, I didn't smoke. In the army, we got two meals a day. Breakfast consisted of black coffee. We got a very good dinner, including such things as meat and peas, but we didn't get any supper at all.

I was a cavalryman in the army. We usually rode our horses in the deserts, and on rainy days we rode them in buildings which were a solid mass of red and yellow colors [German colors]. One day we were jumping our horses indoors over hurdles, when a cruel ring-master made me try a jump that I knew was impossible to make. I fell and the horse fell on top of me. The ringmaster cursed me and tried to make me get up and get on my horse, but I couldn't move, so I was taken to the hospital and soon turned loose to shift for my-self until I was well enough to return to active duty. Still I couldn't go home to my father for help, for he had all that he could do to make a living for himself. So I went to my uncle's house — bent, broken, and hobbling around with the help of a walking cane.

My uncle had a mill where he ground wheat, barley, and oats, and he also took newspapers from America. One day I saw an advertisement in the paper telling of the wonderful land called the United States. In the same issue, a Czech from Lavaca County, Texas had an article in the paper telling about the operation of a beef club. I remember saying to myself how good a life those people in America must have to be able to raise cattle and kill one to eat and to even divide the beef among themselves. Then and there, I thought if I were not crippled and had the money to go to America I would go there rather than to return to Cracow [to complete the five months unserved term in the army].

I wrote for information as to how I could get to America. They [a steamship company] wrote back that all that was needed for the trip was 50 *koruny* [about ten dollars]. But I didn't have that much money: neither did anyone else that I knew. Shortly after that my back began to straighten out and I got a message from Cracow from the army headquarters to report for a physical examination. If I could pass the physical examination I would return to the cavalry, and if I couldn't, I would finish out my time in a telegraph regiment. I redoubled my efforts to reach America.

I asked my father if he could possibly think of anyone who could lend me the necessary money for the trip to America. He said that he knew that my married sister had saved some money, but 50 *koruny* was so much money! I asked my sister to lend me the money, and she refused to do so, for she and her family had worked so hard to save it. Finally, my father ordered her to lend me the money. She did so, but only after I swore on a cross in her presence that I would repay it. So I finally got my chance to come to America without finishing out my term under those . . . Hapsburgs.

Imagine how wonderful America looked to me. The very day that I was ashore, a man in Galveston gave me the ten dollars to send to my sister and also gave me a job that paid enough so that I could easily save as much money in a month as it took most people in the old country years to save.[15]

How did the European peasant find out about Texas? There were several ways, but probably the most common was letters sent by friends and relatives. In fact, Karel Jonáš, the U.S. Consul General in Vienna, stated in 1888,

There can be no question that the emigration from this Empire is, on the whole, free and voluntary, induced undoubtedly in the great

[15] Skrabanek, 55-56, and the *Temple Daily Telegram*, January 31, 1971, 26C.

majority of cases by the favorable reports written by Austrians resid-
ing in the U.S. to the friends at home.[16]

These letters from America reached not only the relatives and
friends of those in America, but whole villages and regions. It was very
common for letters from America to be the talk of the town, especially
in the early years of emigration. Also, newspapers such as the *Moravské
noviny (The Moravian News)* printed these letters, informing large
areas of Bohemia and Moravia about the emigrants' experiences.

Not only did American relatives and friends urge Czechs to come
to America by their letters; they also financially supported such emigration. Jonáš noted numerous cases of Czech-Americans prepaying
for the passage of friends and relatives still in Europe.[17] As Texas came
to be populated by more and more European immigrants, the steamship and railroad companies foresaw an increasing lucrative trade.
Texas Czech newspapers carried advertisements to prepay passage for
anyone in Europe to come to Texas. It was very simple: one only had to
send the passage money (about $30.00) to the company and it, in
turn, would send the ticket to the company's office nearest the home
of the relative or friend. By 1890, 25 to 33% and by 1900, 40 to 65%
of all immigrants to America were traveling on prepaid tickets.[18]

Steamship companies, land agents, and railroads all advertised
Texas to Europeans. Emily Balch remembered seeing an advertisement
in 1910 declaring that Galveston was the best port of entry because
customs agents were less strict there.[19] Indeed, most Czechs came to
Texas through the port of Galveston. The Galveston, Harrisburg, and
San Antonio Railroad published a pamphlet entitled *"Texas co cíl
stěhování"* (*"Texas as a Destination of Immigration"*) in 1888 describing the soil, climate and the crops grown in Texas. Of course not
all the companies were especially truthful in their advertising. One
steamship company had on display in Bohemia an example of what it
called "Texas soil": black topsoil six feet in depth.[20] Many immigrants
were well aware that others had lost their money to all kinds of thieves
and shady operators while on their way to America. The letters home

[16] House of Representatives, *Report of Consul-General Edmund Jussen,
Vienna, 24 July 1888*, 97-98, quoted in William Philip Hewitt, *The Czechs in
Texas: A Study of the Immigration and the Development of Czech Ethnicity,
1850-1920*. Ph.D Dissertation, The University of Texas at Austin (1978), 23.

[17] Quoted in Hewitt, 23.

[18] See Hewitt, 32.

[19] Emily Balch, *Our Slavic Fellow Citizens* (New York, 1910), 80.

[20] R. W. Chervenka, *John Kohut and His Son Josef* (Waco, 1966), 11.

Anthony M. Dignowity
— Photo copied from *Indian Wars
and Pioneers of Texas.*

and the Czech newspapers were replete with accounts of these pitfalls and advice on how to avoid them. In fact, an early Texas Czech hero was Ignác Rusek, a Czech employee of a steamship company who faithfully and honestly helped many immigrants find their way from Galveston to the inland Czech communities.[21]

EARLY INDIVIDUAL AND GROUP IMMIGRATION

Czech immigration into Texas begins with individuals rather than with groups. According to the Texas Czech Catholic history *Naše dějiny*, it is "historically certain" that there were Czechs among the Jesuit missionaries to Mexico in the Seventeenth Century and that they visited Texas soil in their work with the Indians. It is also claimed that bells engraved with the names of Czech saints have been discovered in mission churches. These interesting assertions are undocumented, however.[22]

The first Czechs known to have visited and lived in Texas were restless, adventurous men. First was the wandering writer Karel Anton Postl, who was known only by his pen name Charles Sealsfield for most of his adult life. Postl, whose Czech identity was revealed after his death in 1864, set many of his exciting tales in Texas, especially the Texas-Louisiana borderland, which he probably visited as early as 1823. After living in Pennsylvania for a time, he returned to what is now the Southwest United States as a plantation owner and itinerant businessman, remaining during the period 1828-32. His subsequent articles and stories about the area, written while he lived in Switzerland, attracted Czechs, as well as Germans, Englishmen, and other Europeans, to Texas and helped to generate the myth of the American West in Europe.[23] His single most influential book in this regard was *Das Kajutenbuch* (The Cabin Book) (1841), which presented a somewhat utopian picture of life in Texas. The book went through fourteen editions in German and English. Postl's literature will be discussed further in Chapter 6.

Another early Czech wanderer and adventurer in Texas was Anthony M. Dignowity, who was born in Bohemia in 1810. After fighting with the Polish revolutionaries in their unsuccessful revolt against

---

[21] Narodní svaz českých kotolikú v Texasu, *Naše dějiny*, (Granger, Tex., 1939), 421. Also see Hugo Chotek's novelette *"Zahuba města Galvestonu"* in *Amerikán národní kalendář*, 1906, for a reference to Rusek's work as a railroad company agent.

[22] *Naše dějiny*, 13.

[23] For additional information about Postl, see the discussion of literature in Chapter 6.

Reverend Bohumír Menzl
— Photo copied from *Naše dějiny*.

the Russians in 1830, he fled first to Hamburg, Germany, and then to New York in 1832. In America, he traveled from state to state, working at many different jobs. He invented a machine to clean cotton; worked on a plantation; lived with the Creek Indians and studied their culture; studied medicine at Cincinnati College; became a manufacturer, a land agent, and a writer. After arriving in San Antonio with a group of Arkansas Volunteers for the Mexican War, he decided to set up a medical practice there. Through all his wanderings, Dignowity retained his love for his native land. In 1859 he wrote *Bohemia Under Austrian Despotism*, an autobiography which will be discussed in Chapter 6. During the Civil War, Dignowity's anti-slavery stand cost him many friends and endangered his life.

In 1836 Frederick Lemský came to Texas. He took part in the Texas Revolution, playing the fife in the Texan band at the Battle of San Jacinto.[24] Lemský was also active in the German Union, an organization which supported European immigration to Texas.

Probably the first Czech Catholic priest in Texas was Bohumir Menzl. He arrived in 1840 along with a group of German settlers which included a few Czech families. The group went to New Braunfels and Fredericksburg where Menzl served the Catholic inhabitants and taught school. Menzl also served Catholic settlers in the Castroville and D'Hannis areas. His knowledge of medicine helped not only the European settlers but the Indians, who looked upon him as a benefactor. In 1856 Menzl returned to his hometown of Frýdlant, Bohemia, and died soon thereafter. A huge oak cross was erected not far from Fredericksburg to honor this Czech immigrant priest. A statue of

---

[24] It is sometimes suggested that another figure in the Texas Revolutionary period, George Fisher, was also of Czech descent. (For example, in the audio-visual presentation *Texané Českého Puvodů*, Institute of Texan Cultures, San Antonio, 1971.) This mistake is understandable, because Fisher was at one time known as Rybář (the Czech word for "fisherman" or "fisher") and because he evidently spent some time in Prussian Silesia and northeastern Bohemia (areas which produced early immigrants to Texas) prior to coming to America. It is most probable, however, that Fisher was a Hungarian of Serbian origin. See the description of Fisher in John Lloyd Stephens, *Incidents of Travel in Yucatan* (New York, 1843) I, 84-86. Also see John Livingston, *Portraits of Eminent Americans, Now Living* (New York, 1853-54) III, 441-46. In addition, Fisher left a self-description in a volume of *Memorials* presented to the Fourth and Fifth Congresses of the Republic of Texas in 1840. (The original copy is preserved in the Houston Public Library.) Fisher was a flamboyant and controversial figure whose role in early Texas history deserves further study.

Reverend Josef Arnošt Bergman, wife Marie (nee Berndt), and daughter Otillía in 1863.
                — Photo courtesy of Evelyn Barnum and Albert J. Blaha.

the man and a museum to house his botanical specimens and various artifacts brought from Texas were built in Frýdlant.

Menzl had little or no influence on later Czech immigration, but another religious figure did. The Rev. Josef Arnošt Bergman can be justly described as the "father" of Czech immigration into Texas. He was born in 1797 in Zápudov, Bohemia. Bergman left his studies in a Catholic seminary in Prague, but later studied Protestant theology in Vratislav, Silesia. From 1830 until 1849 he served as pastor of a Czech congregation in an Evangelical Reformed church in Stroužný, Silesia. Bergman was influenced by the Czech National Revival and was acquainted with the works of Karel Havlíček and other Czech patriots of the day. He wanted, above all, a democratic government for his homeland. The continuous ethnic, political, and religious oppression in Austria came to be intolerable for him, however, and after nineteen years of dedicated work in Stroužný, he gave up everything he had worked for and left for Texas. Although frustrated by conditions in his native land, Bergman was optimistic about a brighter future in America, where he would be free to carry out his plans to establish a new Czech Brethren community.[25]

Czech Protestants such as Bergman probably learned of the fabled land of Texas from German Lutheran soldiers. Members of both groups had been stationed in German towns before 1848. The fever for German emigration to the United States and Texas was high at this time, and, undoubtedly, it affected the Czechs as well.[26]

On the day after preaching his last sermon in Stroužný, October 2, 1849, he and his family left for Texas. After landing in Galveston

[25] Actually, Bergman remained a minister of the German Evangelical Reformed Church during his career in Texas. The complicated religious heritage of the Czechs in Texas is discussed in some detail in Chapter 4. The account of Bergman given here is based on the version given in *Letopisy pamatných události evang. Křesťanské obce v Strouzným* (Brno, 1931) and a manuscript autobiographical fragment which has been reproduced in Albert J. Blaha, Sr. and Dorothy Klumpp, *The Saga of Ernst Bergmann* (Private Printing, 1981), pp. 111-17. Bergman's name, like many of the others referred to in this book, appears in different forms in various sources. Josef Arnošt Bergman is the Czech form, Jozef Ernst Bergmann the German. To further confuse matters, the name Ernst or Arnošt does not appear on Bergman's birth certificate, although it was the name he used exclusively in Texas. Possibly he adopted the name to avoid confusion with his father, who was also named Josef. Bergman spent his last years in Corsicana, Texas, and was buried there in April, 1877 (Blaha and Klumpp, 23-24).

[26] *Amerikán narodní kalendář* (1924), 271.

Frederick Lemský at the Battle of San Jacinto in 1836.
— Photo of detail from mural courtesy of Texas Southern University.

on March 2, 1850, he immediately went to the little German community of Cat Spring in Austin County, where he served as pastor and
teacher. (See Map 3.) Since his income was insufficient to maintain
him and his family, he bought a farm and raised wheat, rye, corn, and
cotton. By 1860 he owned 109 acres.[27] Very soon after arriving in Cat
Spring, Bergman began writing to his friends in Europe. His letters
told of the opportunities which awaited future immigrants, and they
provided an important stimulus to the subsequent large-scale Bohemian and Moravian immigration.

In 1851 the area around Nepomuky and Čermna in northeastern
Bohemia was severely depressed after several years of bad harvests. The
people's deprivation was such that they were selling furniture, clothes,
feather beds, almost anything not essential to life in order to buy food.
An official in the district advised them to emigrate to Hungary.[28] One
of the leading citizens, however, was not enthusiastic about this idea.
Josef Lidumil Lešikar had come into possession of a letter from Bergman which described Texas in glowing terms.[29] Lešikar diverted the attention of those desiring to go to Hungary to this exotic place called
Texas. He also sent a copy of the letter to the *Moravské noviny*. This
letter inspired the beginning of mass Czech and Moravian immigration to Texas. Although only seventeen families left Nepomuky and
Čermna in the first group, larger numbers of persons followed them in
the coming years. Bergman and Lešikar had set an irreversible tide into
motion. As oppressed, hungry peasants read Bergman's letters in their
newspapers and then began to receive letters from relatives who had
arrived in Texas, increasing numbers of them decided to leave. Typical
of the letters is a very early one written by Kateřina Herrmann. Her father had known Bergman in the old country and his letters had convinced Kateřina and her husband, along with their children, to come
to Texas. The letter is dated July 10, 1851:

> One cannot call Cat Spring a town or even a village. It is a wildly
> beautiful region with many trees. The hills alternate with a beautiful

---

[27] Hewitt, 40.

[28] A number of Czechs were emigrating to Hungary at this time. Community leader Josef Lešikar, however, had heard that the Banat region, where
they had been urged to settle, was unhealthy and that Hungarians there were
unfriendly toward Slavs (Šilar, 3).

[29] It is not entirely clear how the Bergman letter fell into Lešikar's hands,
but it was common for such letters to circulate widely in districts where the idea
of emigration was popular. Emigration to America was becoming one of the
most popular subjects of discussion among inhabitants of the Lanškroun area.

MAP 3

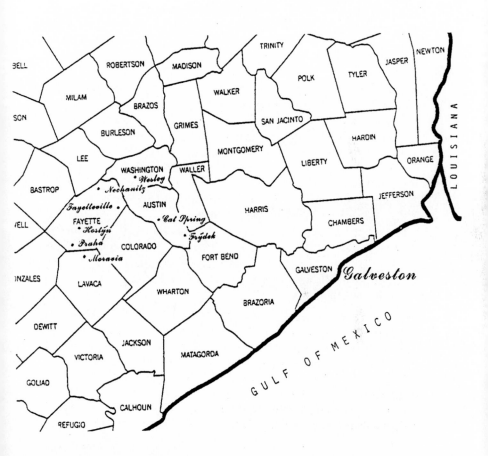

THE LOCATIONS OF SOME
EARLY CZECH SETTLEMENTS IN TEXAS

Galveston was the port of entry for most Czech immigrants. The early groups usually travelled to Cat Spring before dispersing into neighboring areas.

valley. . . . There is a road and I think I would like it here, but everyone says that better soil lies farther inland. Even so the corn grows very well here. From all I can gather, it seems to me that a delightful future awaits us, for, whatever we need, we will surely find it here; what we can't get here we would not look for anywhere else. . . . I must sincerely say that on the confounded Herschel [the boat that brought the Herrmanns to Texas] from time to time I sighed wearily, but what is to be found in this beautiful country makes me not regret our moving.[30]

The first group of emigrants was made up of very poor Czech peasants who wanted more from life than they expected to find in their native country. On August 19, 1851, 118 emigrant passes were granted by the government. The family names were Šilar, Rippel, Pfeifer, Haisler, Sontag, Lešikar, Marek, Votava, Rohsler, Motl, Ježek, Coufal, and Mareš, and they came from several villages around Nepomuky and Čermna. All but two, Jan Šilar, a weaver, and Josef Šilar, a soapmaker, were laborers, the poorest of the villagers. On November 6, 1851, 74 of those that were issued passes started the long trip to Texas. Sixteen of the families were Protestant, one Catholic. The remaining 44 people could not bear to leave. Ironically, Josef Lešikar was one of these. His wife Terezie prevailed upon him at the last minute not to leave their home.

Like most emigrants, these surely had mixed emotions concerning the future. Their past had not been easy, living on very small farms, barely making enough to survive. At present, the potatoes, the staple crop of the area, were rotting in the ground, and the friends and relatives who remained behind faced possible starvation. On the other hand, the future, though full of promise, seemed vague and uncertain, and the emigrants were leaving everything they had ever known. Most of them were never again to see the hometowns, friends, and relatives left behind.

Many did not find a better life, either. The story of this first group is full of misfortune and tragedy; only about half of them were to reach Texas alive. After traveling to Hamburg by train, they met a Mr. Hirman, who talked them into saving a few dollars on their tickets by taking the circuitous route to Liverpool, New Orleans, and finally, Galveston, their intended destination. When they arrived in Liverpool, they found that their ship, the *Maria*, was already overcrowded

[30] Published in František Kutnar, *"Dopisy českých vystěhovalců z padesátých let 19. století ze zámoří do vlasti"* in Josef Polišenký, *Začiatky českej a slovenskej emigracie do USA* (Bratislava, 1970), 228.

Josef L. Lešikar
— Photo courtesy of J. J. Stalmach.
Copy from University of Texas Institute of
Texan Cultures at San Antonio.

with Irish immigrants. The conditions on board ship were so bad that only 38 of the original 74 people remained alive after the 10-week voyage.[31]

Future immigrants were to learn from the experience of this first, ill-fated group. The *Moravské noviny* later printed a letter from Bergman to Josef Lešikar describing the best route to take:

> Tell them to be sure not to try to save money at the wrong time. It is better to pay a little more and buy passage on a German boat from Mr. Valenti in Hamburg. If this is not possible, then pay only a little more in Bremen and buy passage on a German boat directly to Galveston. In the end, this, although slightly more expensive, passage, will be the most economical.
>
> In addition, please advise any future emigrants not to delay long anywhere along the route, but especially not in Houston, that "Texas Graveyard of Germans." Instead move on to higher ground as soon as you can.[32]

The leader of the first group, Josef Šilar, did make it to Texas. His son Josef remembered his experiences as a boy of thirteen:

> In 1851 a large group of Czechs from Nepomuky set out for Texas. Among them were my father Josef Šilar and his family of three children. We went from Liverpool to New Orleans in ten weeks and had a very bad crossing for they were very sick and badly taken care of. Because over one-half were sick when we got to New Orleans, many had to go to the hospital. My parents, brother, and sister were taken there and I alone stayed with my Uncle Ježek in the hotel. We couldn't talk with anyone because hardly any of us knew German, let alone English. There were no Czechs in New Orleans. . . . After a few days I went to see my parents in the hospital. Not having any way to communicate with anyone, I had to wander around the hospital trying to find my parents. When evening came and the sisters had seen me wandering around, they took me to supper, let me wash up, changed me into clean night clothes, and put me to bed. The patients around me were constantly screaming and I couldn't sleep, so about midnight I got up and ran downstairs to get away from there. The hospital was surrounded by a high fence and the only thing I could hear was the wailing of the patients and the barking of dogs outside. I wanted to go through the gate but it was locked. Without hesitation, I climbed over the gate and happily ran into the street where everything was dark. It was about three miles to Uncle's

---

[31] Šilar, 9.
[32] Quoted in Šilar, 9.

hotel and I, chased by the dogs, wandered through the streets of the city, not knowing what to think. Finally, as dawn was breaking, I found the hotel.

After a while those that did not die were released from the hospital. From there we went to Galveston where more of us got sick and some died. The same thing happened in Houston, from where we were hauled on wagons to Cat Spring. It was in the spring of 1852 when we came to the Brazos River which was flooded and about six miles wide. We camped here fourteen days. We found some fruit there which resembled nuts. Some ate the fruit and suffered terribly; a few even died.[33]

For Josef Šilar, Sr., Texas was not to be the promised land. In 1852 he moved to Industry and bought a farm. In 1854 his wife died, and shortly thereafter his house burned down. His spirit broken, he died in 1855, leaving three orphaned children. Josef Šilar, Jr., however, was to survive and prosper.[34]

Although the shipboard conditions for the first group were unusually harsh, most of the vessels which brought the hopeful Czech immigrants to Texas in the early years were definitely not comfortable or even, in many instances, safe. Ship brokers bought space aboard freighters going to the New World and, in turn, sold spaces to emigrants. Of course, the more people the agent could pack into each ship, the higher his profit. The ship owners made money, too, and in the 1850s they looked at the transportation of emigrants much as they would the transport of raw materials or manufactured goods.

The emigrant families were usually given space between the decks of a ship. The area was typically only about six feet in height with six-foot-square berths for living space. This confined space became almost unbearable when rough weather threatened and the hatches were battened down. The stench of squalid water and filth permeated the mid decks, and the area was unsanitary. Many became ill and many died. Julie Škarpa of Snook, Texas, gave this picture of shipboard conditions given her by her parents who came to Texas in 1855.

> The trip on the sailboat lasted three months. Terrible storms drove the ship off course and for an entire week it was continually crushed by the waves as by a nut cracker. Our poor immigrants suffered terribly from sea sickness and each and every moment fully expected the boat to be crushed by the waves. Their only comfort was reading the

[33] *Amerikán narodní kalendář* (1882), 142.

[34] Jan Habenicht, *Dějiny čechů amerických* (St. Louis, 1910), 79.

Kralice Bible [Czech Protestant Bible] and singing songs from the
Kancionál [Czech Brethren Hymn Book]. They were with few exceptions evangelicals, followers of our martyr, Master Jan Hus and the
Moravian Brethren. The food on board was very poor, mostly beans,
bacon, and worm-eaten biscuits instead of bread. The women would
break them open and pick out the worms before feeding them to
their families. They soaked them in a kind of soup made from brown
flour brought from home. Boiling water was poured on the flour and
the biscuits were then soaked in the "soup." How happy they were
when after three months of such suffering they finally reached Galveston.[35]

After the Civil War, conditions on ships began to improve mark-
edly. New ships were designed and built to carry primarily people
rather than cargo. With these improvements, the mortality rate of
those crossing dropped substantially.[36]

About two years after the Josef Šilar group came, a second group
from the same geographical area followed, lured by the same promise
of a better life. The leader was Josef Lešikar, whose wife had finally re-
lented and agreed to leave her troubled homeland. They sailed on the
German ship Suwa from Bremenshaven directly to Galveston, which
they reached a few days before Christmas, 1853. After a short rest in
Galveston, they bought supplies in Houston and proceeded to the Cat
Spring area on foot and by wagon. The most favorable route from the
Czech lands to Texas was now established, and it was used by most of
the Czech immigrants, including groups of Moravians by 1856, in the
following decades.

The earliest groups of immigrants did not found true Czech colonies. Instead, they dispersed among the German settlers around Cat
Spring and nearby New Bremen, New Ulm, and other small Austin
County settlements. Their first priority was to build primitive huts or
cabins for shelters; their second was to buy or rent available land in order to prepare for planting. As William P. Hewitt notes, almost all of
the early emigrants left their European homes in the fall, after harvest
time, hoping to arrive in Texas in time for spring planting.[37]

Czech settlers in Texas remained relatively isolated up until the
time of the Civil War. Overall, the density of the Czech population
was simply not sufficient to support a large, well-organized ethnic
community. The total Czech population in Texas was well under 1,000

[35] *Amerikán narodní kalendář* (1924), 280.

[36] Hewitt, 30.

[37] Hewitt, 47.

until the 1870s, and individual families tended to be somewhat scattered. Neither Czech Protestants nor Catholics had organized stable congregations by the time of the war, and Czech-American schools were only beginning to be organized. No formal Czech "ethnic" organizations existed.[38] On the other hand, the Czechs maintained their European culture and were acculturated into the majority society only in economic terms: almost invariably they sought to accumulate capital and buy farm land.[39]

In spite of the general isolation of family groups, a few real Czech colonies were founded before the war. By 1860, Fayette County was the home of the Czech settlements of Dubina, Bluff (Hostýn), and Mulberry (Praha), and the Anglo and German settlement of Fayetteville was fast becoming a Czech town. A few settlements, such as Wesley in Washington County and Novohrad in Lavaca County, also had distinctively Czech identities.

The Civil War affected the small Texas Czech community in important ways. First, the Union blockade of Texas ports prevented further European immigration from 1861 to 1866. The only net increase from the 700 present in 1861 was from within the community.

Second, the war presented those Czechs already living in Texas with a dilemma. Should they join in the fighting, and if they did, on which side? In general, the Czechs did serve, but they did not volunteer for army duty in large numbers. Only about 40 Czechs served in the Confederate Army.[40] Most Czechs preferred to join the state troops and militia; do their three-to-six months duty, usually within the state; and be through with it. Some, however, did see active duty in Tennessee and other theatres of the Civil War.

One of these was Peter Mikeška:

"In our company there were eleven Czechs and Moravians and of these, as far as I know, four are still alive: V. Votýpka, J. Kruhlík, P. Slováček. On the 9th of August we left Washington County and went to the state of Mississippi. Two months later, we went to Vicksburg for a week and then to Holly Springs. We got our weapons in Jackson. The Yankees made us retreat from Holly Springs and then we had our first battle at Green Woods. A Czech from our company, Ignác Šiller, died there. A musket ball tore off his leg."[41]

[38] A few of the Czechs joined the Cat Spring Agricultural Society, which had been organized by Rev. Bergman in 1856 for the practical purpose of improving the settlers' farming methods. Most members were German.

[39] Hewitt, 70-71.

[40] Hewitt, 96.

[41] *Amerikán narodní kalendář* (1907), 258.

Many Czechs simply tried to ignore the war and the state's desire that they serve. This proved to be a poor strategy, however, because the Confederacy needed manpower, and it and the state of Texas conscripted any man of age 18-50 who was not classified as a temporary alien. Most Czech heads of households were eligible for conscription. The case of Ignác Křenek illustrates the uneasy situation in which many Czechs found themselves.

> He and his son were hauling their cotton to the gin. . . . On the way the conscription officers caught him and despite his pleas took him away, leaving the ten-year-old boy with the wagon and five pairs of oxen. Thanks to the help of a conscientious soldier, the boy got home. Křenek was taken to Columbus (Colorado County) where he was imprisoned for fourteen days. There were other countrymen there, too, who had suffered the same fate. With one, Křenek brought up the possibility of a mutual escape. He would not even listen to Křenek's offer for fear of being caught and shot. Therefore, Křenek decided to try it alone. Early in the morning he crawled outside with his shoes in hand and a blanket under his arm and ran into the streets of Columbus aiming at the brush on the bank of the Colorado River which separated him from home. Without a moment's thought he jumped into the water and happily swam across the river. He ran all day through the forests so as to escape recapture. When he got to Countryman Adamek's farm, he spotted a group of riders bearing down on the farm at full gallop. Křenek quickly hid. By evening, worn out and hungry, he arrived home. He had to hide seventeen weeks, however, before he could be seen in public.[42]

Antonin Štupl and his three brothers "went AWOL" after serving in the Texan outfit guarding Galveston. They took refuge at a "countryman's" farm and on one occasion used a Czech delicacy, garlic, to throw the dogs of the conscription officers off their trail.[43]

Some Czechs used their abilities as teamsters to avoid conscription and to profit financially at the same time. Confederate cotton was much needed as an income producer for the rebel states. Since the Union Navy had blockaded the southern Gulf Coast, the cotton had to be shipped to Mexico by wagon. The pay was good, 10¢ per transported pound, and often the teamsters were paid in gold. The method of payment was an extra bonus because the value of Confederate dollars decreased drastically during the war. In addition, teamsters were officially exempted from military service. It was the good fortune of many Czechs to live

---

[42] *Amerikán narodní kalendář* (1897), 200-201.
[43] *Amerikán narodní kalendář* (1892), 201.

around an important juncture of this Confederate life-line in Fayette County. There the railroad lines stopped and the slow, treacherous wagon journey -to Matamoros, Mexico, began.[44] Although Czechs avoided military duty this way, travel south was not without danger, and some of them died while on these trips to Mexico.

The painful family divisions brought about by the Civil War in many American families were duplicated in a few Czech families. Josef Lidiak, after coming from Moravia and settling in Hostýn, enlisted in Martindale's Company of the Confederate Army. In 1863 his son, Jan, went to Mexico with a friend hauling cotton. While in Brownsville, he met some friends who talked him into joining the Union side. He served in Hammett's Company, First Texas Cavalry, United States Army.[45]

Another example involved young Josef Šilar, the same boy who had been lost in the New Orleans hospital. He joined the Texas state forces and was used to help capture runaways. This situation led to a family confrontation.

I was in Brown's Company, and our duty was to catch all 'conscripts,' that is, men who were called to duty but ran away. Among the runaways were most often found Czechs for their wives did not want them to leave home and family for the war. They didn't have anything to fight for. They weren't afraid of losing their freedom, and they didn't have any slaves. These conscripts usually hid in the forests to which we were sent to search for them. Our company was stationed about two miles from my uncle's house. I knew that he was in the forest and where he was hiding. Since I had not seen him for a long time, I went to visit him. When I arrived at his farm, it was evening and he had just come out of the forest. He asked me in the usual way what I was doing and when he found out he said, 'I am a conscript too — What are you going to do with me?' I answered, 'Dear Uncle, let me stay with you overnight because I have not seen you for a long time. In the morning, I'll return to my company and to my duty, searching for conscripts. If we find you Uncle, I can't help, we'll have to take you to camp.' Uncle answered, 'Well, stay here the night, Son, and tomorrow go do your duty. As for me, be assured that I will not let you catch me.' The next day we were sent for him but couldn't find him.[46]

[44] Hewitt, 94-96.
[45] Hewitt, 93-94.
[46] *Amerikán narodní kalendář* (1882), 143-44.

Šilar's war experience was atypical of most Texas Czechs', but then his whole life was. Immediately after settling in Industry, his father sent him to live with an American family. Later, Josef worked for an American slave owner; he finally became a lawyer in Eagle Lake. It is unfortunate that the war set him against one of his few remaining relatives, for his mother and father had died shortly after arriving in Texas. Šilar does not describe his relationship with his uncle after the war.

Czech women and children suffered greatly during the war. An already hard life was made worse by the absence of a husband or son of working age. Czech women were used to doing farm work, but not the heaviest labor. In addition, the shortage of all consumer goods made it doubly hard to feed and clothe a family. Some wives were forced to defend their homes and families from renegades and outlaws, who preyed especially on "foreigners," while their husbands were away.

The Czech community in Texas grew only slightly during the war years, but once peace—and the flow of Czech immigration—were restored, it began to expand rapidly.

CHAPTER 2

Movement and Growth

The Bohemian farmers have given Texas her
great agricultural industries and have been
largely responsible for her rapid development.
—Lee Roy Hodges, writing in
The Texas Magazine (June 1912)

THE SPREAD ACROSS TEXAS

Fewer than 800 foreign-born Czechs lived in Texas in 1870, but at about that time a crescendo of new Czech immigration began.[1] As Table 2 indicates, the net gain of foreign-born during the period 1891-1910 was about 12,000. It is more difficult to measure the number of second- or third-generation Texas Czechs, but, beginning in 1910, the U.S. Census figures are somewhat more helpful. The 1910 census listed the number of "foreign white stock" identified by the language spoken in the country of origin of the parents: over 41,000 for Czech.[2]

[1] See William Philip Hewitt, *The Czechs in Texas: A Study of the Immigration and the Development of Czech Ethnicity, 1850-1920.* PhD Dissertation, The University of Texas at Austin (1978), 104. Figures are based on United States Department of Commerce, Bureau of the Census, *Eighth Census of the United States: 1860,* Population Schedules for Austin, Colorado, Fayette and Washington Counties; *Ninth Census of the United States: 1870,* Volume I, Statistics of the Population of the United States, Table VI, 337; *Tenth Census of the United States: 1880,* Volume I, Population of the United States, Table XIII, 492; *Eleventh Census of the United States: 1890,* Population of the United States, Table XXXII, 608; *Twelfth Census of the United States: 1900,* Abstract of the Twelfth Census of the United States, Table 49, 59.

[2] For Foreign Born White as well as Foreign White Stock see United States Department of Commerce, Bureau of the Census, *Thirteenth Census of the United States: 1910,* Volume I, General Report and Analysis, Table 15, 981.

"Foreign white stock" could indicate a foreign-born individual or a son or daughter of at least one foreign-born parent. This number, then, which had grown to almost 50,000 by 1920, excludes later generations, and is not a precise count of the number of Texas Czechs.[3] No comparable figures were collected in 1930, but the 1940 census included a "foreign-white-stock" category which more clearly reveals the total number of Czech speakers. The mother tongue was defined as the "principal language spoken in the home at earliest childhood" and did not exclude later generations whose first language was Czech in its total of 62,680.[4]

The mother tongue census figures raise a question concerning the actual number of foreign-born Czech inhabitants of Texas. The United States census figure for those who gave their birthplace as "Czechoslovakia" in 1920 is 12,819.[5] However, in the same year, the number of those who were foreign-born and stated that their mother tongue was "Bohemian" or "Moravian" was 14,871,[6] a difference of

[3] United States Department of Commerce, Bureau of the Census, *Fourteenth Census of the United States: 1920*, Volume II, General Report and analytical Tables, Table 10, 1001.

[4] United States Department of Commerce, Bureau of the Census, *Sixteenth Census of the United States: 1940*, Nativity and Parentage of the White Population. Mother Tongue by Nativity, Parentage, Country of Origin and Age for States and Large Cities, Table 2, 20. As noted in the "Introduction," the number of Slovaks in Texas has always been relatively small, but population data concerning this related ethnic group may be of interest to the reader. For 1910, the United States Bureau of the Census gives the foreign-born Slovak population in Texas as 305. By 1920, it had climbed to 833 (General Report and Analytical Tables, Vol. II, Population, Table 7, 984.) The "foreign-white-stock" figures for the Slovaks are 867 in 1930 and 940 (a surprisingly low figure) in 1940. See the *Sixteenth Census of the United States: 1940*, Nativity and Parentage of the White Population. Mother Tongue by Nativity, Parentage, Country of Origin and Age for States and Large cities, Table 2, 20.

[5] United States Department of Commerce, Bureau of the Census, *Fourteenth Census of the United States: 1920*, Volume II, General Report and Analytical Tables, Table 6, 698.

[6] For 1920 Foreign Born White and Foreign White Stock, see United States Department of Commerce, Bureau of the Census, *Fourteenth Census of the United States: 1920*, Volume II, General Report and Analytical Tables, Table 10, 1001.

over 2,000. This discrepancy can perhaps be explained in three ways. First, Czechs emigrating from Europe did not all go to America, and some of those who went first to other countries later came to Texas. Also, there were substantial Czech enclaves in several European countries. The 1910 census shows that numerous individuals who indicated Czech as their mother tongue did not come directly from the Czech lands: 370 came from Germany, 46 from Hungary, and 36 from Russia.[7] All of these settled in the "West South Central" portion of the United States and were, no doubt, ethnic Czechs. (Unfortunately, these figures are not further broken down into numbers for individual states.) Finally, before the creation of the Czechoslovak Republic, undoubtedly some Czechs were counted as "Austrians" by immigration officials. The main point is that a more accurate count of foreign-born Czech Texans is given by the mother tongue figures of the 1910, 1920, 1930, and 1940 censuses than by the simple category "born in Bohemia."[8]

These figures indicate the magnitude of the Czech immigration into Texas and suggest the vitality of the Texas Czech community, as measured by the number of Czech speakers, up to the time of World War II. They do not, however, describe the internal movement of Czechs within the state nor the location and density of their settlements.

TABLE 2

Population Levels of Czech Ethnics in Texas

	Number of Foreign Born	Number of Foreign White Stock
1860	700	
1870	780	
1880	2,669	
1890	3,209	
1900	9,204	
1910	15,074	41,080
1920	14,871	49,929
1930	11,093	
1940	7,700	62,680

[7] United States Department of Commerce, Bureau of the Census, *Thirteenth Census of the United States: 1910*, Volume I, General Report and Analysis, Table 13, 978.

[8] See notes 2, 3, and 4 above.

Czech immigrants and their descendants settled Texas in a fairly well-defined pattern. The first groups poured into Austin County, but, very soon, large numbers of Czech families were moving west and south, particularly into Fayette, Lavaca, and Washington counties. These counties provided "seed" colonies during the early years. The newly-arrived immigrants before and shortly after the Civil War invariably came to one of these four counties to find friends, relatives, or, at least, someone who could speak Czech. They found sympathy and support in the midst of a strange, new world. After becoming somewhat acclimated to Texas, they either bought land nearby or moved on, usually northeast into Central Texas, establishing either new Czech communities or enclaves of Czechs in and around previously established towns.

The great majority of the approximately 250 Texas Czech communities that had been settled by the early twentieth century lay within the two comparatively fertile Blackland Prairie soil regions of Texas. The most concentrated cluster of communities was found in the southern-most strip, in an area running northeast from Lavaca County through Fayette and the eastern part of Austin County, and into Washington County, with a finger running northward into Burleson before trailing off in Brazos County. Running roughly parallel to and above this strip was a wider and more extensive strip of Blackland Prairie, where Czech communities could be found more loosely grouped in a line running northeast from Williamson, through Bell, into McLennan Counties, with smaller, more isolated groupings northward in Hill, Ellis, and Kaufman Counties. Most of the remaining Czech communities lay in the Coastal Prairie region, with significant clusters in Wharton, Fort Bend, Victoria, and a few South Texas counties. It is evident that the Czechs systematically chose some of the finest soil in Texas for their farmland.

The pattern of Czech settlements after the Civil War can be directly related to the search for good, new farm land at a reasonable price. New immigrants as well as old settlers seeking more and better farming land moved to the north and west away from the old Austin and Fayette County colonies, as new immigration and the domestic birth rate led to an increased demand for land. Farm land that was selling for $5-$10 per acre just before the Civil War had increased to $10-$15 by the late sixties and early seventies.[9] Land could still be pur-

---

[9] See Hewitt, 115. Figures are based on Austin County Abstract of Titles, Books I-M.

chased for the old prices in counties such as Williamson, Bell, and Mc-Lennan. By the turn of the century, Czechs were moving as far west as Runnels County, where land was available for $2-$5 per acre.[10] Although many first-generation Texas Czechs moved two or three times (often remaining in the same general area), the movement was usually part of a larger pattern involving other Czechs, often individuals with kinship ties.

Since Henry Maresh's landmark article of 1946 about the Texas Czechs in the *Southwestern Historical Quarterly*, the "32 contiguous counties" he listed, from the Dallas-Fort Worth area down to Victoria and Calhoun Counties in the south, have been assumed to delineate the "Czech Belt" of Texas.[11] And it is true that at the turn of the century, the great majority of the more than 9,000 Czech-born Texans lived in these counties, with the largest concentration in Fayette County.[12] Even then, however, significant groups of Czechs were pushing into counties northwest, southeast, and west of those traditional ones. This chapter will describe in a general way the spread of Czech settlers through the original Central Texas counties and into Northwest, Southeast, and Southwest Texas. (See Map 4.) More inclusive and detailed information, including dates of settlements, names of prominent early settlers, and dates of early ethnically-related churches and fraternal organizations is given in Appendix B.

Austin County was of course the first to be settled by large numbers of Bohemian and Moravian immigrants. After the Šilar group came, the Lešikar group and others followed. In addition to the groups, some families came individually. All the early groups set out for Cat Spring soon after arriving in Texas; however, most of the families did not stay long in the vicinity. Ironically, the one town which can claim to be the birthplace of the Czech community in Texas was, by 1900, inhabited by only a few Czechs.[13] Even the leaders of the Czech immigration to Cat Spring eventually left: Šilar in 1852, Bergman in 1870. Within the county, the flow was first northwest and later southwest. Industry soon attracted settlers, as did Nelsonville. By 1876, Industry had both a Czech Catholic and a Brethren Church.

The towns of Sealy, Wallis, and Frýdek in the southeast part of Austin County also attracted Czech settlers, but not until the late

[10] Hewitt, 265.

[11] Henry R. Maresh, "The Czechs in Texas," *The Southwestern Historical Quarterly*, vol. 50 (1946), 238.

[12] See Hewitt, 256.

[13] Jan Habenicht, *Dějiny čechu amerických* (St. Louis, 1910), 77.

MAP 4

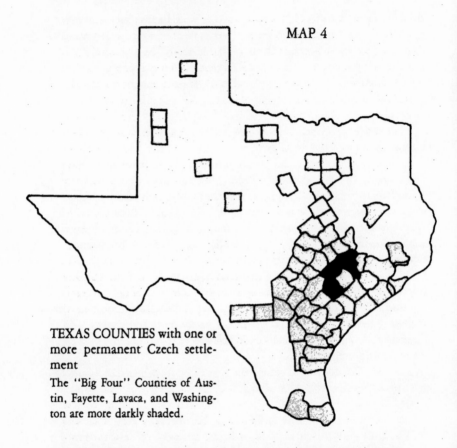

TEXAS COUNTIES with one or more permanent Czech settlement

The "Big Four" Counties of Austin, Fayette, Lavaca, and Washington are more darkly shaded.

1880s. In 1890 several Czech Catholic families left Hostýn and Dubina, in Fayette County, and settled about three miles northeast of a small train depot named Wallis Station, where the Santa Fe and San Antonio & Aransas Pass railroads intersected. Until that time, the land in this area had been used only as grazing land for cattle, but the Czechs began to break up the vast sea of grass and plant cotton. In 1892, a school named Krásná (Beautiful) and a Catholic fraternal society were established. By 1938, 300 families belonged to the Catholic parish at Wallis, only about 20 of which were not Czech.[14] North of Wallis is Frýdek, named for a town in Moravia from which many of the settlers came. The first known settler here was Josef Železník, who came from Jankovice in Moravia in the early 1850s. After at first hiding

[14] Národní svaz českých katolíků v Texasu, *Naše dějiny* (Granger, Tex., 1939), 461-78.

from the Confederate conscription bands, and then voluntarily serving in the Confederate Army, he settled down and urged his friend August Mlčak and his family from Roštění, Moravia to join him. By 1896 there were about 59 Czech families living around Frýdek.[15]

Czech settlers funneled through Austin County and spread northwest into Fayette County at an early date. Although it is unclear who the first Czech was to inhabit the county, Tomáš Hruška arrived in 1855 to find several Czech families already established there. Valentin Haidušek and Josef Petr, Sr., probably were the first Czechs to settle west of the Colorado River. As the tide of mostly Moravian settlers increased, predominantly Anglo and German communities were transformed into Czech communities. The first Czech Catholic priest to serve primarily Czechs in Texas came to Fayetteville in 1872. Rev. Josef Chromčík was literally following his congregation, the majority of which had left Moravia for Texas in 1870 and written letters which persuaded their priest to do likewise. By the turn of the century, there were 220 Moravian families in the church, the Czech Catholic school had enrolled 150 children, and several Catholic societies had been established.[16] Another 60 Czech families around Fayetteville at that time were claimed by the Brethren congregation, which had built a church in 1874. Still other Czech families were members of a local Presbyterian church served by a Czech pastor, Václav Pazdral.[17]

In 1856, the first Czech settler, Matěj Novák, arrived near the community of Mulberry. Other Czechs followed during the next decade, and the town was renamed Praha. Because of the town's name (Praha, or Prague, is the capital of Czechoslovakia) and its later importance to the Texas Czech community as a whole, Praha is called even today *"Matička Praha"* ("Mother Prague"). One of the largest and best-known annual Czech festivals is held there. About the same time that Novák came to Mulberry, Josef Janda and several other settlers from Trojanovice, Moravia, arrived in the community of Bluff. A Catholic church of logs was built in 1856 and a school in 1868.[18] These

---

[15] *Naše dějiny*, 178.

[16] Habenicht, 88.

[17] Habenicht, 88.

[18] See *Naše dějiny*, 242. According to this source, the teacher at the Bluff school, Terezie Kubalová, was the first Czech teacher in the United States. However, Josef Mašík was probably teaching in a home in Wesley as early as 1859 and may have been the first Czech teacher in the United States. According to Estelle Hudson and Henry R. Maresh, in *Czech Pioneers of the Southwest* (Dallas, 1934), Mašík's place in history as the first "has been authoritatively established" (172).

settlers were followed by many others, and eventually Bluff became Hostýn, named after a Moravian town. Similarly, the town of Navidad, on the banks of Navidad Creek, became Dubina (Oak Grove), named by Valentin Haidušek. Many other Fayette County towns were either founded or heavily settled by Czechs in the nineteenth century, although La Grange, the county seat, did not attract many of them, and by 1900 only about twelve Czech families lived there.[19]

Overall, Fayette County deserves its reputation as the "cradle" of Czech settlement in Texas. Although Jan Habenicht's estimate of over one thousand Czech (mostly Moravian) families in the county at the turn of the century may be an exaggeration, Fayette very early became the most populous Texas county for the Czechs, and from here Czech immigrants fanned out all over Central Texas as the search for more desirable farm land continued.[20]

The first Czech reported to have settled in Lavaca County was Alois Klimiček, a Moravian from Frenštát who had lived two years in Fayette County, in 1858. By 1880, there were about 400 Czech families in Lavaca County; twenty years later, there were about 900.[21] The county seems to have been informally divided into two sectors. In his study of the schools of Lavaca County, Theodore Leslie notes that Kopecký School was sometimes called "Boundary Line School" because it was "located on the dividing line between the farming community to the north, owned by German and Bohemian people, and the ranching country to the south owned by Anglo-American people."[22]

Halletsville, the county seat, was not heavily settled by Czechs before 1900, although two important Texas Czech newspapers — *Nový domov* and *Obzor* — were there by the 1890s. Other Lavaca County towns, however, were predominantly Czech. In the 1930s, 425 of the 500 families in the Catholic church at Shiner were Czech. Several Texas Czech priests received their early education at Shiner's St. Ludmila Academy, which was renowned for its Czech language program.[23]

[19] Habenicht, 97.

[20] Habenicht, 85. Habenicht's population figures are generally higher than those given by the United States Census. One reason is that he included in his totals all Czech ethnic families of European and Texas birth. Also, he consistently overestimates rather than underestimates when there is some doubt. Nevertheless, his figures can be used as a rough estimate of the size of the Texas Czech communities.

[21] Habenicht, 102.

[22] Theodore H. Leslie, *The History of Lavaca County Schools*. Masters Thesis, The University of Texas at Austin (1935), 355.

[23] Ludmila is a popular Czech saint.

And several Lavaca County towns have Czech names: Moravia, Novohrad, Komenský, Bilá Hora, Vsetín. Both Bilá Hora and Vsetín were founded by Czech Protestants in about 1876.[24]

Washington County is sometimes considered one of the "Big Four" Texas Czech Counties, along with Austin, Fayette, and Lavaca, not for its total population of Czechs but because it began attracting Czech settlers about as early as the other three. It also has a special significance for Czech Protestants, who began moving to the area around Wesley about 1860. (The name is derived from the Czech *veselý*, which means "happy.") Rev. Josef Opočenský founded an independent Brethren church there in about 1864. Meanwhile, the nearby communities of Latium and Greenvine began to attract Czech settlers.[25] Only a few Czechs settled in the city of Brenham, but they included Rev. Adolf Chlumský, who began to print the Brethren newspaper *Bratrské listy* there in 1902. By the turn of the century, about 250 Czech families lived in Washington County.[26]

At about the same time, Colorado County already had about 400 Czech families and Burleson County had about 500, although the Czech population of these two counties had not been significant until the late 1870s.[27] The case of Josef Labaj and his friends is typical of the more successful Texas Czech farmers during this period of expansion. With his wife and five sons, he bought 1,500 acres of open prairie on the right bank of the Colorado River, near Nada, Colorado County, for $6.40 an acre in 1882. Closely following him were the families of Florian Frnka, Josef Blinka, Martin Hejda, and Martin Holčak, all of whom bought as much land as they could farm from Labaj. Within two years, all owned their land free and clear. The names of Czech villages founded in Burleson County around 1870 are especially interesting: Nový Tabor, Šebesta (later Snook), Frenštát. Tabor in Bohemia is an ancient Hussite city dear to Czech Protestants, Šebesta is a common family name in Moravia, and Frenštát is a city in northeast Moravia from which many emigrated to Texas.

Other Central Texas counties with significant Czech populations by the turn of the century are Bastrop, Lee, Brazos, Milam, William-

---

[24] Habenicht, 105.
[25] *Naše dějiny*, 290.
[26] Habenicht, 111.
[27] Habenicht, 116, 118.

son, Bell, Falls, McLennan, Hill, Ellis, Dallas, Kaufman, and Tarrant. Of these, Williamson is probably the most important, with about 350 families.[28] The city of Taylor saw its first Czech in 1870, but by 1900 the Czech influence was prominent. One of the first Czech settlers describes the process:

> The first Czech business in Taylor was opened on the 15th of September, 1889, under the name of Šťastný and Holub. These two countrymen had at first worked in other businesses in Taylor as salesmen and then founded their own store, which finally went out of business in 1936. Josef Šťastny and Frank Holub were the first countrymen in Taylor. At that time Taylor was just a small town, the street often impassable due to the rain. It often happened that on Main Street a wagon got stuck in the mud for several days. In the 80s, families of countrymen from other counties as well as from Europe began to move to Taylor. Among them were Josef Šafařík; Josef Kašpar; Jan Urbanek, who came here as a bachelor; Jan Zycha with his family; Frank Čuba; and many others. They all settled around Taylor and of the above mentioned only Jan Urbanek is still alive [in the late thirties]. Countrymen Matěj Holub and Zelinka owned a tavern in town for a long time. . . . Now the countrymen in Taylor and the surrounding area occupy prominent positions and are held in respect.[29]

Granger, also in Williamson County, has been one of the "most Czech" of Texas towns. As late as 1938 there were over 200 children of Czech descent in the Catholic school and all reportedly were fluent in the Czech language.[30] In 1919, a bank was founded there, with Jan Bača as president, I. C. Parma, treasurer, and Vilém Bartoš, assistant treasurer, which regularly advertised itself as *vaše česká banka* ("your Czech bank") in Czech-language periodicals.

Turn-of-the-century Milam County had about 300 Czech families, Bastrop about 250, and Brazos about 200.[31] One of the more important Czech towns is West, in McLennan County, and it will be discussed in some detail in Chapter 7. Also important is Ennis, located in Ellis County, famous today in Texas, and even in Czechoslovakia, for its annual Polka Festival. Only a few Czechs lived in the large cities of Dallas and Fort Worth at the turn of the century, though their numbers increased fairly rapidly after about 1910. One of the earliest

---

[28] Habenicht, 120.
[29] Quoted in *Naše dějiny*, 445.
[30] *Naše dějiny*, 204.
[31] Habenicht, 420, 125, 118. *Naše dějiny*, 48.

Czechs in Fort Worth had a very unusual background. After serving as an officer in Maximillian's army in Mexico, August Lebeda returned to his native Bohemia, married, and came to Texas in the 1870s, eventually settling in Fort Worth, where he worked as a saddle maker. He then moved to Mexico City, where he owned a hotel, and after moving back to Fort Worth, he bought the Southern Hotel. He died in Fort Worth in 1915.

In the late 1800s and early 1900s, Czech farming communities were established in several North Texas counties, separated from the contiguous body of counties in the North-Central region. The Czechs who came to these communities were "enticed" *(lákat* is the word used by the Czechs) there by sales agents working for land companies. Some of these land companies were owned by Czechs. In 1905 John Přibyla, John Tobola, Frank J. Novák, and J. R. Čoček purchased 1,476 acres of land for $9.00 an acre in Baylor County to resell. Advertisements for Baylor County land in the Czech-language newspaper *Svoboda* had begun to appear with increasing frequency by 1907. One land agent using this medium to sell land was J. J. Hanuš. Hanuš was born in Moravia and immigrated to Bryan, Texas, in 1882 with his parents. By 1907 he had started to sell land in Baylor County. The J. H. Kohut Land Company was active in Baylor County, too. This company offered railroad trips every week from Waco to Baylor County, where it sold land in 80-, 160-, and 320-acre plots for $16.00 to $20.00 an acre. Similar rail trips were offered to Haskell and Jones counties.[32]

A note of frustration enters many of the accounts by and about the Czechs in these communities for, after all, the soil and climatic conditions were different from those of Central Texas and, obviously, from those of Eastern Europe. A large proportion of the Czech farmers who moved to these new communities quickly became disillusioned and moved back to more traditional Czech farming areas.

Czechs moved to Wichita, Wilbarger, Archer and Baylor counties on the Texas-Oklahoma border as early as the 1880s. A typical comment on the conditions met by Czech settlers in extreme North Texas comes from Bomarton in Baylor County. The writer laments,

> The community of St. John of Nepomuk in Bomarton celebrated in 1936 its silver anniversary. How our people have been tried in that

---

[32] Hewitt, 280-83. Information concerning Czech communities located in Haskell and Jones counties is sketchy or unavailable.

time, how their hopes have been crushed! After the great rains of
1908-1909 the land owners enticed us here. Our countrymen from
counties in South Texas and also from the old country listened to
their appeals. The head land agent was named Bomar and his community took the name Bomarton. The Wichita Valley railroad track
was built between Wichita Falls and Abilene. Soon there were about
60 families here but, alas, they realized that they had settled on arid
soil, not favorable for farming.

Our pioneers had to endure hardships about which today's generation have no idea. Only after many years of work and toil have the
majority of our people rid themselves of debt.[33]

However, those Czechs who stayed, survived and carried on their
traditions. Into the 1930s and even later, church services were in both
Czech and English, and both languages were used in the parish school.
The traditions survived, and some settlers eventually did well financially:

Our people settled the Seymour area for the same reason as those in
Bomarton and Megargel—the land agents of the rich owners enticed
them there. Rev. Karel Dvořák has described it very nicely in one of
his poems.

Our countrymen lived through the hard years, however, and
those who held out are doing well because of it, maybe better than
many of those who moved to the south, because this sandy land is
fertile enough.[34]

The first settler in Seymour, and in all of Baylor county, was Antonín
Mocek, who came from Hostýn, Texas, in 1907. By 1910 there were
about 30 Czech families in Seymour.

Other important Czech farming communities were founded in
Wichita, Wilbarger, Archer, Scurry, Hockley and Lamb Counties.
Farmers also began to settle in Runnels County in the early 1890s after
many cattlemen had gone bankrupt and sold their ranches to land
companies. At this time Czech and German farmers began to buy
farms in the area, especially around Rowena and Ballinger. One of the
first was Jan Žák, from Williamson County.[35]

In September of 1896, Mrs. Mary Baron of Williamson County
bought a section (640 acres) of land from the Nichols Land and Cattle
Company. The price was $2,700 for land with a Sante Fe rail line run-

---

[33] Quoted in Naše dějiny, 42. (Authors' trans.)
[34] Quoted in Naše dějiny, 418. (Authors' trans.)
[35] Naše dějiny, 383.

ning through it. Her husband, P. J. Baron, had gone bankrupt in Granger and, probably for this reason, negotiations to buy the land were made through his wife. He had been a land agent, cotton buyer, merchant, rancher, and trader after emigrating from his native Moravia to Texas with his family. Now he wanted a chance to strike it rich. He founded the town of Baronsville, which was renamed Rowena in 1904. His slogan was "Come West and Prosper. Your Opportunity is Here." He sold land to many Czech and German settlers from Central Texas, including Rev. Adolph Chlumský of Brenham, who bought two blocks of downtown Baronsville for a grand total of $10.00. Others bought farms in Baron's section of land and some, like Jan Martinec, František Šimek and Josef Červenka of Williamson County, bought land directly from the Nichols Land and Cattle Company. It was Baron, though, that caused the area to attract more and more Czech and German farmers. As in other counties outside Central Texas, the cheap price of unbroken land was the magnet which drew Czechs to Runnels County.[36]

The Czech community prospered. The post office was named for Jan Bolf, who settled in Baronsville in 1900 after coming to Texas from Horní Bečva, Moravia, and worked as a land agent. In 1904 Rev. Chlumský established a Brethren church, and six years later, a competing Moravian-Bohemian Presbyterian Church was organized with 22 Czechs as founding members. In 1922 the Czech Catholic community had grown to the point that a Czech priest, Rev. F. J. Pokluda, was sent to Rowena.[37] By 1910, 360 Czechs were listed as living in Runnels County in the U.S. Census; 209 of these were Texas-born but their parents had been born in Europe. There were so many Czechs in Runnels County that they defeated attempts to make the country "dry" until 1911.[38]

An anomaly in the pattern of the spread of Czechs across Texas in search of farmland is to be found in the two North Texas counties of Erath and Palo Pinto. Apparently, the coal mines of Thurber in Erath County and Lyra in Palo Pinto County drew Bohemian miners sometime around the turn of the century. They soon established a local fraternal lodge and maintained their own Sunday School, which was intended not only for religious education but also for teaching the children about their Czech heritage.[39]

[36] See Hewitt, 259-70.
[37] *Naše dějiny*, 384.
[38] See Chapter 5, note 20.
[39] Josef Buňata, *Pamatník Čechoslováků* (Rosenberg, Tex., 1920), 157.

The initial thrust of Czech settlement in Texas in the years following the Civil War was undoubtedly north from the Big Four Czech
Counties of Austin, Washington, Fayette, and Lavaca. The counties
immediately north of these were settled beginning in the 1860s and
1870s. By the late 1890s, however, significant numbers of Czechs in
the central Texas counties were looking for new, fertile land. The ever-
increasing price of land in Central Texas (due to the increasing population) became almost prohibitive for new immigrants and posed a considerable barrier to existing landowners and future second- and third-
generation farmers in either buying farms of their own or increasing
their holdings. Many sharecroppers longed to become landowners. For
landowners, the memory of peasant holdings in Europe that had been
divided and subdivided so many times that one could sometimes literally jump over the several furrows of plowed ground that represented
the width of one's farm land was a disquieting one. While some
looked north and west to the new areas being opened up by the land
speculators, others turned south and east. The counties of Fort Bend,
Wharton, and Waller which were adjacent to the earliest settled Czech
counties, and Matagorda, Brazoria, Galveston, Liberty, and Harris,
which were further east, began to witness the establishment of Czech
communities in the 1890s.

In 1896 František and Jan Buček, along with other Czechs from
Lavaca County, came to look for new farm land in Wharton County.
They bought several hundred acres near Hungerford, and other
Czechs soon followed them. Crops were very poor for the first few
years because of excessive rainfall, but gradually, the farmers' lot improved. By 1938 there were 80 Czech Catholic families in a church
where only the Latin and Czech languages were used in services.[40] East
Bernard was also established in the late 1890s. Despite some pressure
from the local unit of the Ku Klux Klan, which was opposed to the influx of "foreigners," especially Catholics,[41] the Czech community
prospered there. Beginning in 1901, Czechs began to settle around
Needville, in neighboring Fort Bend County, and about ten years

---

[40] *Naše dějiny,* 265.

[41] The Klan experienced a revival in the 1920s and directed its revived energy not only at Blacks but Jews, Catholics and East Europeans as well. The
East Bernard Klan was alarmed by the vitality of the Czech-Catholic community and its ambitious building and educational program. Tensions rose to the
point that Czech men felt they had to carry guns wherever they went. Thanks
to the local constable, the crisis was resolved without bloodshed. See *Naše
dějiny,* 105.

later, Czechs began to buy unbroken prairie land near Rosenberg, the county seat.[42]

The Gulf Coast counties of Matagorda and Brazoria attracted Czech settlers still later, as the movement eastward to the coast continued. A group of Czechs began buying unbroken land in an isolated area known as Damon Mound in 1913.[43] A second Czech community began on the open Gulf Coast prairie in 1920 when several Czech families settled around Danbury and began farming. Soon the Czech Catholic community established a church but had no regular priest. The Czechs were surprised and pleased when Rev. C. Zoepfchen, a German, first held a mass in their new church and asked them to join him in singing *"Tisíckrát pozdravujeme tebe,"* a traditional Czech hymn. "Then tears came to everyone's eyes for indeed up until that time they had not heard a word of Czech from the mouth of a priest."[44] On the other hand, several of the families in the Iowa Colony area, settled by Czechs in the late 20s and 30s, were "freethinkers."[45] Bay City in Matagorda County attracted Czechs in 1925, as did Blessing in the late 1920s. By 1938, over 150 Czech families resided in Blessing alone.

The admonition to avoid Galveston, "that Texas graveyard," issued after the earliest group of Czechs came to Texas was, for the most part, heeded until about the turn of the century.[46] Hugo Chotek's story *Zahuba města Galveston* describes the fictional lives of several Czech families living in the city during the 1900 hurricane. Some Czechs began to work on the docks about 1910. At any rate, a local lodge of the popular Catholic women's fraternal KJZT was not established until 1936.[47]

Harris County had an established Czech community in Crosby by 1912 when I. P. Křenek moved there from Fayette County and found Josef Volčík, F. J. Morávek, Josef Siročka, Karel Machala, Josef Franta, Jan Kristíník, a certain Šťastný, and a man named Clawson who spoke Czech and apparently considered himself Czech.[48] By 1914, when a

---

[42] *Naše dějiny*, 372.

[43] *Naše dějiny*, 87.

[44] Quoted in *Naše dějiny*, 90. (Authors' trans.)

[45] Apparently there were some clashes between local freethinkers and Catholics. See *Naše dějiny*, 275.

[46] *Naše dějiny*, 494.

[47] *Naše dějiny*, 191.

[48] *Naše dějiny*, 81.

Catholic church was built, about 15 or 16 Czech families were parish members. The Czech Brethren first organized a church in Crosby in 1913 with the aid of Rev. Barton.[49] The Czech community in Houston is difficult to describe because of its fragmentation, unlike the cohesiveness of Czech communities in rural areas or small towns. It is known, however, that by 1938 there were about 350 Czech Catholic families with membership in various churches around the city. Some Czechs came to Houston in the early 1900s; for example, Jakub Bujnoch, a shoemaker, moved there from Brenham in 1902. Others became artists, newspapermen, lawyers, doctors, and musicians. Of course, without the reinforcement of a number of other Czechs living nearby, many probably lost their Czech identity much earlier than did their fellow countrymen in the smaller communities. Significantly, *Naše dějiny* reports that some did not want to speak Czech or even identify themselves as Czech.[50]

The only Czech community in deep East Texas is found in Houston County around Lovelady and Crockett. A member of that community described its early years very well:

We came here in 1907 from Petrovice u Čermná, Bohemia. At that time there were five Czech families around Lovelady. They were František Křenek, Jan Slánina, Leopold Šupák, J. Janák, and Josef Farek. They were the first Czech settlers in this area, who came about three years sooner than we. With us came countrymen František and Josef Rosenbaum from Beroun, Bohemia.

When we came here there were coal mines which were being worked and that was a great advantage for us. Everyone found work in the mines, and many made good money.

The country here is hilly, and in the lowlands there is good, fertile soil. The first settlers bought land for $3.00 and $4.00 an acre but later they paid $8.00 and even $12.00 an acre, and later, $20.00 and even more.

In 1931 Rev. Weillot [a visiting priest] suggested that if we built a small church, he could come every two weeks. The members of the community immediately got to work and bought land in Crockett; now we have a pretty little church. But one thing is missing — a Czech priest.

The Czechs here number about 21 families and all are doing well. Most of us are farmers except František Snobela who has a shoe store in Lovelady and Josef Skalický who has a garage and gas station in Crockett. In our church we hear nothing in the Czech language.

[49] Hewitt, 241.
[50] *Naše dějiny*, 268.

Rev. Elias Holub from La Porte has visited us only about two times, but our countrymen are still holding to the faith well.[51]

The isolated Czech communities in Houston County can be compared to those in Erath and Palo Pinto counties, which also do not fit into the normal pattern of fairly rapid but well-defined expansion in search of more high-quality farmland. The Houston County settlements, although they developed into farming communities, were originally settled by Bohemian miners as were the two North Texas counties.

A number of Czech communities were established in South Texas. Some of these are relatively insignificant, made up of a very few families, while others are fairly large, rivaling in population and ethnic solidarity some of the better-known Czech communities in Central Texas. They were found in 21 counties west of Matagorda, Wharton, Colorado, Fayette, and Bastrop Counties. One of the older communities in this region is Svatá Anna Při Yoakum (St. Anne's) in DeWitt County. It was begun in 1886 after the Aransas Pass Railroad started serving the area. At that time land there sold for $6.00 to $8.00, a difficult deal to ignore for the Czechs in neighboring counties to the east.[52] Around the turn of the century, Bishop Forest of San Antonio learned that someone had willed several thousand acres of land in Karnes County, around Hobson and Karnes City, to the Church. When the land was put up for sale at a relatively cheap price, several Czech families eagerly bought farms and settled around these two towns. The local Czech population had reached about 200 families by the 1930s.[53] Significant Czech settlements also developed in Jackson, Bee, Live Oak, Victoria, Wilson, Karnes, Jim Wells, Nueces, and even as far south as Hidalgo and Cameron Counties, on the Mexican border.

The South Texas county most heavily settled by Czechs is Nueces, where nearly 400 lived by the 20s.[54] Settlement plans instigated by, and largely for, Czechs, are primarily responsible. By 1910 over 100 foreign-born Czechs lived in Nueces County in what was called the Bohemian Colony settlement. In 1904 Stanley L. Kostohryz had bought two tracts of land totaling over 7,000 acres. The next year, Kostohryz, who was born in Prague, had moved to Nueces County from his home in Wilbur, Nebraska, and started selling land, most of it to Czechs.

---

[51] Quoted in *Naše dějiny*, 296. (Authors' trans.)
[52] *Naše dějiny*, 423.
[53] *Naše dějiny*, 229.
[54] Hewitt, 298.

Plow used for clearing brush, designed by Tom Mrázek, Robstown, Texas.
— Photo courtesy of Mrs. Stacy Labaj, Granger, Texas.
Copy from University of Texas Institute of
Texan Cultures at San Antonio.

He eventually went back to Bohemia, never returning to the United States. His children, however, remained in Texas.[55] In 1905, Josef Oujezdský and his brother-in-law, Jan Brandejský from Bryan, came to Corpus Christi to look at land in the vicinity. Brandejský, who spoke German, gained the confidence of Frank Kress and other German farmers in the area and bought land from them in the hopes that he could encourage a large number of Czechs to settle there. He was disappointed; however, some, like Alois Čech, "Uncle" Hajný, and František Kocurek from Ellinger, Adolf Rohan from Yorktown, Fred Polašek and a Žežula from Granger, Jakub Koblížek from Cameron, and a few others, did come.

The main credit for helping the Czech community in and around Corpus Christi grow, however, apparently goes to Songin Folda and his son Lamar. Songin and others bought the "Kostohryz renč" (ranch), as it was known by 1920, renovated the dilapidated housing, and reworked the fields before renting them to Czechs. Later he sold land to Czechs. His son, Lamar, was called "adviser and friend to our countrymen."[56] Robstown also attracted Czechs, and Tom Mrázek moved there from Williamson County in 1907. Then came František and Stanislav Procházka from Fayette County and John Řektořík from Lavaca County. In 1909 Tom Staněk arrived from Williamson County, having driven a team of oxen the whole way. Staněk's action was unusual because, by the late nineteenth century, most settlers came by train. Time and time again, Czech accounts of the founding of settlements throughout Texas describe settlers arriving only after a railroad line had been laid into an area which had previously been only range land. The Czechs there did very well, aided by a special plow invented by the first settler, Tom Mrázek. The new plow enabled them to break the ground more efficiently after it had been laboriously cleared of brush.[57]

Czechs moved to Live Oak County between George West and Three Rivers after a ranch owner, George M. West, decided to divide his 30,000 acres into 80-acre tracts and sell them to Czech and Polish farmers. The first Czech to settle in Skidmore in Bee County was Josef Rusek, son of Ignác Rusek, the shipping line agent who had helped many of the early Czech immigrants find their way safely from Galves-

---

[55] Hewitt, 290-98.
[56] *Naše dějiny*, 79.
[57] *Naše dějiny*, 369.

Farm scene with early (steam-powered) tractors near Granger, Texas, ca. 1920. — Photo courtesy of Mrs. Stacy Labaj. Copy from University of Texas Institute of Texan Cultures at San Antonio.

ton to the Central Texas settlements. In a tragic accident, the younger Rusek was gored to death by a bull and did not live to see the Czech community there prosper.

At one time the land around Crystal City in Zavala County was hailed as a "new Czech community" but, as in other areas outside the principal Czech counties of Central Texas, many were soon disappointed and moved away:

> Even here [Crystal City], as to the majority of the other newer communities, our countrymen were enticed and quite a few came. Unfortunately, they did not find the paradise *[zemský raj]* which the land agents painted in their sales pitches. After some bitter experiences, one after the other moved away until only one was left, Josef Solanský, with his family and his married son Bedřich, who was for several years a supervisor on a big vegetable farm.[58]

Josef Solanský had come to Texas from Velké Karlovice in Moravia in 1906 as a young bachelor. After a year here he sent for his fiance and married her in Temple. They rented land near Cyclone, cleared it and, probably, would have stayed there but for František Hanák. In 1918, Hanák, working as a land agent, convinced Solanský to move to Crystal City. After first renting land, Solanský bought ten acres on which he raised vegetables. Others, like Václav Šramek, who moved from Kansas to Crystal City and then back to Kansas, did not do as well.[59]

The story was repeated in Frio County, around Dilley. In the 1920s, Jan Hruška and Jan Chupík from Temple; Valentin Sládeček from Flatonia; František Kuběna from Wied; and Josef Valíček, Josef Urban and Jan Merečka from Gonzales bought land in Frio County. Others moved there, too, but most soon left. Also, a syndicate from Dallas bought several thousand acres 16 miles from Dilley with plans to build a completely Czech community. Due to a drop in farm prices, however, the plan never materialized.[60] Del Rio, in Val Verde County, was founded by Anthony Dignowity's son František. He also became sheriff of Val Verde County. Czech families lived there in 1938, but never in any great numbers.[61]

Most of the Czech families in South Texas settled in groups, or at least in proximity to other Czechs; however, Matěj Novák of Goliad County, reported to the writers of *Naše dějiny: "Zde není Čech. Jsem zde sám s rodinou."* ("There are no Czechs here. I am here, alone,

---

[58] *Naše dějiny*, 125. (Authors' trans.)
[59] *Naše dějiny*, 82-83.
[60] *Naše dějiny*, 92.
[61] *Naše dějiny*, 92.

with my family.'')[62] Some Czechs did, however, live in Charo, about 19 miles from the Novák home at Goliad. The first Czech resident of San Antonio, and of Bexar County, was of course Anthony Dignowity, as described in Chapter 1. Although San Antonio was not heavily settled by Czechs, the city was important to Czech Catholics because the seminary St. John's was located there. In 1938, 12 Czech-American seminarians graduated from St. John's.[63]

WORLD WAR I AND BEYOND

The advent of World War I brought new challenges for all the Czech communities of Texas. Being "foreigners" in Texas presented problems to many ethnic groups in the state, but for the Czechs, the war also brought the opportunity to combine the desire for a free and independent Czech state with patriotism for their adopted country.

The Czechs' compulsion for joining organizations and clubs served them in good stead during this time. In the August 12, 1914, issue of *Osvěta americka*, (American Culture)[64] the editor called his readers' attention to the example set by Czech soldiers (fighting under the "yoke" of Austrian oppression) deserting *en masse* to the allies. Many Czech Texans responded to the editor's call for the American "branch" of the Czech nation to help their brothers in Europe.

The result of this and other articles, plus the contributions which began to flow in, triggered the creation of the *České narodní sdružení* (ČNS), the Czech National Alliance. The Texas division was first organized at the SPJST Convention in Galveston in 1916. At a public meeting, Vojta Beneš, a well-known Czech educator from Chicago, addressed the crowd, and representatives at the meeting returned to their individual communities to set up local chapters of the ČNS. The national headquarters was located in Chicago. A regional office for Texas was first located in Houston, but due to a lack of enthusiastic support there, the regional headquarters was moved to West, Texas, where the organization prospered. All the groups of the multifaceted Czech community put aside their differences to accomplish their task. Among the leaders were Augustin Haidušek, prominent statesman and editor of *Svoboda;* J. R. Kubéna, one of the founders of the SPJST; E. Bažant, a Texas Czech poet; Josef Tápal, editor of *Věstník;* A.J. Morris, editor of *Westské noviny;* J. R. Vilt, a Czech Presbyterian

---

[62] *Naše dějiny,* 192.

[63] *Naše dějiny,* 388.

[64] *Osvěta americká* (American Enlightenment) was a Czech-American periodical published in Omaha, Nebraska.

minister; Antonín Václav Tesař, editor of the Catholic newspaper *Nový domov;* and F. G. Kupec, editor of the Czech Brethren paper *Bratrské listy.*[65]

Because of such unity and support, the ČNS in Texas was a stunning success. In 1916, the local chapters raised $2,662.73; in 1917, $11,884.65; and in 1918, $78,214.93. The figures, added to separate Texas contributions sent directly to the national headquarters in Chicago, total almost $100,000.[66] These dollars were raised in a variety of ways. Speakers, including Czechs from the northern states like Beneš, travelled to the Czech towns and delivered patriotic speeches about freeing the homeland. Then, the hat would be passed, and almost everyone present gave what he could. The various local chapters also held "bazaars" to raise money. Farmers would donate bales of cotton to be auctioned. The buyers would then donate the bale previously bought.

The crowning achievement of the Texas region of the ČNS came in 1918 at the statewide bazaar held in Taylor, Texas. At this *Den Svobody* (Day of Liberty), which actually lasted November 20-22, the ČNS collected about $54,000. Virtually every local chapter of the 87 in Texas and the two in Louisiana participated in some way, by either sending donations or delegates with items to sell at the bazaar.[67]

Near the end of the war, the regional officers of the Texas branch commissioned Josef Buňata, a well-known Czech-American editor, to write a history of the Texas ČNS groups. This record, *Pamatník čechoslovaků,* published by the Narodní Podník in Rosenberg, Texas, is revealing not only for the information concerning the individuals from all over the state who contributed their time and money, but also in the group photographs of many of the members' local chapters. These pictures often evoke the loyalties felt by the participants. Frequently a United States flag is displayed, along with a flag depicting some feature associated with Czech nationalism, such as the ancient symbol of Bohemia, the rearing lion. Slogans on banners appeal to fighting men to come to the defense of the people: the ones in English call for the aid of the American people and democracy, the ones in Czech call for the liberation of the motherland. The photograph of the El Campo ČNS local features two posters urging Czechs to join the Czech Legion. One compares the modern warriors to the *Boží bojovníki* (warriors of God), or Hussite warriors of 400 years before. The banner design over

---

[65] See Buňata, 17-24.

[66] Buňata, 3.

[67] The two Czech communities in Louisiana were Lubuše and Kolin. Buňata, 135-37.

Č.N.S. local at Hallettsville, Texas. The banner on the left reads, "let's fulfill our American and Czech duty." The other, "For our independence, to the fight."   — Photo copied from *Památník Čechoslováků.*

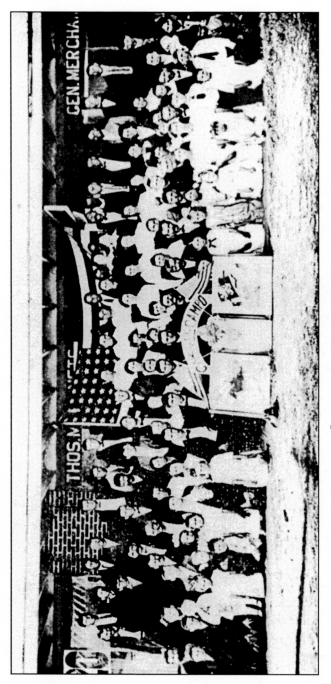

Č.N.S. local at El Campo, Texas.

— Photo copied from *Památník Čechoslováků.*

Č.N.S. local at Westhoff-Yorktown. The sign says, "Our goal is honorable and great. He who is against us is a traitor."

— Photo copied from *Památník Čechoslováků.*

Josef Buňata

— Photo copied from
Památník Čechoslováků.

the picture for the Westhoff-Yorktown local reads, *"Naš úkol čestný a velký jest. Kdo proti nám zradce jest."* ("Our goal is honorable and great. He who is against us is a traitor.") Prominently displayed in this photograph is a large American flag. In the Skidmore-Beeville photograph, an English language poster urges citizens to buy war bonds "to make the world a decent place to live in."[68]

Perhaps the most straightforward statement of the Czechs' loyalty to the two causes, which were definitely not seen as conflicting, is made in the photograph from Hallettsville: *"Konejme svoji americkou a Českou povinost [sic]"* ("Let's fulfill our American and Czech duty.")[69]

Indeed, Texas Czechs did fulfill what they saw as their Czech and American duty. Many enlisted in the United States Army and fought in some of the major engagements of the war, such as Verdun and Argonne. Some also served in the United States Navy. One was so anxious to get into the war that he went to Canada to enlist. Dominik Naplava was rejected by the United States Army because he was not a citizen. Therefore, he rode the train from Houston, where he lived with his brother, to Winnipeg, Canada, and joined the Canadian Army. On November 12, 1917, Naplava was killed by shrapnel in a German air attack, the first Texan to die in the war.[70]

Some Czech Texans felt they should serve the homeland in a more direct way, and they were given that opportunity. As the war progressed, more and more Czechs serving in the Austrian Army began to defect to the Allies. Since many leaders of the Czech nationalist movement had escaped from Austria and were living in Western Europe, they determined to establish a Czech government in exile. Tomáš Masaryk, who was to become the first President of Czechoslovakia after the war, and the other Czech leaders persuaded the Allies to let them form a Czech Legion composed of any Czechs who could make their way to Allied lines. Once the disgruntled Czechs in the Austrian Army got wind of this development, they deserted in droves. Whole divisions would simply abandon their positions and walk over to the "enemy." At first the Allies did not know what to do with them, but later, through the efforts of Masaryk and other Czech resistance leaders, the Czech Legion was formed. Most of the Legionnaires fought on the Eastern Front because of Austria's geographical proximity to Russia. Some, however, did see action alongside the French and English

---

[68] See Buňata, 131, 43, 47.

[69] Buňata, 82.

[70] See Hewitt, 308-309.

troops on the Italian and Western Fronts. The Czech Legion gave some Czech Texans the opportunity to serve in the armed forces of their soon-to-be liberated homeland. One was Jerry Baletka, whose Legion uniform is prominently displayed in the SPJST Museum in Temple, Texas.

After Russia made peace with Germany in 1918, that part of the Legion on the Eastern Front fought its way across Russia to Vladivostok, where it embarked for the Western Front which was half a world away. On their trip across America, they stopped in Houston and were received by a delegation of Czechs from the surrounding area.

Though Czech immigration to Texas was far below the pre-war levels in the twenties and thirties, as already seen, Czech nationalism in Texas remained a popular, emotional force until the time of World War II. American participation in the Second World War was, of course, widely supported by the Czechs in Texas. Again a popular Czech cause — the liberation of Czechoslovakia from Nazi domination — was in unison with American interests and goals. The forties, however, were to usher in an age of more rapid assimilation and the weakening of emotional ties with the European homeland. Chapter 7 will explore the assimilation of the Texas Czech and related issues in greater detail.

Even in the late 1930s, the overwhelming majority of Texas Czechs lived in rural areas, and the most recent immigrants continued to disperse into the network of small Czech-American farming communities rather than cluster in the cities. 8,630 foreign-born Czech farmers lived in rural areas in 1930. Another 1,765 held non-farming occupations in rural areas, while only 1,887 lived in the cities. The 1940 U.S. Census still classified 77% of the foreign-born Czechs as "rural."[71] It is not surprising that the social structure of the Texas Czechs was closely related to their system of agriculture, as the next chapter will show.

[71] United States Department of Commerce, Bureau of the Census, *Sixteenth Census of the United States: 1940*, Nativity and Parentage of the White Population. Mother Tongue by Nativity, Parentage, County of Origin and Age for States and Large Cities, Table 3, 31.

Anna Švadleňáková. Chosen queen of the ČNS Bazaar in Taylor, Texas, 1918.
— Photo copied from
Památník Čechoslováků.

Dr. Josef Kopecký. Born in Ruttersville, Texas, 1886. Joined U.S. Army in 1917. Sent to Siberia where he treated wounded American soldiers and Czech legionaires.
— Photo copied from *Pamätník Čechoslovāků.*

Dominik Naplava
— Photo copied from *Czech Pioneers of the Southwest.*

Jaromir Ulč from Galveston, Texas. Served in the 22nd division of the Czech Army. Wounded twice in the battle of Voziers in France. Later returned to Texas.
— Photo copied from *Pamätník Čechoslovāků.*

Jan Polašek. Born in Hošťálkova, Moravia. Later came to Texas. Member of SPJST Lodge #42, Moravan. Joined Czech Army in 1918; after war returned to newly created Czech state.
— Photo copied from *Pamätník Čechoslovāků.*

William Blaha and his future wife, Albina Hejtmančík, near Hranice school, ca. 1912.

— Photo courtesy of Albert J. Blaha.

CHAPTER 3

Social Structure

Všude je dobře, ale doma je nejlíp.
(Life is good everywhere, but it is best at home.)
—Czech proverb

The social structure of the Czech ethnic community evolved as the Czech settlements in Texas went through the stages of development traced in Chapters 1 and 2: the settlement of the old colonies prior to the Civil War and the continual expansion into new ones afterwards. Emerging from this growing community in the final decades of the nineteenth century was an increasingly complex and sophisticated social structure. Despite constant growth and change, however, there was a strong sense of continuity and coherence in this development.

The Czech settlers did not originate primarily in one or two isolated villages nor in widely dispersed regions. Instead, they came from a number of villages and cities located in well-defined geographical districts. In the mid-nineteenth century, the national culture of Bohemia and Moravia, despite its diversity, was fairly well integrated. In addition, the great majority of the Texas Czechs came from particular regions — especially northeastern Bohemia and eastern Moravia — and from a particular social class within those regions. The underlying unity of their folk culture will be examined in Chapter 5. They settled in a particular area of the United States primarily due to personal contact with countrymen who had come before, beginning with the "Bergman connection," and continuing with a steady stream of letters from more recent emigrants as time went on. Their settlements spread rapidly, but, with a few exceptions, along well-defined lines, so that their population, while always relatively sparse because of the rural environment, became concentrated in certain areas. Out of the 254 counties that make up Texas today, only Fayette County had more than 20

Czech settlements, while Lavaca had 13 and Austin, Burleson, Fort Bend, McLennan, Wharton, and Williamson had 9-10 each.[1] They came in family units. Men and women came in approximately equal numbers,[2] and they brought many young children with them as well. Many of the family units were related, so that the "extended family" among the immigrants was more the rule than the exception, and, of course, many personal and family ties of friendship were brought from Europe to Texas. Religious and other differences within this group, on the other hand, led to an internal diversity that was probably advantageous in meeting the demands of a new life in a new land. The social structure of the Texas Czechs was flexible enough to make the necessary adaptations to the new environment and, at the same time, retain its integrity.

Before examining the superstructure of clubs, cooperatives, and other organizations that make the typical Texas Czech look like a very socialized human being, it is instructive to consider two basic social characteristics which lie at the heart of his social identity and which to some extent set him apart from the general Texas population, in particular, the Anglo-Americans. Most important is the extremely close-knit family unit. The second is closely related to the first and must be discussed together with it: the Czech attitude toward the land. The major social institutions which define the distinctive identity of the Texas Czech— the ethnic churches, the fraternal organizations and social clubs, the musical orchestras — did not really emerge until fairly late in the century, but their seeds were planted at the time of the first major group migrations in the 1850s. When the two essential factors of family and land are understood, the archetypal Texas rural community, with all of its social institutions, can be better accounted for.

THE FAMILY AND THE LAND

It is appropriate that Czech culture is noted for elaborate wedding ceremonies, for the family unit was all-important. There can be little doubt that individualism was generally less highly prized by the Czech than by his Anglo counterpart. Little František's and Františka's would

---

[1] Henry R. Maresh, "The Czechs in Texas," *The Southwestern Historical Quarterly*, vol 50 (1946).

[2] This is true of the Czech immigration in general. See Tomáš Čapek, *The Čechs (Bohemians) in America* (Boston and New York, 1920), 29.

naturally grow up to be much like their parents and grandparents.[3] One's individual identity was closely related to his family identity.

Although the percentage of unmarried and divorced individuals was probably lower than that for the general population,[4] unmarried children of both sexes tended to remain at home with their parents after maturity rather than establish their individual households. Married children of both sexes, on the other hand, were encouraged to maintain close ties with their parents, and extended families were often the result. It was not uncommon for even cousins to maintain a strong sense of family loyalty toward one another.[5] The Old World custom of having the eldest son bring his bride home to live in his parents' home was made optional by the relative abundance of land, but it was nevertheless customary for sons of all ages to cultivate and maintain all or portions of the parental homestead with a view toward the time they would inherit it. Often sons would purchase adjoining tracts of land — perhaps with the aid of family loans — and continue to help with the parental homestead in a system of teamwork with other family members. Daughters were encouraged to marry sons of neighboring Czech families. For the first century in Texas, a "mixed marriage" was the marriage between a Czech and a German![6] Of course, a mate from just any Czech family might not be desirable, but there is evidence that intermarriage between Catholic and Protestant Czechs was relatively common from the beginning, despite some conflict between the two groups.[7]

The typical Czech farm family cannot be adequately discussed outside the context of its function as a somewhat self-contained eco-

[3] The name František and its female form Františka were, in fact, the most popular given names among the early Texas Czechs, and it is common for a favorite given name to run through several generations of a family.

[4] See Robert L. Skrabanek and Vernon J. Parenton, "Social Life in a Czech-American Rural Community," *Rural Community*, vol 15. no. 3 (Dec. 1949), 225. Snook, the subject of this study, was an almost "purely Czech" community and probably typical.

[5] See, for example, František Branecký, *"Tři švagři poděli farmu"* in *Amerikán narodní kalendář* (1886).

[6] Interview with Mrs. Mary Haisler (nee Mynar) at farmhouse near Providence, Burleson County, March 9, 1975. See Chapter 7 for a discussion of interaction between Czechs and Germans in Texas. The majority of first-and second-generation Texas Czechs were of course also opposed to intermarriage with Anglo-Americans and other ethnic groups.

[7] See the discussion of Catholic-Protestant relations in Chapter 4.

nomic and social unit whose main purpose was to cultivate the land. The great majority of the immigrants thought of themselves as farmers, and they were moving to a vast rural land where they expected to remain farmers. Farming was a way of life, not clearly separated from other life goals and certainly not seen merely in terms of a market economy as a way of making money. Although soil, climatic, and economic conditions in Texas were somewhat different from those in their native land, certain cultural factors associated with farming practices — attitudes and traditions — continued to prevail in the new land.[8]

According to the last census prior to World War I in Bohemia and Moravia, over one million small farming families each held five or fewer acres of land. On the other hand, over seventy percent of all landowners owned only 6.5% of the land area.[9] As explained in Chapter 1, by far the greatest number of emigrants to Texas came from the *chalupník*, or cottager, class. The cottager typically owned only a few acres, perhaps fewer than ten. In Moravia in the 1840s, there were about 40,000 parcels of land measuring between five and ten *joch;* one *joch* is equivalent to approximately one and one-half acres. About 7,000 holdings consisted of 24-90 *joch,* and over 130,000 smaller than five *joch.* The ratios were similar in Bohemia.[10] Of course, some of the immigrants came from the *nádeník* (landless, day-laborer) class and a few from the more prosperous class of *rolník* (farmer), who might own up to 200 acres of land. Generally, the more prosperous farmers who emigrated to Texas came relatively late — after they had sufficient evidence that Texas was after all a land of considerable opportunity. Obviously, the *rolník* was not driven by the same sense of economic and social urgency as the *chalupník*.

The intense economic and related social pressures which led to mass migrations from the homeland have already been discussed. The important point here is that the special case of the *chalupník* helped to define the characteristics of the typical Texas Czech farmer. He generally had only a taste of land ownership and he craved much more in a country where such ambitions were virtually hopeless. And more than

---

[8] See Skrabanek, "The Influence of Cultural Backgrounds on Farming Practices in a Czech-American Rural Community," *The Southwestern Social Science Quarterly,* v. 31, 1951, 258-66.

[9] Cited in Edgar E. Young, *Czechoslovakia: Keystone of Peace and Democracy* (London, 1938), 137.

[10] Figures are cited in Jerome Blum, *Noble Landowners and Agriculture in Austria, 1815-1848* (Baltimore, 1948), 393-94. Bohemia, however, had fewer of the smallest holdings (fewer than five *joch*): 62, 131.

economic security was involved. The fact that political rights and social prestige were invested in property holders led to the valuing of land ownership above almost everything else, a kind of "land worship."[11] Perhaps "reverence" is a better term, but these people saw farming as their rightful occupation and were idealistic about "the good mother earth." It is easy to see why the average holding of about one hundred acres or a bit less for the typical early Texas Czech farmer was regarded as a very significant property.

The ownership and maintenance of the farm land and its buildings were from the beginning the criteria of success for the majority of the Czech immigrants. Most of these families were poor, and many of them had actually gone into debt in order to pay for their passage to America. Thus, it was not easy to buy land, though it was relatively plentiful and inexpensive; it was common for first-generation renters to work ten or twelve years before buying their own land, since farm labor, their chief source of income, was also very cheap.[12] Some of the immigrants were, of course, able to purchase tracts of land soon after their arrival in Texas.[13] Land ownership was the common goal, at any rate, and most of the tenant farmers rented land from relatives, land which they often expected to inherit.[14] Ownership of land was characteristic not only of full-time farmers, but also of the minority of craftsmen and even professional men in the early days as well. With very few exceptions, first and second-generation Texas Czechs who became school teachers, preachers, doctors, and lawyers, not only owned farm land, but worked at farm labor for a significant part of their lives.[15] The same was true of tailors, blacksmiths, and most other craftsmen.

A passage in *Czech Pioneers of the Southwest,* describing the family of a man who like many other Czechs was employed as a team-

[11] See Skrabanek, "The Influence of Cultural Backgrounds," 263.

[12] According to Le Roy Hodges, "Slavs on the Southern Farms," in *Senate Documents,* XXIX, No. 595, 13-14, more than 60% of the Czechs in Texas were property holders, and about 50% of them had their property free from debt in 1912.

[13] See records of early land sales made to Czechs in William Philip Hewitt, *The Czechs in Texas: A Study of the Immigration and the Development of Czech Ethnicity, 1850-1920,* PhD Dissertation, The University of Texas at Austin (1978), 59-60, 115-16.

[14] See Skrabanek, "The Influence of Cultural Backgrounds," 261-62.

[15] Josef Bergman, himself a preacher-farmer at Cat Spring, began the tradition.

ster hauling Confederate cotton to Mexico during the Civil War is archetypal: ''The gold was hoarded in an old coffee-pot in the Hruška home at Rutersville. When the pot was full enough, the family bought a farm.''[16]

Even after the family was able to buy its farm, it was generally too poor to hire much, if any, labor; besides, central to its culture was the concept of the family farm in its truest sense. The success of the farm — and of the family — depended upon the cooperation of all family members, with the resultant interdependence of individuals and family loyalty. Each family member primarily functioned as a part of the group rather than as an unattached individual. Family solidarity without conscious consideration of individual self-interest or demand for remuneration was the norm. Conformity, not only in farming practices, but in family values, attitudes, and behavioral characteristics of all kinds, was part of the overall pattern.

The fictional Podhajský family, which will be discussed in Chapter 6, is in some ways a picture of the ideal: it is large, and, although patriarchical, it functions as a cooperative unit in which each individual freely gives of himself for the good of the whole.[17] Not emphasized in this portrait, however, are the effects of the gruelling physical labor characteristic of a relatively primitive agricultural environment.

The father was recognized as the head of the family, but to a greater extent than in Anglo families (and, perhaps, German-American families, as well) there is a balance between masculine and feminine values. Children are expected to be loyal, yet are given a great deal of attention and open signs of affection. There was, of course, a division between male and female roles in terms of the farm-work. The husband supervised work in the field and construction on the farm and represented the family in business contacts with the outside world. The house and, in particular, the kitchen, was the wife's domain. The daughters' work was largely composed of the lighter tasks — housework, milking, picking eggs, gardening, and so forth. However, from the age of about ten, every able-bodied child of both sexes was expected to contribute to the family welfare by working in the fields. The fact that virtually all family members worked side by side in the fields contributed to the family comraderie and overall feeling of

[16] Estelle Hudson and Henry R. Maresh, *Czech Pioners of the Southwest* (Dallas, 1934), 134.

[17] See Hugo Chotek, *''Z dob utrpení,''* *Amerikan národní kalendář* (1900), 33-77.

Mazoch Brothers Truck Line. Granger, Texas, 1932.
— Photo courtesy of SPJST Supreme Lodge, Temple, Texas.

unity, as well as perhaps to a less-strict division of sexual roles. The husband and wife normally shared the responsibility for making important decisions, and a woman, particularly a *stařenka* (grandmother),[18] could wield considerable influence in the household and in the community.

Perhaps the most important differences between the Czech and his Anglo neighbor are related to family structure and work habits. Anglos commonly thought it odd or even morally wrong that (white) women and children should work in the fields along with the adult males.[19] On the other hand, the Czechs sometimes saw their Anglo neighbors as lazy and shiftless, and the use of slaves to work a family's land tended to strike them as being very strange, as well as immoral (one reason the majority of the Czechs felt they had no stake in the Civil War).

The concept of *hospodářství* is central to the overall ethic of Texas Czech rural family life. This word can be translated as either "husbandry" or "economy." The term *hospodář* (which gives its title to an important Czech-language publication still being published in Texas today) can be translated simply as "farmer," but a connotation associated with the little-used English term "husbandman" is important. A whole complex of attitudes toward the land, the family, and the community, is suggested by this term: intensive farming, the utmost use of resources, conservation, careful attention to detail, and an overall conservative view of the world. Diaries of farmers from early times illustrate the careful documentation of economic expenditures, utilization of land, crop figures, and so forth.[20] Typical accounts by Czech settlers are laced with comments on the availability and cost of food and supplies and other practical details.

At its worst, such an ethic can lead to pettiness, parsimony, and a narrow view of the world. At its best, however, it can lead to success in adapting to a relatively harsh, new environment and the establishment of a harmonious, fulfilling way of life. There is evidence that the typical Czech farmer of the turn-of-the century, despite his deprived background, was considerably more successful than his Anglo neighbors holding similar acreages. In a time when the typical farm con-

---

[18] *Stařenka* is the Moravian word for "grandmother," and was therefore the usual Czech term used in Texas. The corresponding Bohemian word is *babička*.

[19] Personal interview with Marvin Hegar, November 14, 1975; Temple, Texas.

[20] See Chapter 6, note 53.

J. Ježek, cotton buyer, standing beside scales outside Louie Albert's store in Nelsonville, Texas, early 1900s.

— Photo courtesy of Doris Fischer Obsta.
Copy from University of Texas Institute of Texan
Cultures at San Antonio.

sisted of about 100 acres[21] and the only nonhuman source of energy in farmwork was provided by work animals, the typical Czech family, with its love of the land, its ambition and willingness to work hard and cooperate, and its sense of *hospodářství,* was well equipped to succeed. Knowledge gained and passed down from generations of farming small plots of sometimes poor soil in Bohemia and Moravia led to very satisfactory results when applied to Texas farms with more fertile soil.

Of course, some initial errors were made. At first the Czechs were confused by the grain they called *turecká pšenice* (Turkish wheat)[22] and later *kukuřice* (Indian corn). They planted the seeds too close together and made poor crops. Similar mistakes were made with cotton.[23] The advice of Anglo and German farmers and the experience of one or two years generally corrected these problems, however, and, after the first Czech settlements were established, new immigrants could learn from the experienced Texas Czech farmers and avoid making the mistakes. Overall, the Czechs adapted quickly to a land that was generally hotter and drier than their homeland, with a much longer growing season.[24]

Inevitably, there was evolution in the typical Czech farmer's way of life from 1851 to 1939. The most important factor of change, however, was the farmer's increasing prosperity. Often there is a wide gap between the experiences of the first-generation farmer and his son. In general, the Czech immigrants were willing to undergo tremendous physical and psychic strains because there was a very strong feeling of continuity between generations. To sacrifice for one's children was both an unquestioned duty and a source of pride and satisfaction.

Although there was some advancement in the use of farm machinery, the wholesale mechanization of farming methods did not occur until the 1940s.[25] After oxen, once the indispensible possession of every farm family, were phased out, mules and horses commonly pulled plows and other farm implements even in the thirties. Personal trans-

---

[21] See Lee Roy Hodges, "The Bohemian Farmers in Texas," in *The Texas Magazine,* VI, 87, 90.

[22] See František Kutnar, *"Dopisy českých vystěhovalců z padesátých let 19. století ze zamoři do vlasti"* in Josef Polišenský, *Začiatky českej a slovenskej emigracie do USA* (Bratislava, 1970), 228.

[23] Hudson and Maresh, 85.

[24] Thadious Polášek illustrates some of the unpleasant aspects of the new environment from the point of view of the Czech immigrants in "Early Life in Moravia, Texas," *The Czechs in Texas: A Symposium,* ed. Clinton Machann (College Station, Tex., 1979), 53-59.

[25] See Skrabanek and Parenton, 223.

portation was at first furnished by an ox-drawn, wooden sled, or if the family was more fortunate, a wooden cart, upon which the family would ride to visits, to town, to church. Later came the wagon, perhaps a buggy, and, eventually, the automobile, in the twentieth century. The one-room log cabin with no windows gave way to the wood frame house with glass windows. The local spring or dug-out water hole was succeeded by the family well. Tallow candles were replaced by kerosene lamps and an outdoor fire by an indoor stove. It was not until after World War I, however, that electricity was made available to most Czech farm families.

Cotton was still the major cash crop, as it had been at the time of the Civil War. That crop reporting district of Texas which includes Ellis, McLennan, Bell, and Williamson counties saw cotton account for 75% of its combined farm-ranch income in 1935. For the district including the counties of Burleson, Washington, Austin, Fayette, and Lavaca, the corresponding figure was 65%. Also in 1935, just as seventy-five years before, corn was the second-most-popular crop, second in acreage planted only to cotton.[26] The Czech, like his Anglo counterpart, knew that his prosperity was tied to the fluctuating price of cotton, but, from the beginning, the Czech farmer had maintained a considerable degree of diversification. He kept various kinds of poultry and livestock, maintained a large garden and perhaps a "truck" patch and a fruit orchard, and, if possible, dug a pond and stocked it with fish. To a large extent he was self-sufficient, although he would probably never become very wealthy. The percentage of cleared and productive land on his farm was likely to be higher in 1935 than in 1865, but his farm was still likely to be relatively small. (In the nineteenth century, it was not unusual to have only fifteen or twenty acres in cultivation on a 100-acre farm.)[27] After all, almost 80% of the Texas farms in 1935 had fewer than 175 acres.[28] Truly the Texas Czech's way of life was tied to the "family farm" concept, and the accelerated trend away from that concept in the forties helps to explain the rapid decline of Texas Czech culture.

[26] Agricultural figures for 1935 are taken from Texas Department of Agriculture, *Texas in the Field of Agriculture* (Austin, 1939).

[27] The rest of the area would consist of woods or open prairie (where livestock would graze).

[28] Texas Department of Agriculture, *Texas in the Field of Agriculture* (1939).

THE COMMUNITY

The typical Czech farming community can be seen as a network of extended families, characterized by a common way of life, a common ethnic identity, in many cases a common church, as well as various kinship ties. Much of what we have said about the nature of the Czech family can be applied to the community as well.

Acceptable standards for behavior in the community were in some ways tied to *hospodářství*. It was a serious condemnation to say of a man that he allowed weeds to grow in his cultivated land or that he permitted his farm buildings or fences to deteriorate or that he did not properly care for his livestock. Generally, such a fault was much more serious than getting drunk in public or failing to attend church.[29]

Largely due to powerful family constraints and the fear of social pressure in a general sense, juvenile delinquints and runaways were comparatively rare. As might be expected, divorce and separation rates, as well as the rate of illegitimate births, were probably much lower than for the general population. Although it is difficult to document, the violent crime rate among the Czechs was almost certainly lower than for the general population.[30]

The chief means of informal recreation was visiting between families. Picnics, barbecues, and dances, attended by everyone in the community without regard to age or status, were popular from the beginning. Almost any social activity was likely to include some form of musical entertainment. The smallest children commonly attended these functions, including the dances. Often they would sleep on blankets under tables and benches while the adults danced and talked.

Whether it was established in a comparatively isolated area or one already settled by Anglo-Americans or members of other ethnic groups, the Czech community in Texas, like the individual family unit, was in many ways self-sufficient. A community was likely to have its own merchants and craftsmen that were necessary to a rural way of life. More significantly, the local residents typically joined together in various kinds of cooperative ventures in order to serve the needs and desires of the community.

Many Czech immigrants probably intended to simply transplant their native society to the Texas plains. Anthony Houšt, an early Czech-American historian, wrote in 1904 that the culture of Fayetteville,

[29] See Skrabanek, "The Influence of Cultural Backgrounds," 265.
[30] Low rates of crime, juvenile delinquency, etc. are reported by Skrabanek and Parenton, 225, 228.

Texas, was very much like that of a Moravian village.[31] Of course, conditions in Texas made the full re-creation of the typical Moravian farming village impossible. The very factor which made the new country most attractive—the relative abundance of land—was largely responsible. Houses in Texas tended to be more widely separated, usually located amidst the farm land itself, rather than clustered together in a village. Despite the increased isolation of individual households by distance, however, a great deal of interfamily visiting took place. Due to the relatively small size of the average farm, at least some neighbors were likely to be within an easy wagon's ride away for a Saturday night or Sunday afternoon visit. Social activity revolving around a community center, often a church or a lodge hall, helped to maintain a strong sense of community cohesiveness. This center did not completely replace the intricate farmer-village association of the homeland but it partially did so and allowed a continuity of cultural evolution rather than a sharp break with the past. Economic establishments such as the local grocery store and cotton gin often supplemented the local tavern as the focal points for socializing, especially among the men.

Cooperative activity among the people took various forms and was pervasive. Robert L. Skrabanek's study of the almost "purely" Czech town of Snook provides many typical illustrations.[32] For example, a cooperative general merchandise store was founded in Snook in 1886, before the local church or school. The "swapping" of farm equipment on a cooperative basis was common. When a local farmer was sick, it was customary for his neighbors to work or harvest his crops at no cost. The local Brethren church provided a Czech-language school: it was nondenominational, and some Catholic children were usually in attendance. Also associated with the local church was the Ladies' Aid Missionary Society, which helped to coordinate the work crews for the relief of the sick or disabled farmers and made such work a social event. The Society even had its own cotton crop, harvested by volunteers from land owned by a local farmer, and the proceeds were used for church projects.

In the late twenties and the thirties, groups analogous to that of the Snook ladies began to provide similar functions to meet the needs

[31] Anthony P. Houšt, *Kratké dějiny a seznam Česko-Katolických osad ve spoj. státech amerických.* (St. Louis, 1890).

[32] In addition to "The Influence of Cultural Backgrounds," "Forms of Cooperation," and "Social Life," all cited above, see Skrabanek's 1950 Ph.D. Thesis entitled *Social Organization and Change in a Czech-American Rural Community* (Louisiana State University, 1950).

of a growing urban Czech population. For example, the *Kroužek českých žen* (Circle of Czech Women), was founded in Dallas in 1935. Originally, the members gathered in each other's homes to strip feathers (for bedding) and other chores, but gradually they became involved in charitable and cultural work, working with both local Czech organizations, such as the *Sokol,* and national organizations such as the American Red Cross.[33]

Another of the cooperative institutions in Snook described by Skrabanek was the "beef club."[34] Because the local beef club was one of the most common forms of cooperative community organization throughout the Texas Czech community, at least beginning in the late nineteenth century, it will serve as a typical example and be discussed in some detail here. The purpose of the beef club was to provide each member family with a supply of fresh beef each week, especially during the spring and summer months. (Beginning in early winter, about the time of the first freeze, each family would normally butcher its own hogs and substitute pork for beef during the colder months of the year.)

In most cases, the club would own a small wooden structure from which to operate. One of the individual members would be designated "butcher," usually for a term of one year, and he would coordinate the club's activities. The members would draw lots to determine the order in which they were to provide the animals for slaughter. It was customary for the farmer to make his fattest, most desirable calf available. Arriving early each Saturday morning, the butcher, usually with helpers, would kill and dress the animal, cut up the meat, and distribute it to the members, keeping careful records of the amount of meat and the quality of the cut given to each. At the end of the season, the books were balanced. Those families receiving more than contributing would have to pay the balance to the club (normally at a rate well below market cost). Those who had contributed more would receive compensation in cash. Because this system is most efficient on a relatively small scale, sometimes several beef clubs would operate in the same community.

Almost always it was the male head of the household who would arrive on Saturday morning to claim his family's portion of the meat. The beef club was often an informal meeting place where these men

---

[33] The *Kroužek českých žen* is discussed in Calvin C. Chervenka and James W. Mendl, *The Czechs of Texas* (Unpublished manuscript, 1975), 149.

[34] Skrabanek, "Forms of Cooperation," 186-87.

discussed among themselves the crops, weather, and issues of the day. Thus, the beef club serves as a good example of a relatively informal social institution among the Texas Czechs, illustrating the typical combination of utility with social interaction.

A strong sense of egalitarianism is central to the kind of society described in this chapter. To be "common" was seen by the majority of the Texas Czechs to be a virtue rather than otherwise, and they found American ideals of political freedom and equality very congenial. There are several obvious reasons for this attitude. Although the Czech immigrants who came to Texas can be described as ambitious for material success, there was very little "class consciousness" among them. As pointed out before, the majority came from the *chalupník* class of small landholders, some with a strong consciousness of their family's origin among the peasants. The native Czech nobility had been largely suppressed since 1620 by the Hapsburgs, and Czech and Moravian citizens tended to associate class privilege and prerogative with the oppressive Hapsburg rule. In general they were hungry for land and economic security, not class superiority.

Too, their homesteads in Texas generally did not vary a great deal in size. Due to their primary interest in the kind of intensive farming described earlier in this chapter, the kind of "empire building" sometimes associated with large-scale cattle ranching in Texas was largely alien to them although some Czechs deviated from this stereotype. Although he might have been self-conscious about the cultural and, perhaps, social differences between himself and his Anglo neighbor, then, the typical Texas Czech looked upon fellow members of his ethnic group as social equals. No doubt this egalitarianism contributed to the remarkable stability of the Texas Czech society and culture.

Studies suggest, in fact, that small Czech farming communities are much more stable than their Anglo counterparts.[35] This greater social stability appears to be closely related to the closer relationship between the farmer and his land: greater adherence to the goal of self-sufficiency (while taking the realities of the marketplace into account),

[35] Skrabanek's generalizations concerning the stability of the Texas Czech rural community parallel those put forward by Russell Wilford Lynch in his study of a Czech-American agricultural community in Lincoln County Oklahoma: *Czech Farmers in Oklahoma* (Stillwater, Ok., 1942). Lynch's study is especially interesting because he statistically compared the Czechs with neighboring native American groups in a variety of ways and found the Czechs to be not only more stable as a social group but significantly more successful in their farming practices. See especially his "Conclusions," 104-107.

decreased tenancy, better soil conservation, overall increased production, and more improvements to the land. The symbiotic relationships among the individual, the family, the community, and the land must be central to any analysis of Texas Czech social structure.

EDUCATION

Despite their rural orientation, the Czechs in Texas from the beginning placed a high value on education, a value that was to greatly enhance their success in being accepted by the general community and which, of course, hastened the process of assimilation as well. In terms of cultural values, education was venerated, and the internationally known seventeenth-century scholar and exiled Brethren bishop Jan Amos Komenský (Comenius) was a major national hero. In practical terms, the illiteracy rate among the Czech immigrants was extremely low, partly due to compulsory education in their homeland.[36] Like Americans in general, these Czechs saw education as a stepping stone to social and economic success, and the most important community leaders, such as Augustin Haidušek, whose career will be discussed later, often began their careers as country school teachers.

Organized education in the Czech language began early in Texas. The Rev. Josef Bergman was conducting lessons in both Czech and German in his home and in the church building at Cat Spring as early as 1855. In 1859, Josef Mašík became the first formal Czech teacher in the United States when he opened his school at Wesley—held first in the home of a Mr. Šupak outside of town and later in the community church building. As many as one hundred pupils are reported to have attended during the school term, and Mašík was joined by F. B. Zdrůbek, who came to take his position as teacher there in 1872. Although the first Czech school was located in Washington County, Fayette County, with a very large Czech population, soon took the lead. Several public schools were organized there soon after the Civil War and the Catholic school built in Bluff (Hostýn) in 1868 — with Terezie Kubálová as the first teacher[37]—was probably the first of its kind in the

---

[36] See Tomáš Čapek, *The Čechs (Bohemians) in America* (Boston and New York, 1920), xi.

[37] See Hudson and Maresh on Mašík and Zdrůbek, 172-73. On Kubálová, see Národní svaz českých katolíků v Texas, *Naše dějiny*, (Granger, Tex., 1939), 242.

United States. Czechs were also especially active in establishing schools in Lavaca County late in the century.[38]

The early Czech schools probably resembled other small, rural Texas schools in most respects. Usually all grades (five or six) were housed in a small building, perhaps in one large room of a church or private home until local residents could afford to build a separate structure. One schoolmaster (in the case of the Czech schools, at least, usually a man) would run the school by himself until the enrollment grew large enough to warrant the hiring of an assistant. In the early years, the one-teacher, one-room school was the rule. The teacher would be paid by the local residents, and in some cases, was formally elected by them. His income was seasonal and generally very low. Accounts by some of these early educators attest to their poverty.[39] It was, of course, common for the teacher to hold additional jobs — usually farm labor — or to farm for himself.

Conditions in the early schools were primitive. In some cases, no Czech-language textbooks were available. In 1868 at Ross Prairie, teacher A. M. Koňakovský used the Czech-American newspaper *Slavie* as a class reader.[40] In other cases, "crayons" consisting of broken bits of chalk brick, a few pieces of paper, a single book from which to copy lessons, and sticks for counting were the only supplies available. Occasionally, books were ordered from Europe at great expense.[41]

During the heat of the summer, classes were often taught under shade trees. The school buildings were usually made of logs. Sometimes the door would be cut out above the bottom three logs in order to prohibit wild hogs and other animals from wandering into the building. According to some accounts, class sometimes would be broken up by wild animals or fighting bulls. The teacher and his pupils would climb to the roof of the schoolhouse for protection.[42]

The Texas public school system as a whole received very little financial support and was poorly organized until the 1870s. As conditions gradually improved, the Czech community schools were incorpo-

---

[38] A good study of these schools is found in T. H. Leslie, *The History of Lavaca County Schools*, Masters Thesis at The University of Texas at Austin (1935).

[39] See examples in Hudson and Maresh, 172-78.

[40] Hudson and Maresh, 175.

[41] Hudson and Maresh, 176. In at least one case, books ordered from Prague cost $10.00 in gold each, plus shipping charges.

[42] See. John M. Skrivanek, *The Education of the Czechs in Texas*, Masters Thesis at The University of Texas in Austin (1946), for additional descriptions of the early Texas Czech schools.

rated into the public school system, and new public schools were established in Czech settlements.

The first Czech-English school was established at Praha in 1870, and the history of this school illustrates the nature of the Czech-language schools and their evolution. In 1869, a Czech-language school opened at Praha with fifteen students. F. J. Pešek, the schoolmaster, held classes in the home of Ignác Šrámek. When enrollment climbed rapidly, a two-room schoolhouse was quickly built. Pešek lived in one room and taught in the other. In the second year, an assistant was hired, and the building was enlarged. The Anglo assistant taught in English and Pešek taught in Czech.

This arrangement was adequate until the Texas Legislature enacted the 1871 law which required all public school teachers to pass an English proficiency examination. Pešek, who was fluent in both Czech and German, but not in English, was not allowed to take a substitute examination in German (ironically, despite the petition of Augustin Haidušek, who would later insist upon English proficiency). Therefore, the assistant became the schoolmaster, and Pešek was demoted to assistant until he was able to pass the examination. Pešek retired from the Praha school in 1883 but, later the same year, took a teaching position in the Lavaca County school of Grieve, where he taught in Czech, German, and English.

Several Czech Catholic parochial elementary schools were organized in the years following the Civil War. It was common to establish a school soon after each new parish was organized. These schools, where Czech-language instruction could not be interfered with by state law, will be discussed in Chapter 4. The majority of Texas Czech school children, however, attended public schools or none at all in the 1870s and 1880s, though conditions in these schools remained very poor throughout this period. In some cases, Czech youths stayed away from the English-language schools because they were afraid of being harassed by the English-speaking students or misunderstood by the teacher. Absenteeism was also caused by the need for children to help with the farm work, a problem shared by many Texas farm children at the time. Very few Czech children went to high school; no Czech-language high school was ever organized.

In many Czech (as well as some German) communities, the 1871 law requiring that English be the primary language of instruction in all Texas public schools was being ignored or circumvented a decade after

---

[43] Hudson and Maresh, 177. Skrivanek, 62.

its enactment. An eventual crisis was probably inevitable. It came in 1883, when Augustin Haidušek, the Czech-American County Judge and *ex officio* school superintendent of Fayette County announced that he was prepared to enforce the letter of the law. English would have to be the *primary*, although not the only, language of instruction in all county schools. Despite the uproar caused by some hard-liners, it was soon apparent that the majority of the Czech community supported the Haidušek position. Haidušek carried the day, not only because he was at that time the most prominent Czech ethnic leader in Texas, but because most Czechs agreed with his philosophy. Czech youths would have to learn English well before they could become successful and effective American citizens. This attitude will be discussed in more detail in Chapter 7. In a few isolated Czech communities, teachers continued to circumvent the law. According to some reports, even in the late nineteenth century, teachers in certain all-Czech schools would call for the English-language textbooks only when a state inspector was expected.[44] This situation was exceptional, however.

In the classroom and the schoolyard, many Czech children learned English for the first time, and the public school was surely the most powerful institution which promoted assimilation. Czech continued to be taught as an accredited modern language in various Czech communities throughout the twenties and thirties, however, and churches and other organizations continued to sponsor Czech "summer school" in some communities, in addition to the numerous Czech Catholic schools.

Furthermore, even though many of the old Czech schoolteachers had been disqualified by the state language requirements, the Czechs continued to take an active interest in public schools. In the 1890s, teachers of Czech origin in Fayette County organized the Komenský Society, with the aim of improving public education among the Czechs. About 1890, a movement to establish a high school in which the Czech language would be taught began to gather strength. The Č.S.P.S. lodge at Velehrad even pledged $1,200 toward the construction of the building.[45] Texas Czech teachers failed to support the idea, however. They argued in articles published in the newspaper *Svoboda*

[44] For example, see Skrabanek, *Social Organization and Change in a Czech-American Rural Community*, 72.

[45] Mollie Emma Stasney, *The Czechs in Texas*, Masters Thesis at The University of Texas at Austin (1938), 87. Also see *Svoboda*, January 28, 1892, on the plans for a Czech-language high school.

that conditions in the already existing elementary schools in Czech communities should be improved before building a high school.

Studies of the public schools located in Lavaca County Czech districts illustrate the extensive Czech involvement in community schools throughout the period of this study.[46] At least fifteen Lavaca County schools can be described as "Czech." That is, Texas Czechs founded them and predominated among students, teachers, and school trustees through the years. The Vyšehrad School, for example, was founded in 1887.[47] J. F. Kutach, Sr. donated the land for the site of the original one-room building. A two-room building was constructed in 1905. Through the efforts of local residents František E. Konvička, Jan Mičan, and Jan Čada, a three-room structure was erected in 1935, still on the original site. The first teacher was František Jakubik. A non-Czech served as teacher during the period 1889-1893. After that time, a series of about thirty Czech and only two non-Czech teachers taught at Vyšehrad up until 1935. (After the time of World War I, two, and later, three teachers were commonly employed at the same time.) Only during the period 1905-1911 did a non-Czech serve as schoolmaster. Three school trustees served each year. During the entire period 1887-1935 every trustee had a Czech surname.

"Czech clubs," designed to fill social needs as well as to preserve the Czech language and culture, began to appear at Texas high schools in areas heavily populated by Czechs, such as West, East Bernard, and Wallis. Czech clubs were organized on the college level, too, and members began to agitate for the inclusion of the Czech language in the curriculum. In the year 1909 alone, such clubs appeared at The University of Texas, Southwestern University, and the Catholic Seminary in La Porte.

Čechie, the club at The University of Texas, is of particular interest. The founders—C. H. Chernosky, E. E. Křenek, M. J. Breuer, Louis Mikeška, and J. Kopecký—lobbied for the establishment of the Department of Slavonic (later, Slavic) Languages at the University, which took place in 1915. The alumni extension of Čechie, the Czech Ex-Students Association of Texas (CESAT), began about this time to solicit funds in order to promote higher education among young Czechs in Texas, many of whom lacked the necessary financial resources. A CESAT loan fund which offers loans to qualified college and university students of Czech origin at very low rates of interest still exists today.

---

[46] See especially Leslie and Skrivanek.

[47] The following account is based on Skrivanek, 82-85.

CLUBS AND ORGANIZATIONS

Other organizations with a cultural or educational purpose were common in the late nineteenth and early twentieth centuries. The musical organizations — bands, choral and dance societies — will be discussed in Chapter 5. Also very popular were the amateur theatrical organizations, though some were separate entities. In 1875, a theatrical society was organized by Jindřich Parma and František Lidiak in Bluff. Money from admissions was donated to the local school. Two years later, the *Kajetan Tyl* society was formed by Marie and Anton Kulhanek for the Praha school, and in 1890, I. J. Gallia founded a similar society at the Engle school. Early in the twentieth century, theatrical societies could be found in almost every large Czech community in Texas.[48] Up until the time of World War II, Eduard Miček, Chairman of the Department of Slavonic Languages at The University of Texas, produced one play a year, and student-players travelled to various Texas Czech communities for Sunday evening performances. Some small communities, such as Moravia, also maintained amateur theatrical groups.

Cooperative libraries or "reading clubs" were also common. It was practical to pool limited financial resources for buying Czech-language books, which were, of course, difficult to obtain. The first formally organized club of this type was probably the *Českoslovanský čtenářský spolek* (Czechoslovanic Reading Club) in 1867 at Wesley, followed by another at Ross Prairie in 1871.[49] The procurement and maintenance of Czech-language collections on a larger scale eventually became the province of the college and university Czech clubs and the Czech fraternal organizations.

Before discussing the extremely important state fraternal and mutual aid organizations, however, it is necessary to examine one important national Czech society which has also had some influence in the state. The *Sokol* was founded in Prague in 1862 by Miroslav Tyrš and Jindřich Feugner. Although officially banned in modern Czechoslovakia, the society continues to function in various nations today. The society's symbol, the *sokol*, or falcon, represents "swiftness, vigor, strength, heroism, daring, and high flight." The society combines studies for the development of the mind with systematic training for the body, and the organizational motto is "a sound mind in a sound

---

[48] I. J. Gallia, *"Jaký podíl brali czechoslovane* [sic] *na vybudování lepších poměru ve státu Texas"* in *Věstník,* July 22, 1936.

[49] Hudson and Maresh, 179.

Granger Sokol Team, ca. 1910.
— Photo courtesy of Mrs. Stacy Labaj; Granger, Texas.
Copy from University of Texas Institute of
Texan Cultures at San Antonio.

body." It has always been known chiefly for its gymnastic program and the *slet* (gymnastic "flying" meet) which features displays of competitive skills, along with special group dance drills with colorful costumes.

The American branch of the *Sokol, Narodní jednota sokolská,* was one of the most popular Czech organizations in America. It had a relatively late start in Texas, however, and it was already twenty-five years old when the first state unit was organized in Ennis in 1908.[50] Dogobert Novák was instrumental in persuading the local members to join the national organization. In 1909, local units were organized in Shiner, Hallettsville, and Granger, and by 1936 Texas had about twenty units which belonged to the National Sokol Society. The Catholic counterpart of the *Sokol,* which was open only to Catholics, was organized in Texas about the same time. By 1934, sixteen local units existed in the state. The *Sokol* halls usually served as social and civic centers as well as gymnasiums. Almost all members were Texas Czechs, and the Sokols helped strengthen a sense of ethnic solidarity. Like the fraternal and mutual aid societies, they sponsored Czech language classes and choral and dance clubs.

At this point it should be obvious that the pervasive social, cooperative spirit of the Czechs within the family unit and within the local community characterized the statewide ethnic community as a whole, as it began to take shape during the years of rapid growth following the Civil War. Later chapters will deal with the ethnic religious institutions of the Czechs and the overall issue of ethnicity. The remainder of this chapter will be devoted to those organizations called "fraternal" and "mutual," which have been so crucial to the history of the Czechs in Texas.

Strictly speaking, a "fraternal" organization is a mutual aid society which offers life insurance protection for its members, who are affiliated with a particular ethnic group, religion, or occupation. A "mutual protection" association is similar, except that it serves to insure members' property against damage or loss. The fraternal organizations have been by far the most popular and influential among the Texas Czechs. They are organized around local lodges, each with its own lodge hall, which serve not only as headquarters to administer the insurance needs of the local members, but, more importantly, as centers for important social activities: meetings, dances, picnics, and various ethnically-related festivals, many of them held on an annual basis.

[50] For an account of the Sokol in Texas, see Stasney, 102-104.

I. J. Gallia. First President of the SPJST.
— Photo courtesy of the
SPJST Supreme Lodge, Temple, Texas.

Local lodge officers are often identical with local Czech community leaders.

Fraternal and mutual orders are non-profit corporations without capital stocks. Delegates elected by the local lodges meet in a convention—in most cases, every four years—to elect state administrative officers and make changes in the operation of the societies. Fraternal orders generally operate on a legal reserve basis, use mortality tables, and have fixed insurance premiums. Mutual orders require that members pay insurance premiums in the form of assessments which vary and are based on the member's losses and the resulting claims paid by the organization.

The fraternal order was ideally suited to the needs of the Texas Czech. His egalitarian and fraternal spirit was satisfied in several ways. The business sessions served as forums for parliamentary debate and democratic decision-making. Although blatantly political and religious issues were excluded from discussion, these meetings served as a training ground for participation in the American political system, a particularly cherished activity because of the background of political and social suppression under the Austrian Germans. Records of the lodge meetings show a willingness to debate among members that might even be called contentiousness. The fraternal lodge was thus the center for most large-scale social activities of both a serious and leisure nature, and the emphasis was on family participation.

The proliferation of these organizations is staggering, and it led to a labyrinthine structure of more-or-less autonomous groups in which some Czechs held two or more concurrent memberships. The old adage seems quite appropriate: "Where there are two Czechs, there are three clubs."

The *Česko-slovanský podporující spolek* (Č.S.P.S.) was one of the earliest fraternal orders in the United States, beginning informal operation in a St. Louis tavern in 1854.[51] Following the Civil War, it was incorporated under U.S. fraternal laws and grew to include about 5,500 members and 93 lodges in 1884, the year the first Texas lodge was founded in Ellinger. Lodges in Praha, Caldwell, Nelsonville, and Dubina followed, and the Texans sent their first representatives to the ČSPS national convention in Cedar Rapids, Iowa, in 1891. Most of the ČSPS lodges were located in the Midwest and the Northeast. The only Southern lodges were those located in Texas. At the 1891 convention, however, the Texas representatives — Josef Peter, Augustin Polach,

---

[51] On the history of ČSPS, see *Organ československých spolku v Americe*, vol. LXII (March 1, 1954).

J. R. Kuběna

— Photo copied from
Památník Čechoslováků.

and I. J. Gallia—fell into a natural alliance with representatives from some of the ČSPS lodges who were demanding organizational reforms. The representatives from western states thought it was unfair to assess the same fees for all members, regardless of occupation or age. They also wanted to admit women into the organization on an equal basis with men. The Texans were particularly drawn to the argument that eastern members from highly industrialized areas of the country had higher mortality rates than members from rural, western areas, and that insurance rates should be adjusted accordingly. The western proposals were voted down by the eastern majority, however, both in 1891 and again in 1895, at a convention in St. Paul. The Texans, as well as their western allies, gave up their futile attempt at ČSPS reform. Instead, a secessionist group headed by Frank Čihal, J. R. Kuběna, and L. V. Vaňek met in La Grange in December, 1896. The result was a new fraternal organization, the *Slovanská podporující jednota statu Texas* (SPJST), known in English as the Slavonic Benevolent Order of the State of Texas, which began operation in July, 1897.[52] Although the ČSPS, which survives today, after a series of mergers, as part of the *Československé spolky v Americe* (ČSA), maintained a minimal membership in Texas (some of the original SPJST members maintained joint membership) and a few lodges, the SPJST began with 822 charter members and 25 lodges which had dropped out of ČSPS, and rapidly grew into the most powerful and influential Texas fraternal and probably the most important organization in the history of the Czechs in Texas. The first SPJST lodges (in order of their official numbers) were located in Fayetteville, Rožnov, Moulton, Hallettsville, Ammansville, Cottonwood, Caldwell, Weimar, Snook, Shiner, Praha, Dubina, Dime Box, Wesley, Buckholts, Bílá Hora, New Tabor, Elgin, Velehrad, Granger, Engle, Cat Spring, Moravia, Cyclone, and Ennis. The number of lodges climbed to 108 in 1912 and 146 in 1931. By 1910, the SPJST reported 5,653 life insurance policies, assets in excess of $135,000, and nearly five million dollars of insurance in force. These figures were nearly doubled over the next decade, and by 1940, the

[52] On the history of SPJST, see *Věstník*, vol. 24, no. 37 (1936) and vol. 44, no. 25 (1956). Also, Marvin J. Slovacek, *A Sixty Year Insurance History of The Slavonic Benevolent Order of the State of Texas*, Masters Thesis at The University of Texas at Austin (1956). Nick Morris, President of the SPJST, was compiling a more complete history of the organization at the time of writing.

Josef Holík, Jr.
— Photo courtesy of SPJST
Supreme Lodge, Temple, Texas.

SPJST had 16,604 current policies, with assets of $3,375,000 and insurance in force of $14,758,658.

The *Západní česká bratrská jednota* (ZČBJ), known today as the Western Fraternal Life Association (WFLA), was another splinter group which broke off from the ČSPS in 1897, and subsequently became very successful in the Midwest and West, with headquarters in Cedar Rapids, Iowa.[53] By 1930, this organization had established seven lodges in Texas but never became very influential in the state. It is important to note that Texas was the only state to form its own independent Czech fraternal, a pattern that was followed in the establishment of other unique Texas Czech institutions.

Three prominent early figures in the SPJST were I. J. Gallia, who served as the first and third state president, J. R. Kuběna, who served as state secretary for the first forty years, and Josef Holík, Jr., who served as second state president. These men, along with Czech Texans such as František Čihal, L. V. Vaněk, Engelbert Pollach, Jan Michal, and Fred Bříska, helped to give this organization its independent, non-political, non-religious character. Gallia and Kuběna, foreign-born with rural Texas childhoods, served, like Augustin Haidušek, as models for later ambitious young Texas Czechs. Gallia was a successful merchant and real estate promoter. Kuběna was a successful banker, who served in the Texas House of Representatives from 1903 until 1909, and later as a member of the board of managers for Texas A & M College. No doubt the men's leadership in the Texas Czech fraternal movement was, in the long run, their most important role.

Parallel to the growth of the non-affiliated fraternal organizations was that of the religious orders. Although the SPJST, the pre-eminent Texas fraternal organization, was careful to exclude both religious and political dialogue from its purview, the parent organization, ČSPS, had its roots in the Freethought Movement more popular in the North and Midwest and, in fact, the majority of SPJST members were Protestant or non-affiliated. When Catholic organizations were formed, they, unlike the SPJST, limited their membership according to sex.

In 1879, a group of Czech settlers met at Bluff (later known as Hostýn) and formed the *První texaský česko-moravský podporující spolek,* the First Texas Czech-Moravian Benevolent Society. In 1883, this society became a local unit of the national *Druhá římská katolická ústřední jednota* (The Second Roman Catholic Central Society). Dur-

---

[53] See Stanislav Klima, *Čechove a slovaci za hranicemi* (Praha, 1925), 214-15. Also see *Protokol prvního sjezdu ZCBJ* (New Prague, Minn., 1899).

ing the same years, another national Czech Catholic Society, *První řimská katolická ustřední jednota,* the First Roman Catholic Central Society, became active in Texas and, by 1888, had fifteen local lodges in the state.[54]

In 1888, however, at another meeting of members of the national Catholic fraternal orders, following the dedication of a new church at Bluff, Rev. Josef Chromčík predicted the decline of the national organizations and urged the formation of a separate, independent union of Texas Catholic lodges. Support for this idea grew, and the *Katolická jednota texaská* (KJT), the Czech Catholic Union of Texas, was incorporated in Bluff in 1889.[55] The Catholic men's fraternal order began with six local lodges: Cistern, Novohrad, Bluff, Ammansville, Hallettsville, and Dubina. The first officers were Rev. John Wronski, Chaplain; Josef Psenčík, President; Anton Slíva, Vice-President; F. J. Janda, Secretary; John Klečka, Treasurer; Vinc Dařilek and Anton Janaček, Directors. There were 150 charter members.

During the late 1880s and early 1890s, support grew among Czech Catholic women in Texas for the *Katolická jednota žen americkych* (KJZA), the Catholic Women's Benevolent Society of America, but Rev. C. J. Beneš and others argued for an independent Texas organization similar to that of the men. The women finally moved in this direction when a group met in Yoakum in 1894 to form the *Podporujíci spolek nanebevzet: Panny Marie* (The Benevolent society of the Ascension of the Virgin Mary).[56] In 1897, a similar organization was formed in Hallettsville and the two united under the name *Česko-řimská katolická podporujíci jednota žen texaských* (KJZT), the Czech-Roman Catholic Aid Union of Women in Texas.[57] The charter members were Anna Jakubik, Klara Najvar, Anna Pivoda, Terezie Šitek, Anna Najvara, Anežka Kuban, Julie Gold, Marie Smykal, Marie Janča, Josefa Hradilek, and Johanna Schindler.

From the beginning, the KJZT was loosely and unofficially associated with the KJT, and the two orders frequently coordinated their social activities; however, they maintained separate organizations with no official connections. Both grew rapidly. By the mid-twenties, each

---

[54] See Jan Habenicht, *Dějiny čechů amerických* (St. Louis, 1910), 50-51; Bohdan Kallus, *Dějiny katolické jednoty texaské* (Taylor, Tex., n.d.), 1, 4.

[55] The most complete history of the KJT is found in *Naše dějiny,* 523-72. Also see Czech Catholic Union of Texas, *Short History of KJT* (La Grange, Tex., 1973)

[56] *Naše dějiny,* 574-75.

[57] See *Naše dějiny,* 573-640 for the most complete history of the KJZT.

From the left, Anna Jakubíková, Josefina Habartová, Marie Yurková. Three early leaders in the KJZT.

— Photo copied from *Naše dějiny*.

had about 3,500 members and 80 lodges, although the KJT assets of over $600,000 were about twice those of the KJZT. In 1938, the membership of the KJZT had mushroomed to 6800 adult and 1200 junior (girl), and the number of lodges had increased to 100. The membership of the KJT stood at about 5,000, with 100 lodges. Each organization had assets of over one million dollars.

Another Czech Catholic men's fraternal organization made its appearance in Texas in 1897. In that year, the first lodge of the *Státní řada katolického dělníka v Texasu* (KD), known in English as the State Council of the Catholic Workers (CW), was established in Bryan.[58] The KD was a state-level branch of the national fraternal order of the same name. The charter members were Jan P. Wolf, Martin Vathuber, Jan I. Wolf, Vincent Luža, Ferdinand Rosprim, Vincent Kapčinský, Jakub J. Wýmola, Alois Slanina, Adolf Šťastný, and Karel Kramoliš. In 1900, delegates from Fayetteville and Ammansville met in Praha to organize the state council. By 1939, the state council included 31 lodges and over 1200 members.

Yet another Catholic men's fraternal organization had a more specific purpose. *Rolnická podporující jednota Sv. Isador* (The Agricultural Benevolent Society of St. Isador) was organized by a group of Lavaca County farmers who met in Worthing in 1901.[59] Ignác Brož was the first president. The primary purpose of the organization was to encourage the improvement of agriculture and horticulture. Also, like the other fraternal orders, the Society of St. Isador offered low-cost insurance to its members. In the mid-thirties it had 37 lodges and slightly over 1,000 members.[60]

Although the existence of the non-affiliated Czech fraternal orders probably made the need for a Czech Protestant fraternal less pressing, members of the Evangelical Unity of the Czech Moravian Brethren of North America laid the groundwork for their own frater-

[58] See *Naše dějiny*, 641-658.
[59] See *Naše dějiny*, 659-660.
[60] In addition to the more prominent, state-wide organizations discussed here, many Catholic religious and fraternal societies, with small memberships, existed on the local level. Josef J. Barton refers to a total of eleven such societies among Czech Catholics of Nueces County alone during the mid-1920s. "Land, Labor, and Community in Nueces: Czech Farmers and Mexican Laborers in South Texas, 1880-1930" in *Ethnicity on The Great Plains*, ed. Frederick C. Luebke (Lincoln, 1980), 199.

nal organization at a 1904 convention in Taylor.[61] At a convention in Shiner in the following year, the official by-laws of the *Podporná jednota česko-moravských bratrů,* the Mutual Aid Society of the Unity of the Brethren (MASUB), were adopted. Membership was open to any member in good standing of the Church. In addition to the purpose of "giving the survivors of its deceased members a certain sum of money," the MASUB, like other Texas Czech fraternals, sponsored a number of charitable and social, ethnic and religious, activities, although it is not associated with "dance" halls. Josef Martinets was the first president of the society. Eventually, local units were organized in each community served by a Unity of the Brethren Church. By 1930, membership just exceeded 900.[62]

In addition to the fraternal orders, the Texas Czechs formed two organizations for the protection of property. These mutual protection associations have also been committed to the preservation of ethnic identity and values, and have sponsored their own journals, although their influence as social institutions has not been as pervasive as that of the fraternal organizations.

Rolnický vzajemní orchranní spolek státu Texas (RVOS), later known in English as the Farmers Mutual Protective Association of Texas, was organized in 1901 by Czech farmers living in the Ocker community of Bell County.[63] The charter members were J. R. Marek, F. V. Schiller, Josef Schiller, Martin Štěpan, J. R. Schiller, F. J. Wotipka, Josef Wentrček, Jan Baletka, and Jan Zabčík. RVOS was founded to provide fire, lightning, and storm protection, all of which were then not available from commercial insurance companies because there were not suitable water systems or fire departments in the area for fighting fires on farm property. One of the early requirements for RVOS membership was the ownership of a ladder for fighting roof fires! By 1935, RVOS had about 7,000 members and $14,466,822 insurance coverage.[63]

Slovanský vzajemní pojišťující spolek proti ohňi a bouři (SVPS), later called the Slavonic Mutual Fire Insurance Association of Texas, was probably modeled after the successful RVOS. Organized in Houston in 1926, it was intended to meet the insurance needs of Texas Czechs living in cities, since RVOS was limited in the amount of city

[61] On the early history of the MASUB, see Joseph Hegar, *Pamatník podporné jednoty česko-moravských bratří* (n.p., n.d.).

[62] The total reserve was less than $16,000.

[63] Farmers Mutual Protective Association of Texas, *Eightieth Anniversary* (1981), 2.

property it could insure under the state laws governing farm mutuals.[64]

The fraternal and mutual aid societies can be seen as the culmination of the Texas Czechs' characteristic enthusiasm for social organization and *hospodářství*. They provide at once the security of practical, economical insurance protection and social cohesiveness, and they have been extremely successful. Instead of declining in membership and assets through the years as assimilation and the changing modes of modern society alter the rurally-based ethic of the past, they have continued to thrive by adapting their own identities to suit modern social and economic needs.

[64] The organization was chartered with 104 members. Original officers and directors included Frank Ančinec, Anton Bílý, Stephen Valčík, Martin Rubač, C. H. Chernosky, Frank Bečan, John J. Kelařek, and Tom Hošek. Private correspondence from Vladimir G. Bílý, President of SVPS, April 1, 1981.

CHAPTER 4

Religion

... *vštípeni jsme v narodu,*
   kde jsme našli svobodu.
Za tu volnost oplací
   naše pevné veřici,
pilná, česká povaha,
   sloužíc vlasti pro Boha.

(... we are implanted in this nation,
   where we found freedom.
And for that liberty our believers
   have resolutely given in return
their industrious Czech nature,
   serving the nation for God.)

— Rev. Alois J. Mořkovský, from
the poem *"Naše dějiny,"* (1939)

EUROPEAN RELIGIOUS BACKGROUND

The curious and complex religious history of the Czech people must be considered in any analysis of Czech society and culture in Texas. The community named New Tabor (Nový Tabor), the Hus School (Husova Škola), the Catholic parishes named for Sts. Václav, Cyril and Methodius, and Jan Nepomuk—all these serve as symbols of the religious heritage of the Czechs.

Both Catholics and Protestants maintained a strong ethnic identity within their churches. In fact, it would be misleading to speak of two separate Czech ethnic cultures based on religion. The great majority of the immigrants — probably over 90% of them — were nominal Catholics in their homeland, although they harbored various personal religious preferences which emerged in the relatively free religious environment of America. Most of the generalizations made in Chapter 3 concerning "social structure" can be applied equally to Catholics, Protestants, and non-affiliated Czechs. Similarly, most generalizations about folk culture would apply about equally to each. It is probably fair, however, to make a few qualifications to this principle: Czech Protestants tended to sponsor less elaborate celebrations (weddings, for example), perhaps dance and drink less (although very few believed in the prohibition of either activity), and assimilate more readily. The fact that many of the Czech Protestants were nominal Catholics in the homeland helps to explain why there would be few sharp differences of this kind. In addition, it must be realized that an indeterminate but considerable number of Texas Czechs simply were not affiliated with any religious denomination, although few were strong advocates of freethought or atheism, positions which were more popular among Czechs who settled elsewhere in the United States.

In many cases, both Czech Catholic and Czech Protestant churches stood in the same community: Fayetteville is an early and typical example. In certain Protestant baptismal records, the religious affiliation of the child's sponsors or godparents is occasionally recorded as "Catholic."[1] This is not to say that the Texas Czechs were free from religious disputes and conflicts. Religious friction often made intermarriage between Catholics and Protestants extremely difficult, for example. In fact, religious controversies among the Czechs were colored by unique considerations which must be seen in historical perspective.

The first major, successful Reformed Christian Church was founded in the Czech lands a century before the time of Luther.[2] The reform-minded priest and scholar Jan Hus (1371-1415), who had been influenced by the rebellious English theologian John Wycliff, was burned at the stake after having been found guilty of heresy by the Church at the Council of Constance. Hus, who had built up a large popularity among the Czech people as an articulate advocate of a simpler, more egalitarian Church purged of clerical corruption, was immediately seen as a martyr, and the similar fate of his follower Jerome of Prague, one year later, further infuriated Czech dissidents. The Hussites, widely supported by both nobility and peasantry, and under the leadership of the ruthless but brilliant military commander Jan Žižka, and later Prokop the Great, beat off one papal "crusade" after another on the battlefield. At the same time, they maintained doc-

---

[1] This is a fairly common case in the baptismal records of Brethren minister Jindřich Juren. (See discussion of the Unity of the Brethren in Texas below.) Albert Blaha and Edmund Hejl have compiled over 2,000 entries by Rev. Juren in records of baptisms, marriages, and deaths, mostly from the 1880s and 1890s. Unpublished manuscript.

[2] For a more complete account of Hus and Hussitism, see J. F. N. Bradley, *Czechoslovakia: A Short History* (Edinburgh, 1971), 49-66. Jiří Otter's *The Witness of Czech Protestantism* (Prague, 1970) tells the story from a modern Czechoslovak Protestant point of view. Virtually every Czech-American Protestant history summarizes the early history of the Hussite movement.

trines which included the administering of both kinds of sacrament (bread and wine) to all and the withdrawal of secular authority from all priests, who were supposed to return to "apostolic poverty." In a compromise Compact of Basle with the Church of Rome in 1434, the Hussite Church, while giving up some of its more radical reforms, continued to administer both kinds of sacrament and refused to acknowledge papal authority, thus ending the absolute rule of Roman Catholicism in Europe.

The Hussite movement provided the Czechs with a strong sense of national as well as religious identity, but its overall effect on the Czech nation was ambiguous. However just the Hussite cause may have been, the resultant wars led to great physical damage: thousands of lives were lost, along with an enormous destruction of property, particularly of churches, monuments, art, and cultural artifacts of all kinds which were associated with the Church. Also, great psychic damage can be attributed to the internecine fighting and factionalism which characterized the movement in all aspects save its common front against the Roman Church. Perhaps most significant was the fact that Czech cultural development remained at a relative standstill for decades due both to the continuous violent turmoil and the determinedly iconoclastic Hussite vision, which allowed little artistic expression except for religious music. In a sense the European Renaissance passed by the Czech lands.

From the radical circles of the peasant-supported Taborite faction of the Hussite movement (as opposed to the more compromise-minded, officially recognized Utraquist Czech Church), a new Czech Reformation movement developed in the mid-fifteenth century, during the reign of King George of Poděbrad. It was called the Unity of the Brethren. Influenced by the teachings of Peter Chelčický, groups of Czechs assembled under the leadership of Gregory of Prague and settled in the remote east Bohemian village Kuňwald. There they attempted to live a primitive Christian life which they felt approximated that of the early Church. Perhaps the outstanding characteristic of Chelčický's — and the Unity's — teachings is insistence on the principle of non-violence. In 1476, the Unity of the Brethren elected its first bishop and officially disassociated itself from the Utraquist Church. By the beginning of the seventeenth century, this church numbered perhaps 40,000 members and had produced the definitive Czech Bible: the Kralice Bible (1579-1593), translated from original Hebrew and Greek texts. Subsequent events were to doom the Unity to near oblivion, but it was never wholly suppressed in eastern Bohemia, its birth-place, and in parts of Moravia.

The Thirty Years War, with the cataclysmic Battle of White Mountain in 1620, effectively ended the flowering of the Czech Refor-mation, which had by then been influenced by other European move-ments, especially Lutheranism and Calvinism. Czech nationalists us-ually consider the date 1620 as the darkest in Czech history. The rein-stitution of the Catholic Church under the Hapsburgs coincided with the suppression of the native Czech nobility, the abolition of many Czech political rights, and the substitution of the German language for most state and educational purposes. At the beginning of the peri-od, the Czech lands were approximately 90% Protestant, and the rein-stitution of the Catholic Church was accomplished to a large extent by force. The population of the Czech lands was cut in half (to less than one million) during the following decades, and thousands of Czech Protestant exiles (the original "Bohemians," in the second sense of the word) were scattered over Europe. The most notable of these exiles was Jan Amos Komenský (Comenius), the last bishop of the Unity of the Brethren, who was offered the presidency of Harvard University in America but refused it. He died in Amsterdam in 1670. Until 1781, all forms of the Protestant faith were banned by state law in the Czech lands, although small groups gathered in secret and were occasionally visited by Czech exile preachers from Poland and Saxony.

In 1722, the descendants of Czech exiles founded the Moravian Church on the estate of Count Nicholas Zinzendorf in Lusatia, Sax-ony. This new organization, which kept alive the traditions of the old Unity of the Brethren, was so named because many of its founders were descendants of members of the Unity from the vicinity of Fulnek, Eastern Moravia.

Beginning with the Edict of Toleration, issued by Josef II in 1781, religious persecution in the Czech lands was less severe. Czechs were allowed to join the Protestant "Confessions of Faith" which were per-mitted at that time in Germany and in Hungary: the "Augsburg Con-fession" or the "Helvetic Confession." The native Hussite and Breth-ren faiths continued to be forbidden until 1918. The Calvinist (Hel-vetic) Church, which the Czechs felt most closely approximated the old Czech Church, was the more popular of the two, and this fact accounts for the relative popularity of the Calvinist-oriented Presbyterian Church among the Czech immigrants in Texas. Nevertheless, senti-ment for the ancient, outlawed Unity was never extinguished, and it was to surface in late nineteenth-century Texas in a remarkable way, though most Texas Czechs remained Catholic.

CZECH CATHOLICS IN TEXAS

It must be stressed that the Catholic Church was largely successful in recapturing the loyalty of the Czech people after 1620, despite the remaining undercurrent of resentment and hatred of Hapsburg German oppression with which it was associated. To some, all the trappings of the Church, from the cult of the native saint Procopius (designed to win back Czech loyalties) to the gaudy baroque church architecture of the eighteenth century, were symbols of Czech slavery, but to others they became symbols of Czech national pride. The Church could also appeal to the ancient Czech Christian traditions far antedating the Hussite times; legends of the saints Cyril and Methodius, who brought Christianity (and literacy) to the Great Moravian Empire during the ninth century, were dear to the cultural memory. Furthermore, in the century following the Battle of White Mountain, despite popular suspicion of "Jesuit intrigues," a certain grassroots support for the Church built up on the local parish level. The Czech village priest became a significant factor in a resurging nationalism, and a few members of the clergy and Catholic intellectuals became instrumental in the National Revival Movement of the late eighteenth and early nineteenth centuries. Significantly, after the liberation of the Czech people in 1918, fully ten million of the nation's thirteen million nominal Catholics opted to stay in the Church while slightly over two million joined various Protestant sects, and slightly over a million declined to affiliate themselves with any church.[3] To be sure, as will be discussed later, a much larger percentage of the Czechs who emigrated to America was made up of Protestants and freethinkers. It seems logical to assume that a larger percentage of those most dissatisfied with the institutions of their native land would emigrate.

As noted in Chapter 1, the first Czech priest known to have come to the state was Rev. Bohumir Menzl from Frýdlant, Bohemia, who stayed from 1840 to 1856. Most of this period stands before the first large (family) group migration of the Czechs to Texas, and Father Menzl ministered to the Germans and Alsatians at New Braunfels, Castroville, and Fredericksburg.

The first Czech settlements in Texas that can be described as Catholic are Hostýn, Ammansville, and Dubina, in Fayette County.[4]

[3] Otter, 45-48.

[4] See Narodní svaz českých katolikú v Texasu, *Naše dějiny*, (Granger, Tex., 1939), 14-15. The most complete account of each Catholic community and parish can be found in this work. Also see Estelle Hudson and Henry R. Maresh, *Czech Pioneers of the Southwest* (Dallas, 1934), 198-210, and A. P. Houšt, *Kratké dějiny a seznam česko-katolických osad ve spoj. statech amerických* (St. Louis, 1890).

These were founded in the period 1855-56, mainly by families from the Frenštát region of Moravia. Some of the group leaders were Josef Peter, František Marak, Alois Klimiček, Konstantin Chovanec, Josef Janda, and František Šugarek. The first Catholic church, a small log structure, was built at Ross Prairie in 1859 and, almost ten years later, moved to Hostýn. The settlers at Praha built a church in 1866.

From the 1860s on, the majority of the Czech settlers identified themselves as Roman Catholics. In fact, the percentage of Catholics wishing to maintain their ties to the Church among the Texas Czechs may have been as high as 75%.[5] Nevertheless, the early Catholic settlers faced a critical problem which hampered their development as a religious community: the absence of Czech-speaking priests. They were mainly served by German and Polish priests. The movement to bring in a Czech priest gathered strength in Fayetteville and other Fayette County communities, and Bishop Dubuis of the Galveston diocese honored a petition in 1872 by sending for Josef Chromčík, a young Moravian priest. It was a good choice. Rev. Chromčík, who arrived at Fayetteville on New Year's Eve, 1872, was the most important pioneer Czech priest in Texas.[6]

A man of remarkable energy and dedication, he carried on his missionary work among the Texas Czechs for thirty-seven years. In addition to serving several congregations in Fayette County, he also worked in Lavaca, Washington, Austin, Burleson, McLennan, Ellis, and Williamson Counties. When he arrived in a Czech settlement, the Catholics would gather in a local home, school, or other building, if no church was available. Father Chromčík would "hear their confessions, offer Mass, give Communion, officiate at their marriages, baptize their children, visit and annoint their sick, and give religious instruction to their children, as well as preach to the adults and on occasion bury their dead."[7]

Rev. Chromčík's influence on the growth of the Texas Czech Catholic community was enormous. Working through the authority of Bishop Gallagher of Galveston, he was able to attract six additional

[5] Henry R. Maresh puts his estimate for Texas Czech Catholics a bit lower — at 70%, with 25% Protestants, and the rest "freethinkers." "The Czechs in Texas," *The Southwestern Historical Quarterly*, vol. 50 (1946), 240.

[6] Rev. Chromčík is discussed in Hudson and Maresh 203-206; *Naše dějiny*, 24-26.

[7] Rev. Alois J. Mořkovský, "The Church and the Czechs in Texas," in *The Czechs in Texas: A Symposium*, ed. Clinton Machann (College Station, Tex., 1979), 88.

Czech priests to the state. He was also instrumental in the movement which supported the break of the Texas Czech Catholic fraternal orders with the national parent organizations. Thus he is an important figure in the development of a distinctive Texas Czech ethnic identity.

Five Czech Catholic priests practiced in Texas by 1890. Four of them were in Fayette County; besides Rev. Chromčík at Fayetteville, there were Rev. Vinc Chlapik at Ellinger, Rev. František Shea at Praha, and Rev. Julius Vrana at Bluff (Hostýn). Rev. Karel Pries was at Frelsburg in Colorado County.[8] Rev. C. J. Beneš, who was to serve in Hallettsville, Moulton, Bluff, and Weimar, was ordained in 1890. He is a transitional figure in Texas Czech Catholicism because he began his studies at a European seminary (Hradec Králové) and finished them at the seminary in Victoria, Texas. Also ordained in 1890, in Galveston, was Rev. Josef Pelnář, who was European-born but had studied at St. John's University in Minnesota. At the same time, products of Czech seminaries, such as Rev. K. Kačer, who studied at Celovec and Klausenburk before being ordained in Vienna and coming to America in 1895, continued to be imported into Texas. By 1920, there were twenty-four priests of Czech extraction in Texas.[9] As late as this, there was no demand for English-speaking priests in Czech parishes.

Of course, the Czech Catholics continued to be served by priests of other national and ethnic identities, especially Polish. (This was a logical arrangement since the Polish language is quite similar to the Czech.) For example, Father Tom Moczygemba, a Polish Texan and the first native Texas Catholic priest, served the Czech community in the San Antonio area.

A product of St. Joseph's Seminary in Victoria, Texas, the same seminary that had produced Moczygemba, Moravian-born Peter Netardus served in several Texas Czech parishes, including that of Praha, and served for a time as the editor of the Catholic journal *Našinec* in Taylor before becoming the first Czech monsignor in the San Antonio Diocese.[10] By the end of the century, at least three Texas seminaries were offering courses in Czech: St. Mary's in La Porte, and St. Anthony's and St. John's in San Antonio. In addition to the more than fifty Czech immigrant priests, about one hundred Texas-born Czechs served in the state in the years before World War II. Many came from small country parishes such as Corn Hill, Praha, and Shiner. Certain

---

[8] See Houšt, 545-47.

[9] Statistical Report in *Katolík česko-americký*, (Českých Benediktin Printing Office, 1920), 179-82.

[10] For a short biography of Rev. Netardus, see *Naše dějiny*, 21-22.

Reverend Josef Chromčík
— Photo copied from *Naše dějiny*.

family names are also associated with the priesthood in Texas: Valenta, Petrů, Bílý.[11] Monsignor Alois J. Mořkovský, who served on the staff of St. John's Seminary 1924-41, was instrumental in maintaining an interest in the Czech language among seminarians, and his brother John Mořkovský became the Bishop of the Galveston diocese in 1975.

The Czech Catholic population of Texas and its institutions steadily grew in size. In fact, it can be said that the Czech Catholics were more successful in Texas than in any other state. Tomáš Čapek reports that in 1917, there were 68 Czech Catholic "centers" (churches, missions, or stations) in Texas. Nebraska, by comparison, had 48, and the third largest number, 28, were located in Minnesota. In 1920, Texas had 77 of the 334 Czech Catholic centers in North America. By 1938, Texas had 113 "major centers" and 33 "lesser centers."[12] Although the large area of Texas should be taken into account, it must also be remembered that the Texas Czech Catholic population was clustered in a few major counties (a large percentage of the churches were located in Fayette Co. alone) and that Texas ranked only sixth among the states in total Czech population.

In his study of the six-state region of Nebraska, Texas, Kansas, South Dakota, North Dakota, and Oklahoma, Bruce Garver concludes that only in the states of Texas and North Dakota was the total number of Czech Catholics greater than that of Czech freethinkers and Protestants combined.[13] The implications of this important statistic will be considered in greater detail toward the end of this chapter.

Czech Catholic elementary schools prospered in Texas. As seen in Chapter 3, perhaps the first such school in the United States was established in Bluff (Hostýn) with Terezie Kubálová as teacher in 1868. Czech Catholic elementary schools began to flourish a few years later. Between 1874 and 1904, schools were founded in West, Praha, Dubina, Ammansville, Industry, Corn Hill, and Fayetteville.[14] By 1920,

[11] See Mořkovský, 91.

[12] For comparative numbers of Czech Catholic centers in various states, see Tomáš Čapek, *The Čechs (Bohemians) in America* (Boston and New York, 1920), 247. Also see Statistical Report, *Katolík česko-americký*, 182-92. 1938 figures were compiled from listings in *Naše dějiny,*. A comparison of the total number of first- and second-generation Czechs in various states will help place these figures in perspective. The 1910 United States Census gives the following figures: Illinois — 124,225; Nebraska — 50,680; Ohio — 50,004; New York — 47,400; Wisconsin — 45,336; Texas — 41,080.

[13] Bruce Garver, "Czech-American Freethinkers on the Great Plains, 1871-1914," in *Ethnicity on the Great Plains*, ed. Frederick C. Luebke (Lincoln, Neb., 1980), 153.

[14] See Jan Habenicht, *Dějiny čechů amerických* (St. Louis, 1910), 86-125.

Celebration of the 25th anniversary of the ordination of Reverend C. J. Beneš, October 18, 1915. St. Mary's Church, Hallettsville, Texas.
— Photo by Albert J. Blaha. Courtesy Institute of Texan Cultures.

schools had been added in eighteen additional towns.[15] Not only was the Czech language used for classroom instruction in most cases, but in some of these schools, the Czech National Anthem *(Kde domov můj)* was sung daily. Catholic fraternal organizations were also prominent in the prodigious development of the Czech community. By 1938, the principal Catholic societies had a combined membership of well over 15,000.[16] With the founding of the Catholic *Nový domov* in Hallettsville in 1914, the Czech Catholics in Texas obtained their own press, and this newspaper was joined by the Granger *Našinec* in 1914.

Czech Catholics were involved in Czech cultural development in the state in other ways. Many of the reading libraries, as well as choral and dramatic groups discussed elsewhere in this book, were founded and supported by Czech priests and laymen. Catholic Czech immigrants such as Peter Stavinoha and Marie Nováková added to the meager store of original Czech-American literature with devotional prose and poetry.[17] Nováková is the most notable Texas Czech poet and will be discussed in that context in Chapter 6.

The evidence suggests that Czech Catholics, no less than Protestants, preserved the Czech cultural heritage in Texas. Carrying on the tradition of the local parishes in the Czech homelands, Czech Catholic clergy and lay leaders sought to maintain a distinctively Czech Catholic tradition. The culmination of this cultural tradition came with the publication of the 718-page *Naše dějiny (Our History)* in 1939, inspired by the Texas Centennial of 1936. This volume provides a historical sketch of each Czech Catholic "center" in Texas, biographies of major clergymen and lay leaders, and histories of the Czech Catholic organizations.

Non-Czechs generally describe the Czech Catholics as being more "clannish" than the Czech Protestants. That is, the Catholics tended to "keep to themselves" rather than interact with Catholics of other national groups, while the Czech Protestants were more open to interaction. This phenomenon seems logical in view of the greater number of Catholics among the Czechs and their more extensive social organization. An even more important factor was the Anglo-Protestant majority culture in Texas; pressure to assimilate and "Americanize"

[15] See Mollie E. Stasney, *The Czechs in Texas*, Masters Thesis at The University of Texas at Austin (1938), 89. The towns were Bomarton, Bryan, Cameron, Cistern, Ennis, Frýdek, Granger, Hallettsville, Marak, Moulton, Nada, Rowena, Shiner, St. John, Taylor, Wallis, Weimar, and Yoakum.

[16] See the discussion of these societies in Chapter 3.

[17] Mořkovský, 91.

meant pressure to conform to a basically Protestant ethic. Texas Catholics other than Czechs also tended to be non-English speaking and "foreign" to the Anglo culture. To put it another way, Czech Protestants had one fewer barrier to cross on the road to assimilation. Ironically, however, the most important voice for assimilation and Americanization within the Czech community came from Augustin Haidušek, a nominal Catholic.

CZECH PROTESTANTS IN TEXAS

Rev. Josef Bergman, the Czech pioneer who encouraged many of the early immigrants to come to Texas, was a Protestant minister, and the earliest family groups, such as the Šilars and Lešikars from eastern Bohemia, also described themselves as Protestants. Bergman, a former Catholic seminarian, had been the pastor of a Czech Protestant community in Stroužný, Prussian Silesia. In Texas, he preached primarily to Swiss and German Evangelical Reformed Protestants,[18] and felt a personal allegiance to the old Unity of the Brethren. Czech Protestants therefore figure early in the development of the Czech community in Texas, although they were soon in a minority as Catholic groups began to immigrate.

In 1855 at Fayetteville, Rev. Josef Zvolanek held the first Czech-language Protestant services in America. He did not, however, organize any church units.[19] That distinction was left to Rev. Josef Opočenský in Wesley, in 1864, and after the end of the Civil War, in

[18] See the discussion of Bergman in Chapter 1. For a discussion of the loosely organized German Evangelical Protestants in Texas, see Terry G. Jordan, "A Religious Geography of the Hill Country Germans in Texas," in *Ethnicity on the Great Plains,* 111-12. Bergman preached to the German and Swiss settlers he accompanied to America, but there is no doubt of his Czech identity. Like almost all of the early Czech Protestant ministers, he described himself as "Evangelical Reformed." Most of the independent Czech Evangelical Reformed congregations in Texas eventually became part of the Unity of the Brethren, although a few became Presbyterian, as the denominational boundaries were drawn early in the twentieth century. Although the Czech language contains an equivalent for the English word "Protestant" (*protestantský*), nineteenth-century Czech Protestants usually used the word *evangelický* ("evangelical") to describe their religion, regardless of specific Protestant affiliation.

[19] Rev. Zvolanek, like some of the later Czech Protestant preachers in Texas, was a colorful and somewhat controversial figure, who moved to Wisconsin after playing his brief part in Texas Czech history. Habenicht describes this preacher-doctor as "immoral" (*"nemravný"*), 78.

1866, a church was built. Opočenský lived with Arnošt Schuerer, one
of his church members, who ran a general merchandise store and restaurant in his home. The resultant noise was unbearable to the quiet,
nervous Opočenský, who insisted that his congregation build him a
parsonage. They refused. The frustrated preacher went so far as to
travel to Europe to solicit funds for this purpose—apparently from the
German Emperor William I—but came back empty-handed. When
the Rymershoffer family of Galveston subsequently offered to donate
the required sum of money, the embarrassed Wesley congregation refused the gift and finally decided to raise the money itself. Ironically,
Rev. Opočenský died before his parsonage was completed in 1870. It is
not surprising that discord within the Wesley Protestant community
was credited with undermining Rev. Opočenský's health and leading
to his death.[20]

The subsequent history of this oldest organized Czech Protestant
congregation in Texas continues to be intriguing.[21] In 1872 the congregation called to Rev. F. B. Zdrůbek of Cleveland, Ohio, who was soon
dismissed due to "heresy" or irreverence. In fact, Zdrůbek, another
Protestant minister who had once been a Catholic seminarian, was in

[20] The Opočenský story presents a case of muddled and contradictory
sources. According to Hudson and Maresh, 213, the minister went to Europe
to solicit funds for a church building, not a parsonage. The parsonage version,
related in The Christian Sisters Union Committee, *Unity of the Brethren in
Texas 1855-1966)* (Taylor, Tex., 1970), 40, agrees for the most part with Habenicht's account in *Dějiny čechů amerických*, 106-108. Hudson and Maresh
merely state that Opočenský appealed to "friends" in Europe, but the *Unity
of the Brethren* work has him appealing to the "Emperor of Austria-Hungary."
It is much more likely that, as Habenicht reports, Opočenský actually made the
appeal to the German Emperor William I, who had previously donated money
to help the minister establish a Protestant congregation back home in Zadveř-
ice, Moravia. (Even this version is amazing, of course, and one is not surprised
that the German leader was not interested in supporting churches in America.)
According to Habenicht, some of the members of the congregation accused
Opočenský of "pocketing" some of the money he claimed he could not obtain, when he returned to Wesley. In addition, some insisted on debating the
relative worth to the congregation of Rev. Opočenský and the local teacher
(Josef Mašík, as discussed in Chapter 3), apparently with the aim of combin-
ing the two functions in one individual. According to Hudson and Maresh,
Opočenský joined the Confederate Army during the Civil War, but Habenicht
and *Unity of the Brethren* both have him traveling to Mexico in order to avoid
involvement in the war.

[21] See Habenicht, 109.

The restored Brethren Church at Wesley as it appeared in 1972.
— Photo courtesy of the Institute of
Texan Cultures at San Antonio.

the process of evolving into " the arch-propagandist of atheism," as he was to be called by his fellow Czech-Americans.[22] After his Texas adventure, he founded the influential daily *Svornost* with August Geringer in Chicago (1875) and served as editor of the paper for thirty-three years, becoming one of the leading Czech-American journalists and spokesmen for "freethinkers."

Despite its stormy history, the Wesley congregation, which included members of well-known Czech pioneer families such as Šilar, Mikeška, Škřivanek. Šebesta, Rypl, Zabčík, Baletka, Psenčík, Rubač, Chupík, Ježek, and Mašík, continued to grow. In 1874, when young Rev. Louis Chlumský left his native Moravia to become church pastor, 42 families belonged to the church, and over the next few years, the number grew to 114. In 1881, the homesick Chlumský left Texas, after inducing another young clergyman, Rev. Jindřich Juren, to take his place. Rev. Juren settled in Fayetteville and began a long, difficult career as circuit minister to hundreds of Czech Protestants in several small rural communities.[23] In 1888, he was joined by Rev. B. Lacjak, who died after a few years of service,[24] and by Rev. Adolf Chlumský, the older brother of Louis, who had spent over twenty years as a minister in Bohemia. The younger Rev. Chlumský was to organize the Texas Czech evangelicals into a coherent Czech-Moravian Brethren Church.[25]

Rev. Chlumský was a strong-willed man. As a child, he was taught by his father, a poor Protestant minister in Moravia, because no Protestant schools existed in his homeland. Later he studied in evangelical gymnasiums in Těšín, Silesia and Levoc, Hungary, before going on to Basle, Switzerland to study theology. Two years later, he studied both theology and medicine for one year in Vienna. Ordained in 1866, he served as a Reformed minister in Krabčice, Bohemia. He

[22] On the subject of Zdrůbek, see Čapek's *Čechs (Bohemians) in America*, 132-33; 196-98. Zdrůbek was one of the most important, and one of the most controversial, Czech-American intellectuals of the nineteenth century.

[23] Juren's background is impressive. He had studied at the theological centers of Basle, Bonn, and Edinburgh. See Rev. Adolf Chlumský, *History of the Brethren in Texas* (Brenham, Tex., 1907), 34.

[24] William Philip Hewitt, in *The Czechs in Texas: A Study of the Immigration and the Development of Czech Ethnicity, 1850-1920*, Ph.D. Dissertation at The University of Texas at Austin (1978), discusses Rev. Lajcak's rather unusual design of the Wesley Church's interior, including the pillar, balcony, and brick wall motifs, which are supposed to have symbolic meanings (221-22).

[25] See Hudson and Maresh on Chlumský, 214-18.

Czech summer school for the Unity of the Brethren Church in Granger, Texas, 1910. Reverend Josef Barton in middle.

— Photo courtesy of Mrs. Stacy Labaj; Granger, Texas.

also edited a religious newspaper in Krabčice called *Straž na sionu (Guard of Zion)*, advocating that his colleagues stay in their homeland and strengthen the Czech Brethren Movement, rather than go to foreign lands. He finally emigrated to Texas himself in 1887, however, and took up farming near Brenham, Texas. In 1893, he was already visiting evangelical communities in the area.

By this time, Rev. Juren's missionary work had paved the way. As many as twelve localities, as distant as Industry, Austin Co., and Shiner, Lavaca Co., were being served, and these congregations already thought of themselves as "Czech Brethren." Chlumský continued this work, organizing parishes at Granger, Taylor, Vsetin, and Caldwell. As Juren had done (and as the early Czech Catholic priests did) he travelled a wide circuit, alternating between distant congregations, by train when possible, by wagon or horseback when necessary.

Rev. Chlumský's unification movement resulted in a convention in 1893 in Wesley, which included delegates from Industry, Shiner, Caldwell, Ocher, Fayetteville, and other communities, but the move proved to be premature. Although a temporary union was formed and a protocol was signed by many of the delegates, there was no real unified activity for a decade. The congregations did, however, continue to multiply.[26] Added to the Wesley (1864) and Fayetteville (1890) congregations organized by Rev. Opočenský were 12 others by 1901.[27]

In 1903, Rev. Chlumský tried for unification again, organizing a convention of 11 congregations in Granger. This time a permanent, functional union was formed. During this fateful meeting, the delegates had to decide whether to join an already existing denomination or to organize a new independent church. Rev. Pavel Dyck of the Texas District of the Evangelical Synod of North America attended as an "advisor," but the delegates voted unanimously for the second

[26] Resistance to unification was primarily based on the argument that early Christian congregations had been, for all practical purposes, autonomous. A strong "primitive Christian" tradition is implicit in the Brethren legacy. For a fuller account of the growth of the Unity, see Chlumský's book as well as *Unity of the Brethren in Texas (1855-1966)*.

[27] The twelve congregations, with their founders and date of organization are as follows: Industry (Rev. Ludvík Chlumský, 1875) Snook (Rev. A. Chlumský, 1891), Shiner (Rev. Juren, 1891), Granger (Rev. A. Chlumský, 1892), West (Rev. A. Chlumský, 1893), Nelsonville (Rev. Anton Motyčka, 1893), Smithville (Rev. Juren, 1894), Taylor (Rev. Motyčka, 1895), Elgin (Rev. A. Chlumský, 1900), and Rosebud (Rev. Motyčka, 1901).

Reverend Adolf Chlumský
— Photo copied from
Czech Pioneers of the Southwest.

choice.[28] Several factors influenced their decision. The Czech-speaking delegates did not want to be dominated by German-speaking or English-speaking Protestants. Their most powerful argument for independence, however, was the possibility of reviving the ancient Unity of the Brethren.[29] Czech nationalism and religion were intertwined from the beginning in the Czech-Moravian Brethren denomination.

A survey of Czech Protestant activity in the United States in 1900 reveals the unique situation in Texas that was to lead to this development.[30] Of the 23 Czech Presbyterian congregations that were active at that time, only one was located in Texas (Fayetteville), while Wisconsin and Nebraska each had five. The Congregationalist and Methodist-Episcopal groups, which together had organized twenty-one Czech-American congregations, had one in Texas. On the other hand, Texas had 12 of the 15 independent or non-aligned congregations. These formed the nucleus of the new Brethren denomination three years later. It is remarkable that the Brethren heritage that had been relentlessly suppressed in the Czech homeland for nearly three centuries would re-emerge so powerfully in the American Southwest, without benefit of a pre-existing church organization. It did so nowhere else in the United States.[31]

The Presbyterian Church was the only major U.S. Protestant denomination with significant success in organizing Texas Czech congre-

---

[28] The Evangelical Synod of North America later became part of the Evangelical Reformed Church and, still later, a member of the United Church of Christ in America. Although the Texas Brethren maintained their independence in 1903, they asked for recognition by the Evangelical Synod and permission to send Brethren theological students to the Evangelical school in Elmhurst, Illinois, and their theological seminary in St. Louis. These requests were honored. See Chlumský, 39.

[29] See *Unity of the Brethren in Texas (1855-1966)*, 32.

[30] Vilém Šiller, Václav Prucha, and R. M. De Castello, *Památník českých evangelických církví ve Spojených Státech* (Chicago, 1900). The figures given here omit "preaching stations." The Fayetteville Presbyterian congregation actually had a majority of Germans, along with some Moravians from Vsetín and Frenštát.

[31] The Moravians who established religious colonies in eighteenth-century Pennsylvania and North Carolina were descendants of Czech exiles who had fled to Saxony, as described earlier in this chapter. They continued to trace their origins to the Unity of the Brethren and, ultimately, to Hus, but they had become Germanized to a large degree.

gations in the following years.[32] Due to the early efforts of Rev. Václav Pazdral, a Presbyterian missionary, and later, of Rev. John Schiller, Rev. V. Losa, and several Czech-American missionaries sent by the Department of Immigration, Board of Home Missions, of the Presbyterian Church in the United States, several congregations appeared in the first decade of the twentieth century. Churches were established at Kovar, Sealy, Rowena, and Brownwood, along with several missions. The Presbyterian Church of the South also maintained missionary stations among the Czechs. The Presbyterians generally cooperated closely with the Brethren in Texas, and this fact probably helps to account for their relative success. Interaction between the two denominations was common.[33]

Also at the first Brethren convention in Texas, *Bratrské listy (The Brethren Journal)* was adopted as the official church organ. This religious journal, which Rev. Chlumský had already edited for about a year, had been a major factor in the success of the unification movement. At the second convention, held in Taylor in 1904, a committee was appointed to plan a benevolent association, and the Mutual Aid Society was established at the 1905 convention in Shiner.[34] By 1919, 11 more congregations had been formed and two young ministers, Rev. Joseph Barton and Rev. Joseph Hegar, had become active in the denomination. In that year, the congregations of New Tabor, Rosebud, Nelsonville, Seaton, and Shiner, which had been loosely organized in an "Independent Unity," joined the Evangelical Unity of the Czech Moravian Brethren in North America, as it was then called.[35] At the

---

[32] On the Presbyterians in Texas, see Hilda S. Stalmach, *History of the Ministers and the Churches of the Southwest Czech Presbytery* (Smithville, Tex., 1962.)

[33] The affinity between Presbyterian and Brethren theology has already been pointed out. Brethren minister Henry E. Beseda, Sr. was a "transfer" from the Presbyterian Church. The small Brethren congregations at Wallis and Rowena eventually merged with local Presbyterian congregations. Before the Brethren denomination was formally organized, however, relations between the independents and the Presbyterians were not always cordial. In the "controversy of Barden's Creek," in the Kovar community in 1895, Rev. Chlumský and some Brethren-minded residents were locked out of the local Presbyterian church (which they had helped to build) when they attempted to hold Brethren services there. See *Unity of the Brethren in Texas*, 48, and Hewitt, 231.

[34] See the discussion of the Podporná jednota česko-moravských bratrů (Mutual Aid Society of the Unity of the Brethren) in Chapter 3.

[35] *Unity of the Brethren in Texas*, 35.

same time, however, several "preaching stations" which had been organized in far-flung Texas towns in addition to six in Oklahoma and one in Kansas, had to be discontinued.[36]

Rev. Chlumský continued his organizational and evangelical missionary work, which involved a great deal of travel (especially to and from the preaching stations), his editorship of *Bratrské listy*, and other duties, including the writing of a *History of the Czech-Moravian Brethren in North America* (1907), until his health failed. He died in 1919 at the age of 76, but the Unity continued to prosper, adding nine congregations in the period 1919-1936.

The origins of The Brethren Hus School can be found in Rev. Chlumský's practice of taking a few girls, selected from various congregations, into his home near Brenham. He gave them training in Bible and Sunday school management, while his wife, a talented musician, gave them music lessons. The young women in exchange helped with the housework. Meanwhile, West, Taylor, Granger, and other congregations were organizing Sunday schools. The first annual convention of the Sunday School Union was held in 1909, with John Hunka as first Superintendent. The fourth convention in 1912 reported 17 Sunday schools with 350 members. By 1914, a teacher training school of eight weeks was held in Granger, under the leadership of Rev. Barton and Rev. Hegar. This group of 18 young students was known as the *Husova Škola* (Hus School) and began a longstanding tradition.[37] Classes were taught in the Czech language, of course. In 1924, a permanent building in Temple was acquired for this unique Texas Czech institution. Membership in the Sunday School Union had increased to 933 by 1922.[38]

The Brethren fraternal organization and Sunday School Union were joined to the Christian Sisters' Union in 1926, as several independent Brethren ladies' groups were unified in one organization. They became especially active in missionary work and promotion of the Hus School. By the 1930s, the Czech-Moravian Brethren Church, with its associated institutions, was a well-established, growing denomination.

In his study of the Czech-language *Bratrské listy* from 1906 to 1969, Richard Machalek concludes that until about 1945, "ethnicity

[36] See the "Chronology of Congregations" and "Chronology of Preaching Stations" in *Unity of the Brethren in Texas*, 66-67.

[37] See the account of the Hus School's development in Hudson and Maresh, 219-23. Cf. *Unity of the Brethren in Texas*, 111-18.

[38] *Unity of the Brethren in Texas*, 95.

clearly occupied the vital center of the life of the Unity."[39] Using the
letters, editorials, essays, business reports, and other items in this official organ as a "socio-cultural record," Machalek notes a general eth-
nocentrism, and Czech nationalism, especially in references to the
"sweet mother tongue" of Czech, but also in accounts of national history, commerative events, political and military heroes, and so on.
Like other Texas Czech institutions, the Brethren Church supported
efforts to teach the Czech language at all levels with gifts and scholar-
ships. Machalek, calls the church an "ethnoreligion."

For the Czech Brethren in Texas, then, religion was even more in-
timately associated with Czech ethnic identity than it was for Czech
Catholics. It has been seen, however, that an intense Czech ethnicity
was characteristic of both groups. Through the years, the organizational strength of the Czech Catholic fraternal organizations became a medium of Texas Czech ethnicity at least as powerful as that of the Brethren Church. In fact, it is revealing to look at Texas Czechs as a whole
and compare them with other Czech-Americans in terms of religion.
When seen in the context of the overall pattern of immigrant Czech
culture in America, it must be concluded that the religious orientation
of the Texas Czechs makes them unique. Texas was, according to the
best available estimates, by far the leading state for *both* Czech Catholics and Czech Protestants. That is, Texas had the largest number of
members of both groups, in spite of the fact that Texas, in the early
decades of the twentieth century, ranked only sixth among the states
in total population of Czechs and had only about one-third of the
Czech population of Illinois.

RELIGION AND ANTI-CLERICISM

It was obvious from the beginning of the large-scale immigration
of Czechs to America that they, in contrast with many other groups,
displayed a strong tendency to break away from the majority faith of
their homeland. Tomáš Čapek estimated that although the last official
Austrian statistics listed over 96 percent of the Czech population as
Catholic, about 50 percent or even more of the Czechs in America had

[39] Richard Machalek, "The Ambivalence of Ethnoreligion" in *The
Czechs in Texas: A Symposium,* 104. Also see his 1972 Masters Thesis at The
University of Texas at Austin, entitled *Intra-Organizational Conflict and Sch-
ism in an Ethnic Minority Church: The Case of the Unity of the Brethren in
Texas.* Machalek traces the sharp rise of assimilation and increasing controversy
within the church in the period following that covered by *Krásná Amerika.*

withdrawn from the Catholic faith by 1920.[40] Although Čapek, like most Northern and Midwestern Czech-Americans, was a freethinker himself, more recent scholarship has confirmed and amplified his observations about the whole-sale defection from the Church in America and the central importance of rationalism among the Czech immigrants. The Czech Freethought Movement had its origins in the Czech lands (especially the cities), but it was free to develop in America.

Karel Bicha has traced the movement in America, which had begun to organize in the 1860s and reached its peak of power by about 1920, when it began to decline fairly rapidly.[41] A few statistics will illustrate the striking weakness of the Catholic Church among the Czechs. By 1883, Chicago, with its Czech population of 35,000, the most important Czech-American city by far, had 52 freethought societies, a freethought school, and only three Catholic parishes. In 1920, 62 percent of the Czechs living in New York professed no religious affiliation. Also in that year, freethought-oriented bodies claimed close to 80 percent of the approximately 156,000 members of Czech ethnic societies in the United States.[42] Large scale defections from the sixth largest Catholic foreign-language group in America were a scandal within the Church.

Apparently large numbers of the Czechs who came to America had weak or perfunctory ties to the Catholic Church. The tragic religious history of the Czechs and its complex associations with Czech nationalism undoubtedly were important factors in making the Czechs the only major immigrant group among whom the majority became freethinkers and abandoned all ties with organized religion. Jan Habenicht in his 1910 history of the Czechs in America *Dějiny čechů amerických* found religious dissension among the Czechs, especially as represented by the anticlericalism of the Freethought press, to be disgraceful and destructive.[43]

[40] Čapek, *The Čechs (Bohemians) in America,* 119. Čapek cites J. E. Salaba's estimate that the figure may be as high as 70%.

[41] Karel D. Bicha, "Settling Accounts with an Old Adversary: The Decatholization of Czech Immigrants in America," *Social History,* vol. 4 (Nov. 1972), 45-60.

[42] Figures are taken from Bicha, 53, 57. The figure for total membership in freethought organizations includes that of Texas' own SPJST which, while it had its origins in the freethought movement, was not an anti-clerical organization.

[43] In his "Preface," Habenicht writes that the religious difference was used by the newspapers so that "our Czech people were set one against the other." Although Habenicht might justifiably be charged with prejudice against anti-clerics, his general assessment of the fragmented state of Czech-American culture in the early twentieth century can hardly be questioned.

It can be argued that the great majority of the freethinkers, seeking a "scientific" and "rational" approach to life, simply drifted away from the Church, without any particular hard feelings. It is true, however, that some influential freethought intellectuals, most of them journalists, saw the movement as something of a crusade and that the freethinkers, until the 1920s, were composed of highly organized, if intensely factional and rebellious, Czech ethnocentric groups.[44]

By a remarkable coincidence, three future leaders of the movement arrived in America, independently of each other, in 1869: Ladimír Klácel, František B. Zdrůbek, and Václav Šnajdr. Klácel was an ex-Augustinian monk, and the other two men were former Catholic seminary students. Klácel, who had a reputation as a philosopher, in 1870 helped organize the popular Freethinkers' Union *(Jednota svobodomyslných)* and founded its official journal, *Hlas jednoty svobodomyslných* (Voice of the Freethinkers' Union). He even wrote a formal creed for the organization, composed of 14 articles of faith, including adherence to "natural laws" and "universality."[45]

From the beginning, the Czech-American press had had a decided anticlerical bias. Zdrůbek, who is especially interesting because of his brief career as a teacher and a Czech-Moravian Brethren minister in Wesley, Texas (after a similar short term as an evangelical pastor in Caledonia, Wisconsin) subsequently took up the editorship of the anti-clerical Chicago weekly *Pokrok*, and, after its demise, that of the influential and long-lived *Svornost* in 1875, which he edited until his death in 1911.[46] About the same time that *Svornost* appeared on the scene, Václav Šnajdr founded the *Dennice novověku* (Morning Star of the New Age) in Cleveland and edited it for 33 years.[47] The list of freethinking intellectuals who served as newspaper editors and journalists — although they often quarrelled among themselves — includes Karel Jonáš (the influential editor of the *Dictionary slavie* of Racine, Wisconsin, which had a reputation for steering clear of religious disputes),[48]

---

[44] See Bicha, 50-60. Garver stresses the "generally tolerant majority" among the freethinkers (149).

[45] The full text is given in Bicha, 51-52.

[46] Čapek, *The Čechs (Bohemians) in America*, 198.

[47] Čapek claims that the *Dennice novověku* had more intelligent and well-informed, though fewer, readers (129).

[48] Karel Jonáš was perhaps the most respected and influential Czech-American man of letters. See Čapek, *The Čechs (Bohemians) in America*, 183-86, and Karel D. Bicha, "Karel Jonáš of Racine: 'First Czech in America,'" *Wisconsin Magazine of History*, vol 63, no. 2. (Winter 1979-80), 122-40.

Hynek Sládek, J. B. Erben, L. J. Palda, Jan Borecký, Josef Pastor, and many others.

It is clear, then, that the Czech-American population, seen as a whole in the period 1860-1920, was dominated by the Freethought Movement. Not only were a decided majority of Czech community leaders, intellectuals, and journalists freethinkers, but a majority of the general population was as well. It is doubtful that a majority of them adhered to any specific "rationalist" doctrines such as those advanced by Klácel, and it can only be conjectured what percentage of the freethinkers were true atheists. And although such figures as L. J. Palda, the "father of Czech socialism in the United States," and Johann Most, a more radical socialist, found a sympathetic audience among urban Czechs, especially in Chicago, New York, and Cleveland, and although four socialist Czech newspapers were still alive in 1914, most freethinkers were not socialists and many socialists in fact wrote off the moderate freethinkers as hopelessly middle classed. This group was for the most part non-militant and must be defined in a negative way as the Czechs who simply dropped out of organized religion. Generally, the majority of them advocated the policies which had gained momentum in the Czech lands with the political revolutionary period of 1848 and discontent with the reactionary policies of Pope Pius IX (1846-78): more civil liberties, partial emancipation for women, universal suffrage, and absolute separation of church and state.[49]

It is equally clear that the Texas Czechs are atypical of the Czech-American population in general during the period under study. Čapek himself believed that Catholics outnumbered freethinkers only in the states of Texas, Wisconsin, and Minnesota. The evidence cited earlier in this chapter suggests that the Catholic Church was indeed stronger among the Czechs in Texas than among those in any other state with a substantial Czech population. Furthermore, Czech Protestants were not only more numerous in Texas (they accounted for only about 5 percent of the total Czech-American population),[50] but, unlike other Czech Protestants, they were successful in organizing a truly ethnic denomination which carried on the uniquely Czech reformist tradition.

Obviously, developments in urban centers of Czech population such as Chicago, New York, Cleveland, and St. Louis, would not nec-

[49] See Garver, 149.
[50] Garver, 148.

essarily influence relatively isolated and overwhelmingly rural Texas. More interesting comparisons between Texas Czechs and Czechs living in other states are implied by Bruce Garver's study of the freethinkers in the six predominantly "Great Plains" states of Nebraska, Texas, Kansas, South Dakota, North Dakota, and Oklahoma. In 1910, about 40.3 percent of the 125,140 Czechs in this region lived in Nebraska, 32.5 percent in Texas, and 27.2 percent in the other states.[51] These six states held about 23 percent of the Czech-speaking population of the United States. Except for the residents of Omaha, the fifth largest Czech city in the United States, the Czechs lived almost exclusively on farms or in small towns. Farming was by far the most popular occupation in all of the states. In none of these states was socialism a vital factor.

Garver traces the influence of the Freethinking Czech-language press in these states, particularly in Nebraska, where Jan Rosický (1847-1910), editor of the Omaha *Pokrok západu* (The Progress of the West), gained a reputation as the leading Czech freethinker in the western United States. He goes on to discuss the "Free Congregation," the Czech-language "Free Schools," and, most importantly, the Czecho-Slovanic Benevolent Society and the other fraternals which were spawned by the Freethought Movement.[52]

Freethought was a powerful influence, the most important identifiable cultural force within the Czech community in the Great Plains region area in the period 1871-1914, as Garver convincingly shows. Freethinkers from this area were, next to Chicago Czechs, the principal supporters of the national Freethought Union, from 1907 to about 1917, and produced many leaders of the movement.

Once again, however, the Texas population is an exception. Only in Texas and North Dakota (with its much smaller population) among this group of states, were freethinkers in the minority. It must not be supposed that freethinkers had no influence in Texas, however. A few Texas correspondents contributed to the monthly *Svobodná škola: Obrazkový časopis pro výchovu mládeže české v duchum svobodomyslném* (The Free School: An illustrated magazine for educating Czech youth in the spirit of Freethought,) published in Chicago.[53] Freethought newspapers such as *Svornost* had a fairly wide circulation in Texas during these years; prominent liberals such as Zdrůbek visited the state and a few liberal free-lance journalists such as Josef Buňata

[51] Garver, 152.
[52] Garver, 155-161.
[53] In the summer of 1904, five of the correspondents were from Texas; Wisconsin had six; South Dakota, seven; Nebraska, fourteen.

lived in Texas for long periods of time.[54] The memoirs of priests and other pro-Catholic writers refer to occasional harassment by unbelievers.[55] The secular fraternal movement, with its origins in Freethought, was very successful in the state. In spite of these factors, however, in the context of Czech-America, 1860-1920, Texas, among the states with significant Czech populations, was the least affected by the extremes of the Freethought movement, and, in a positive context, was much more congenial to organized religion, both Catholic and Protestant. In communities such as Fayetteville, Catholic churches, Protestant churches, and "freethinking" fraternal lodge halls stood in close proximity and symbolized an easy coexistence.[56]

At least two major reasons can be found for the uniqueness of the Texas Czechs. The rural environment of the Texans is not necessarily important in itself: the Freethought Movement was strong among rural Nebraska Czechs just as it was among Czechs who lived in Chicago. The Texas Czechs were nevertheless remote, physically isolated, from the Northern cultural centers. Also, most of the Texans had been more or less directly transplanted from their small Moravian (or eastern Bohemian borderland) villages with a minimum of disruption.[57] Moravians, who exhibit subtle cultural differences from Bohemians, outnumber them only in Texas. At any rate, the religion of the Texas Czechs is only one aspect of a distinctive culture that will be examined more fully in Chapter 7.

[54] Buňata was one of the most important links between Texas and the larger Czech-American community. See the Bibliography for a list of his articles dealing with Texas and Texans contributed to the *Amerikán národní kalendář*. He is also important for having documented the activities of the Czech National Alliance in Texas during the time of World War I. (See Chapters 2 and 7.)

[55] See Mořkovský, 91, for example.

[56] For typical examples, see Habenicht's descriptions of the early Texas Czech communities. Evidently, some Catholics were members of the SPJST, even in the early years.

[57] In any given year, total Bohemian immigration to the United States dwarfs the totals from Moravia and Silesia. In 1861, for example, the totals were 1927 for Bohemia, 88 for Moravia, 64 for Silesia. In 1867, 7430 for Bohemia, 371 for Moravia, 126 for Silesia. See Čapek, *The Cechs (Bohemians) in America*, 31. The Moravian majority in Texas (with a generous sprinkling of Silesian Czechs) can thus be seen as something of an anomaly.

The ČSPS Hall in Praha, Texas. Built in 1894.
— Photo courtesy of Roger Kolar.

The KJT Hall in Fayetteville, Texas. Built in 1910.
— Photo courtesy of Roger Kolar.

CHAPTER 5

Folk Culture

Co Čech, to muzikant.
(Every Czech is a musician.)
— Czech proverb

The celebration of folk culture in the Czech lands reached its high-point in the late eighteenth and early nineteenth centuries and gave impetus to the Czech National Revival.[1] The terms *národ* (nation) and *lid* (people) have special significance among the Czech people and carry strong connotations of peasant or folk culture.[2] During the centuries of Austrian oppression which saw the diminution and even the near oblivion of the Czech language and culture at the official and academic levels, the Czech "folk" of the countryside had kept alive the Czech national traditions and language. The group migrations to Texas began at a time when pride in these traditions was strong.[3]

Certain aspects of Czech folk culture crossed the Atlantic to Texas almost intact and showed a remarkable vitality here while others were

[1] See Vera Hasalová and Jaroslav Vajdas, *Folk Art of Czechoslovakia* (New York, 1974), 9-10. Also see Arne Novák, *Czech Literature*, trans. Peter Kussi (Ann Arbor, Mich., 1976), 113-60. The Czech National Revival was, of course, part of the rise of romantic nationalism throughout Europe.

[2] Although peasant or folk connotations are still current in the term *lid*, today it carries additional associations, especially of industrial workers in a socialist state.

[3] Folklorist Linda Degh has written that "elements of local heritage seem to be stronger than those of the national stereotype. . . . peasant immigrants represent the culture of their native village, town, or region more than that of their nation." "Folk Religion as Ideology for Ethnic Survival: The Hungarians of Kipling, Saskatchewan," in *Ethnicity on the Great Plains*, ed. Frederick C. L. Luebke (Lincoln, Neb., 1980) 129. This may be true to some extent of the Texas Czechs. Many were very conscious of being Moravians rather than Bohemians, for example. Nevertheless, they also exhibited a strong Czech national consciousness that was especially evident during the time of World War I.

left behind or arrived in a severely weakened state. This chapter can provide only a general survey of this very large and complex subject. The folk culture of the Czech lands is diverse, although general Czech and Slovak national characteristics run throughout. To divide Czech culture into distinctive Bohemian, Moravian, and Slovak groups is only the beginning. Differing geographical, economic, political conditions; ancient tribal distinctions; and influences from neighboring areas led to the development of sub-cultures that can often be identified with a specific district or even a specific village. An authentic folk costume or *kroj*, for example, by its shape, colors, and patterns of embroidery reveals its particular origin: approximately 500 *basic* designs have been catalogued, and additional flourishes may identify the trade and the family tree of the wearer.[4] Folk songs are identified with particular regions, and each village has its own song or songs as well. Generally speaking, as one moves from west to east, from the western borders of Bohemia, through Moravia, into Slovakia, one finds an increasing level of such differentiation.[5] As might be expected, regional distinctions were blurred early in the history of the Texas Czech settlements. Nevertheless, distinctive folk motifs associated with areas producing the greatest number of Texas immigrants naturally predominate in the state.

ARCHITECTURE AND FOLK ARTS

The earliest Czech settlers in the mid-nineteenth century built *loksáky* (log cabins), with thatch or rough shake roofs and packed dirt floors.[6] Cracks in the walls were often filled with moss or clay. A large family would sometimes live in a 10' x 12' cabin. Later, similar structures were built of rough lumber cut at a nearby mill. As the family's situation improved, the original one-room building might become the kitchen, as a larger, unconnected house would be built in close prox-

---

[4] See the descriptions of *kroje* in *Věstník*, October 30, 1974 and November 27, 1974.

[5] Obviously, the degree of urbanization and "Westernization" are vital factors. Any discussion of Czechoslovak folk art must be careful to define this differentiation. See Hasalová and Vajdas, 7-11.

[6] Several of the narratives recorded in Estelle Hudson and Henry R. Maresh, *Czech Pioneers of the Southwest* (Dallas, 1934) briefly describe the *loksáky* and other early homes; see, for example, 106, 125. Also see Thadious Polášek, "The Early Life of Moravia, Texas" in *The Czechs in Texas: A Symposium,* ed. Clinton Machann (College Station, Tex., 1979), 64.

imity. (Kitchen heat would thus be isolated from the main house.) These early houses bear a resemblance to some of the more primitive houses in Moravian villages, with their rough (unpainted) timber construction.[7] However, clay was never adopted as a major building material, as it had been in Moravia, and as the Texas Czechs enlarged and improved their farm houses, they looked much like those built by other Texans. The two-part "dog trot" structure (two rooms connected by an open porch in the middle) gave way to multi-room frame houses, typically painted white, usually with an attic, and with a second story if possible. (Upstairs bedrooms were desirable because they were breezier and therefore cooler at night.) Red tile roofs, baroque decoration, bright colors on exterior stuccoed walls, and other features of prosperous farm homes in the Czech lands were almost entirely lacking in Texas. Of course, the Texas Czechs, like many other Texans, retained the Old World custom of maintaining a prominent larder, a smokehouse, and other features of a largely self-sufficient farm.

On the other hand, the meeting halls built by the Texas Czech fraternal organizations were characterized by a greater number of ethnic architectural features. Actually, these buildings were more often known as "dance halls," and their central importance in the typical Texas Czech community has been noted. Roger Kolar has studied the distinctive qualities of these halls and their progression of style.[8]

The ČSPS Hall in Praha (1894) is a frame building built in the form of a gabled rectangle, about 25'x52', with a gabled porch on one end and a stage on the other. It is finished on the inside with horizontal tongue-in-groove wood paneling, and the ceiling is a continuation of the wall material. Kolar points to the manner in which the side walls and ceiling meet. "The walls curve at the top (with an approximately two-foot radius) to meet the ceiling, so that the pattern of the beaded wood is continuous and unbroken up the walls and across the ceiling."[9] He speculates that this design is an attempt to reproduce in wood one feature of the more elaborate baroque interiors that are so characteristic of the Czech homeland. Most of the halls built around the turn of the century are similar to, but "more austere" and "less refined" than the Praha Hall. The SPJST Hall at Fayetteville (1910) illustrates the evolution to larger structures. (It is a rectangle of about 48'x80'.) Unlike the Praha building, it is almost totally unfin-

---

[7] Czech farm houses are illustrated in Hasalová and Vajdas, 17-23.

[8] Roger Kolar, "Early Czech Dance Halls in Texas," *Perspective*, vol. vii, no. 1; reprinted in *The Czechs in Texas: A Symposium*, 122-27.

[9] Kolar, 123.

Mrs. Anna Horáčková (left) and Mrs. Františka Mendlová (right) wearing *kroje*, traditional costumes, ca. 1920.

ished inside. It features a ventilating cupola on the roof, which becomes an ornamental device in many of the later halls.[10]

Kolar also notes several distinct deviations from the typical pattern among the more than one hundred halls built between 1880 and the beginning of World War II. Particularly interesting is the "Baroque Facade" group, illustrated by the KJT Hall in Praha (1922) and the SPJST Hall in Taiton, Wharton County (1924), which may have been influenced by the more elaborate but similar form of Moravian houses.[11] The octagonal hall is another notable variant. The octagonal plan permits a dance floor that is especially conducive to the circular patterns of traditional Czech dancing. The KJT Hall in Fayetteville (1912) is a good example. Other halls were uniquely built to accommodate very large crowds. The SPJST Hall at Taylor (1934) has two complete floors, the upper for dancing and the lower for dining.

Probably the most interesting church building is St. Mary's Catholic Church in Praha. This 1895 structure replaced the original 1886 frame building and is still standing today. The simple, Gothic-inspired church maintains a stately position atop a prominent hill. The interior employs tongue-and-groove planks which rise to a classic ceiling vault. The plank ceiling and upper walls have been painted to suggest the ribs of medieval stone vaulting, while wooden pillars suggest Gothic columns. Decorative details of vines and flowers in the *art nouveau* style of the 1890s are exhibited on wall and ceiling panels. A painting of St. Vitus Cathedral in Prague hangs over the altar.

Prominent among the artifacts displayed at the Czech pavilion of the Texas Centennial exhibition of 1936 were the folk costumes known as *kroje*.[12] These colorful costumes were highly prized in the Czech homeland and were worn on special occasions such as weddings, funerals, and festivals. The costumes of linen and woolen homespun were made by the family of the wearer. The following description of a typical *kroj* from Kyjov in Moravia will illustrate the appearance of *kroje* which were brought to Texas and, in many cases, reproduced there.[13] The woman's basic costume consisted of a full red skirt embroidered with flowers and white puffed-sleeve blouses. The accompanying shawl was embroidered in black and edged in black lace, and the close-

---

[10] Kolar, 124.

[11] Kolar, 125.

[12] Národní svaz českých katolíků v Texasu, *Naše dějiny*, (Granger, Tex., 1939) describes the exhibits and illustrates a *kroj* (673).

[13] This description is based on *Věstník*, November 27, 1974.

fitting vest was red and trimmed with beads. The black apron was embroidered and had beige-colored lace at the bottom. Starched, lace-trimmed, white petticoats were worn under the skirt. The woman generally wore black stockings and boots, also. It was traditional for unmarried girls to wear a half-wreath of flowers in their hair, while married ladies wore beaded and embroidered caps. Ribbons trimmed the caps and were also worn around the waist. The man wore fitted, braid-trimmed pants with boots. His blouse was full-sleeved, embroidered and lace-trimmed, while the vest, decorated with ribbons, was red.

In Texas such basic patterns were preserved, although the women gradually substituted black shoes for the traditional boots. The men, in addition to the substitution of shoes for boots, tended to substitute plain black trousers for the traditional braid-trimmed ones and omit the vest altogether. No doubt the men were responding both to the hot Texas climate and the American taboos against overly ornate men's clothing.

Texas Czechs were quick to substitute standard American "dress clothes" for most special occasions, but the custom of wearing the *kroje* to Czech festivals, particularly when the *beseda* or other folk dances were danced, never completely died out, and it has enjoyed a resurgence in the late twentieth century. Texas Czech seamstresses also preserved the *kroje* patterns in miniature, on children's dolls and puppets.[14]

For ordinary dress, the men wasted little time in adopting the typical style of the American farmer. Ethnic modes of dress persisted longer among the women, and the dress of a typical Czech farm wife in the nineteenth century might include a full skirt, about eight widths, gathered at the waist; a closely-fitted basque waist; and an embroidered apron tied behind in a large bow.[15] Her hair was typically parted in the middle and braided behind in two braids, which were wrapped around her head or rolled and pinned back. Over her hair she often wore a large, diagonally-folded kerchief, with two corners hanging down her back and two tied under her chin. In order to combat the hot Texas sun while working outdoors, she added a bonnet over the traditional kerchief. Young ladies often dispensed with the kerchief. Little girls wore dresses similar to those of their elders, but their skirts were longer, sometimes reaching to their ankles.

The ornamentation and embroidery used in making decorative

[14] The finest and largest collection of dolls dressed in authentically reproduced *kroje* is owned by Agnes Houdek of Dallas.

[15] This description is based on Mollie E. Stasney, *The Czechs in Texas*, Masters Thesis, The University of Texas at Austin (1938), 120-21.

fabrics, including the *kroje* and miniature costumes for children's dolls and puppets, represents one of the highpoints of the folk art preserved in Texas. The intricate glassware, ceramics, iron engraving, and other folk arts for which the Czech homeland was famous were, for the most part, not produced in America, although, of course, some families were able to preserve a few precious artifacts from the "old country."

One of the most ancient and popular Czech folk arts is the painting of Easter eggs, which were called by their traditional name *kraslice* as early as the fourteenth century. The art of producing the brightly-colored decorative motifs, which like the *kroje*, often represent specific geographical regions of the Czech lands, was preserved in Texas and survives up to the present day. Some of the designs are produced by a process of batik-like wax painting. More exotic folk arts, such as the sculpting and painting of Moravian beehives into fantastic gnome-like forms, were rare in Texas, however. The painting of designs on the wooden interiors of churches and homes and on wooden furniture was more common. Various floral designs predominated. A few Texas Czech "folk artists" painted designs of flowers, birds, farm animals, and stylized peasant children on door moldings, furniture, pottery, and almost any exposed surface around the home, but this practice was comparatively rare.[16]

Several distinctive "folk crafts" survived among the Texas Czech farm families. Women continued to make the kind of feather bed known as the *peřina*, which was stuffed with goose down. Men sometimes made wooden toys and musical instruments, from a simple flute to the sophisticated dulcimer *(cymbál)* discussed later in this chapter. Children learned to make many of their own toys. Perhaps most popular were those made by a complex process of paper folding. Noise makers were made from walnuts, toy birds from egg shells, whistles from willow twigs.

FOOD

Surely food has been one of the most distinctive features of the Texas Czechs, both within and outside the ethnic community. In spite

---

[16] One prominent "folk artist" was Peter Paul Drgač of Burleson County, who lived into the 1970s. His house in Caldwell was filled with examples of "naive" art, as described here.

of the increasing popularity of barbecue and fried chicken among the Czechs in the twentieth century, they continued many of their ethnic culinary traditions.[17]

Czech pastries are perhaps most important. Today the only Czech word that many Texans know is *koláč*—the term for the famous circular tart made of a special double-risen dough whose center is topped or filled with a sweet sauce made of *mák* (poppy seed), cottage cheese, prunes, peaches, or another fruit. Less well known are the *buchta* and *houska* variations with fruit or fillings baked into a loaf or square-pan form of *koláč*-type dough. (The *koláč* is equally popular in Bohemia and Moravia, but the *buchta* is especially characteristic of eastern Moravia.) Among various other pastries are the deep-fat fried *kobližky* and *smažency*.

Traditionally, pork is the favorite meat among the Texas Czechs, especially *vepřová pečeně* (roast pork) with the usual trimmings of *knedlíky* (dumplings) or *zemáky s máčků* (potatoes with gravy) and *zelí* (sauerkraut), usually flavored with carroway seed, in addition to cooked garden vegetables. Fresh pork was consumed only during the winter months. Almost every farmstead had its own smokehouse, where the meat was preserved in the form of bacon, ham, and most importantly, various kinds of *klobása* (sausage), which like the Czech pastries, gradually gained recognition among non-Czechs, especially as it was sold at legendary meat markets such as Nemeček's in West and Maňas's in Caldwell. A special delicacy among the Czechs was *jitrnice* (a kind of liver sausage). Beef was consumed in great quantities during the summer months, as the prominence of the ''beef club,'' described in Chapter 3, indicates. Lamb was also an important meat source, although not so popular as in the homeland. The favorite poultry were goose and duck, although the standard American chicken became more prominent over the years. Like his German and Anglo neighbors, the Czech also prepared his own dairy products at home. In general, the Czech cook preferred roasting and boiling to frying but gradually accepted the American custom of frying steak, chicken, fish, and even vegetables.

Soup *(polevka)* was an important part of the noon meal *(oběd)*. Rolled-out, paper-thin egg noodle dough, spread on a table or draped over chairs, was a common sight in a Czech home. After drying, the sheet of dough was rolled and cut into thin strips, to be used in various

[17] Probably the most complete Czech recipe book in Texas was compiled by the Czech Club Historical Society of Dallas in 1980. It is entitled *Generation to Generation*.

kinds of noodle soup. Another favorite was liver dumpling soup. Fresh beef liver was crushed and mixed with flour and seasoning. Little balls were fashioned with the fingers and dropped into boiling broth. Various kinds of *guláš* (stew) were also common.

As in many cultures, bread was the most venerated food, and special customs were associated with it. In some families, a loaf of bread was blessed before and after baking, and the sign of the cross made upon it was supposed to cause it to last longer. Another superstition prohibited cutting a loaf of bread from both ends.[18] The early Czech settlers preferred rye bread, but in Texas they learned to accept corn bread as an occasional substitute for rye and wheat bread.

Cuisine was extremely important to the Czechs, and good cooks were venerated. Because many of the traditional foods tend to be high in starches and fats (recipes frequently call for lard, goose fat, heavy cream, butter), they are not always favored by modern cooks, but they were standard fare among the Texas Czechs until recent times.[19]

The Czech has the reputation of being a beer drinker, and the early Czechs did practice home brewing. More characteristic of the Moravian immigrants, however, (as opposed to the Bohemians) was wine-making. They found the wild Texas varieties of mustang and post oak grapes and even dewberries and blackberries suitable for the purpose and began to cultivate domestic varieties of grapes as well. One of the mysteries of the Czech culture in Texas is the absence of *slivovice*. This potent plum brandy is popular all over Moravia but is produced in greatest quantities in the area surrounding Vizovice, the home of many emigrants who came to Texas. Home distilling of this liquor is still commonplace in Europe, but apparently never caught on in Texas, despite the availability of plums. (Opposition to the prohibi-

---

[18] Olga Pazdral, *Czech Folklore in Texas*, Masters Thesis, The University of Texas at Austin (1942), 160.

[19] Of course, during times of great hardship, such as the first years of settlement and, especially, during the Civil War years, the Texas Czechs — like everyone else — ate whatever was available, perhaps little other than corn bread. In general, however, even during the Great Depression, the nearly self-sufficient Texas Czech farmer had plenty to eat even when he had little money to spend.

tion of alcoholic beverages among the Texas Czechs was almost universal.)[20]

BELIEFS, CUSTOMS, AND FOLK LITERATURE

The Czechs brought with them a large body of superstitions to Texas. It is difficult to ascertain just how seriously they were believed. Their most important functions were probably as a source of playful conversation and reference to a common cultural heritage. This is no place to attempt to explain their origins or study them in a systematic way. No doubt some are "universal," while others may be culturally specific. The examples included in this chapter would have been familiar to many or most Texas Czechs as late as the 1930s.[21]

Not surprisingly, many of the most common superstitions are related to animals, domesticated animals in particular. If a swallow builds its nest in the eaves of a roof, good luck will roost in that home as long as the swallow stays. If a rooster crows while standing on a person's steps or porch, that person will have visitors during the day. When a beekeeper dies, someone must knock three times on each hive and say in a loud voice, "Bees, your keeper has died"; otherwise, the bees will follow their keeper and die.

Predicting the weather is a favorite pasttime on any farm, and the Texas Czech farmers knew a number of superstitions related to this activity. If it rains on Easter Sunday, it will rain for six weeks. If it rains on Good Friday, the following year will be a dry one. Rain during a new moon means that there will be rain within three days. If the sun sets behind clouds, there will be rain the next day, but if it sets behind clouds on Sunday, rain is predicted within the next three days. It is supposed to rain on the third day after a frost. If hens go to sleep early or if a spider spins a web, fair weather is expected. Fair weather on Christmas Day is expected if a cow is heard mooing on Christmas Eve. The weather of the first twelve days of the year represents the weather that the twelve months will have.

[20] It was estimated that only five of 1,400 Czech voters in Fayette County voted for Prohibition in the election of 1887. (See *Svoboda*, September 8, 1887). Decline in the influence of the popular Texas Czech Judge Haidušek (see discussion in Chapter 7) was probably at least partially attributable to his support of the *prohibitionist* Governor Hobby. See Jesse Johec, *The Life and Career of Augustin Haidušek*, Masters Thesis, The University of Texas at Austin, 103.

[21] Pazdral, 144-66.

Auguries concerning death and marriage were also common. A member of the family will die soon if a hummingbird is trying to get into the house or if cedar trees around the house grow taller than the roof. A baby may die if he is measured. Many children will die if the forenoon of Ground Hog's Day is cloudy. If four persons shake hands crosswise, some member of their families will soon get married. If a person sitting on the floor throws a shoe over his right shoulder and it lands with the toe pointing toward the door, that person will soon marry. However, if a girl looks into a mirror on the last day of the year, she will not marry during the coming year. Rain on one's wedding day promises wealth. If two sisters have a double wedding, one of them will have much bad luck. If the wedding procession meets a funeral procession, either the bride or the groom will soon die. Additional superstitions have been compiled in Appendix B.

Earlier this century, Arne Novák wrote, "The Czech, Moravian and Silesian people have long been settled in their flat or gently hilly country and have lost contact with supernatural beings; the pale imitations of such beings bear only the faintest resemblance to the supernatural powers of the ancient cult."[22] The point could be made that these supernatural beings became even paler after being transported to the New World, and in fact, they have all but disappeared today. Prior to World War II, however, a pantheon of supernatural creatures analogous to the leprechauns, faery folk, and *lloronas* of other ethnic groups, was still preserved in many Texas Czech communities.[23]

One of the most prominent supernatural creatures in the homeland and by far the most important in Texas was the *Vodník* or *Hastrman*. It was common for parents to warn their children against open wells, rivers, and other dangerous bodies of water by telling them that this water sprite would drag them down into his watery palace. The Texas *Vodník* was described as dressed in one or a combination of the colors red, green, and yellow. He may have a long, white beard, perhaps long green hair, perhaps a wreath of seaweed on his head. His feet and hands are usually webbed, although he may have cat-like claws. When he is out of the water, water continuously drips from his left foot. In order to lure his victims into the water, he may transform himself into a white horse, a dog, a wolf, or another animal. Olga Pazdral reports two supposedly authentic cases in Texas in which the in-

[22] Novák, 105.

[23] See Pazdral, 38-71. Information on the *Vodník* is reinforced by an interview in 1975 with Andrew Prikryl of Austin, whose grandfather was a noted Texas Czech storyteller.

tended victim of a *Vodník* (in his transformed animal state) was able to escape.[24] Little children, when going to the well to draw water, were sometimes taught to sing a song in order to protect themselves. One variant is

Hastrmane, tatrmane, vylez z vody ven.
Dej nam kozich na buben.
Budeme ti bubnovati až vylezeš z vody ven.
(Hastrman, buffoon, come out of the water.
Give us a coat [head?] for a drum.
We will beat on the drum until you come out of the water.)

The European *Vodník* could sometimes be a pleasant fellow who brought good luck, but in Texas he was almost always an evil spirit. Other supernatural creatures, including a type of Czech vampire, are described in Appendix B.

Many of the most exotic customs among the Texas Czechs are closely related to superstitions. The custom of announcing the death of the beekeeper to the bees was evidently fairly common. (Pazdral notes that the word *umírati* [to die] was used in speaking of bees, the same that was used to describe the death of humans, instead of the usual *zhynouti and scípnouti*, which were reserved for other animals.)[25] Several other customs concerning death are worth noting. The mirrors in a house where a coffin was lying were sometimes covered due to the superstition that anyone seeing the reflection of a coffin in a mirror will himself die soon. Also, when a person died in a house, a window was sometimes opened so that the soul could escape. In some communities, when an unmarried man or woman died, attendants analagous to the "bridesmaid" and "best man" of the wedding ceremony would escort the coffin to the grave.[26]

The Texas Czechs had dozens of exotic cures for various ailments.[27] A sty, for example, could be relieved by rubbing it with a gold ring or by looking through a hole in the wall. To cure a head cold a person could leave a trace of refuse from his nose on the side of a door as he passed through. To cure a sore throat, he could swallow a piece of bacon. A sweaty sock tied around the neck would also cure a sore throat.

It was customary for Texas Czech farm families to plant their crops — especially garden vegetables — "according to the moon."

[24] Pazdral, 41-42.
[25] Pazdral, 145.
[26] Interview with Henry Haisler; farmhouse near Providence, Burleson County; March 9, 1975.
[27] Pazdral, 163-66.

Anything that bears above the ground was planted in the light of the moon; anything that bears under the ground was planted in the dark of the moon. If potatoes are planted during a new moon, each plant is supposed to bloom much but yield few potatoes. Roses should be transplanted during a full moon to insure full blooms.

A few special customs were observed for holidays such as New Year's Day, May Day, and St. John's Day, although old Czech traditions such as the burning of brooms on St. John's Day to commemorate the ancient practice of burning witches and the construction of the *majka* (May Pole), a practice still current in many Czech villages, never caught on in Texas. Celebration of the Easter and Christmas seasons in Texas continued to be quite elaborate. In the early days of the Czech settlements, Smrtelná Neděle, the Sunday two weeks before Easter, was observed with a special ceremony. A "Goddess of Death" was constructed from a doll's head, a pole, and ribbons. Then a group of boys and girls, each holding the end of a ribbon, would travel from house to house, singing a song which began *"Smrt lesem za lesem"* ("Death in the woods beyond woods . . ."). The residents of the houses thus serenaded gave the singers eggs, cakes, money, and other little gifts.[28] Then, as Easter Sunday approached, a series of washing ceremonies was practiced by some families. Anyone who washed his feet in a stream on Maundy Thursday was not supposed to get sick for an entire year. On Good Friday, girls got up before sunrise to wash their faces in cold water: it was supposed to make them pretty. On Easter Sunday, it was traditional for the boys to wash the girls' faces. On the following Monday, the girls washed the boys' faces. Another custom observed on this Monday, apparently much rarer than the washing of faces, was for the boys to make willow whips and switch the legs of their favorite girls. The girls could switch the boys on the following day. More common was the giving of the *kraslice* (decorated eggs) and "Easter egg hunts" on Easter Sunday.[29]

Observance of the Christmas holidays began earlier for the Czechs than it did for most Texans. St. Nicholas Day was observed on December 6, and that is the time little children hung up their stockings, although it was not an occasion for large gatherings or feasting.[30] On the night of December 6, the Czech household was traditionally visited by three costumed figures: St. Nicholas, an angel, and a devil. St.

---

[28] Pazdral, 170-71.
[29] Pazdral, 171-72; Stasney, 126.
[30] Pazdral, 172-73; Stasney, 125-26.

Nicholas would ask the children if they knew their prayers and if they had obeyed their parents during the previous year. If they had, he presented them with gifts; if they had not, he called for the devil to whip them. In a variant of this tradition, St. Nicholas was supposed to visit on the night of December 6, and that is when the stockings were left in the window to be filled with little gifts. Then on December 8, the house was visited by *Matička* (Little Mother) and a devil figure. The devil waits outside while *Matička*, dressed in gold or white, goes in to question the children, as St. Nicholas does in the other variation, calling in the devil if a whipping is needed. If they have been good, she gives them candy and fruit. It is difficult to say when the majority of little Czech children began to receive their gifts on Christmas Eve or Christmas Day, like other American children. Remnants of the December 6 tradition still existed in some Czech families in the 1940s.

During the Christmas season, it was common for groups of carolers to go from house to house, serenading the residents. In addition to the usual Czech carols, however, they sang *koledy* (gift songs). One of the most popular *koledy* began *Svatý, svatý Štěpane, co to neseí ve džbáně?* ("Holy, holy Stephen, what are you carrying in your pitcher?") Another common custom was the baking of special Christmas cookies in the shape of animals, people, Christmas trees, hearts, etc. Each cookie was decorated with icing and a special picture, that, according to Pazdral, was often ordered from Czechoslovakia before World War II.[31]

A large number of special customs and games are associated with the celebration of Christmas, and many of them relate to superstitions.[32] If a child fasts all day, he will be rewarded with the glimpse of a *zlaté prasátko* (golden pig) on Christmas Eve. Some families placed a candle by each member's supper plate on Christmas Eve; the member whose candle went out first was to be the first to die. The crumbs of the Christmas Eve supper were divided among the well, the garden, trees, and animals to make them produce well during the coming year. Several games were played with nuts and apples. Each girl peels an apple and keeps the peeling intact. Then she throws it either over her shoulder or over the heads of a line of girls. The letter formed by the peel is the initial of the boy she will marry. In another game, each player is given seven nuts, and he is allowed to choose three of them to crack. The player who cracks the best nut will receive seven years of good luck. Members of a family would sometimes each crack twelve nuts,

31 Pazdral, 173-75.
32 Pazdral, 175-79.

each representing a month. Each bad kernel would predict illness for the month it represents. Several other common Christmas games deal with "good luck — bad luck" or with approaching marriage.

The Czechs brought many children's games with them that were played the year round, of course. They will not be described in detail here, as most of them resemble Anglo-American games.[33] Among the most popular were *prstýnek* (ring), *slepá baba* ("Blind Woman," a form of Blind Man's Bluff), *anděl a čert* (angel and devil) or *barvy* (colors), *na šáteček* ("drop the handkerchief"), *schovávačka* ("hide and seek"), *mrkati* (wink), *zlatá brána* ("Golden Gate," similar to "London Bridge"), *na kozla* ("goat," a kind of leap-frog), *kokeš* ("*Co chceš?*" "What do you want?"), and *hoří, hoří* ("It's burning, burning"). The special rhymes and chants used in these games could also be included in the category of folk literature. Card games included *taroky, durák,* and *Černý Peter* (Black Peter). The game of *taroky* (played by young and old alike) has maintained its popularity over the years, and order forms for the special deck of cards used in the game can still be found in Texas Czech journals. Dominoes was also, and still is, a favorite game.

As is the case with certain other ethnic groups, the best-known customs of the Texas Czechs are related to the elaborate rituals of the wedding ceremony. Traditionally the Czech wedding is a very large event. Every relative and every friend in the community was usually invited, and preliminary plans included the raising of additional poultry and slaughter animals for the wedding feast.

Two of the groom's attendants, who were chosen well in advance, would visit each family to be invited and extend verbal invitations. A special ritual was involved. Both men would dismount their well-groomed horses outside the house and remove their hats. The best man would walk forward and deliver the standard invitation which began (in Czech, of course):

> Do not feel offended that we so daringly entered your home. It is not our will nor yours that we are here but the will of Miss _____
> and Mr. _____. They have resolved to forsake their single state. . . .[34]

Special friends of the family would arrive a few days ahead of the wedding to help with the baking and other preparations.

[33] Pazdral, 106-11.

[34] Stasney, 122. Undoubtedly there were many variations of the wedding rituals and customs described here, but these are typical.

Painting of the wedding of Josef and Františka Laštovica in Hostýn, Texas, 1861.
— Photo copied from *Naše dějiny.*

After breakfast on the day of the wedding (at which only the immediate family members were normally present), guests began to gather in the parlor or the largest room in the bride's house. She walked into the room, accompanied by her parents, and was greeted by an elderly man who had been designated *starosta* (literally, "mayor"). The *starosta* formally introduced the bride to the groom and gave each of them advice about leading a good married life. Then the wedding procession was ready to go to the church.[35] After the church ceremony, the wedding procession returned to the bride's house. When they arrived, however, they were likely to find two men guarding the front gate. When the wedding guests paid them some money, however, the men moved aside and let everybody pass through. (This money was later given to the newlyweds.) It was then time for the feasting and dancing to begin. Sometimes, a doll was passed among the guests at the dinner table by a person who asked for a collection to buy a cradle for the couple's first child. The feasting and dancing went on late into the night. At midnight, there might be a special ceremony for removal of the bridal veil. Either the song *"Už mou milou"* ("Now My Dear One") or *"Svobodo, svobodo"* ("Freedom, Freedom") was sung at that time.[36]

As more fraternal lodge halls became available for the purpose, the wedding feast and dance were more often moved to a hall in order to accommodate a greater number of guests. Some of the "quaint" rituals, such as the formal oral invitation of guests, were probably rare by the 1920s. The bridal unveiling ceremony was apparently still fairly common in 1940. An unchanging feature of the Texas Czech wedding down to the present day, however, is the gala polka dance. In general, Catholic weddings tend to be more elaborate than Protestant ones.

In the early days of the SPJST fraternal organization, a member's funeral often included a flag ceremony (with the SPJST flag) similar to the U.S. flag ceremony that is traditional in a military funeral. In addition, members of the deceased's lodge would not hold a dance or other entertainment for thirty days after his death.[37] These funeral customs illustrate well the group solidarity and implicit nationalism in the early Texas Czech community. Of course, other common customs,

---

[35] Stasney, 123.
[36] Pazdral, 169.
[37] Interview with Henry Haisler; see Note 26.

such as the house raisings, communal farm work in times of distress, feather strippings, quilting bees, and other social activities discussed earlier in Chapter 3, also illustrate these characteristics.

The various kinds of oral literature did not fare equally well among the Czechs in Texas. The folk songs, which can be considered as folk poetry, have been justly called "the most precious single heritage of Czech national culture."[38] Although the preconditions for true folk composition of songs were probably absent in Texas, the existing songs were preserved very well, and new popular songs based on folk models continued to be produced. These songs will be discussed later in this chapter as part of the Czech musical heritage. Czech proverbs are next in longevity; many of them were, and still are, current in Texas. As long as there are "native" Czech speakers, at least some proverbs which are almost incorporated into the fabric of the language and represent habitual ways of thinking in Czech will surely be preserved.

The vast body of children's literature brought with the Czechs to Texas, however, like the legends of fairies and other supernatural creatures with which it is often associated, deteriorated much more quickly. By the time of World War II, it could not be assumed that the Texas Czech child received the traditional lullabies and fairy tales along with his mother's milk, even if the Czech language was used in the home. However, in some of the Czech communities, a number of grandmothers, and sometimes grandfathers, continued to give their grandchildren large doses of folklore. As late as 1941, Pazdral was able to collect a substantial body of folklore, including folk tales and children's rhymes, from high school students in West.[39]

She records several lullabies or cradle songs. One version of a popular song is:

Spi, děťátko, spi	Sleep, baby, sleep;
zavří očka svy,	Close thy little eyes.
anděliček bude spáti,	The little angel will sleep
a matička kolebati,	And the dear mother will rock.
spi, děťátko, spi.	Sleep, baby, sleep.

Among the many poems and songs for small children, several versions of a swinging song begin:

Houpy, houpy,	*Houpy, houpy,*
kočky snědly kroupy.	The cats ate the barley.

[38] Novák, 100.

[39] For children's rhymes and songs, see Pazdral, 84-106.

See Appendix B for other rhymes, riddles, and tongue twisters.

Among the best-known Czech folktales in Texas are those about Hloupý Honza (Stupid John). In some of his tales, he is portrayed as a "wise fool."[40] For example, he tags along with three men who are looking for happiness, but in the end happiness comes to him only (because happiness can never be found if actively looked for). Many of his stories are humorous. In one, he and his father go to the woods to look for wild berries and firewood. As they leave the house, the father says, *"Ber z tebe dveře, Honzo."* The colloquial meaning of the phrase is "Close the door behind you," but it literally means "Take the door behind you." Honza took the door off its hinges and carried it with them. Later the door saves them, when Honza drops the door from the tree where he and his father are perched and stuns the robbers who are stalking them. In other stories, Honza is simply a silly fool. For example, when his mother asks him to carry some butter to his aunt, he puts the butter on his head under his hat, and, of course, the butter melts and runs all over him. His mother tells him that he should have wrapped the butter in cabbage leaves and cooled it in the spring. The next time Honza goes to see his aunt, she gives him a little dog. After wrapping it in leaves and cooling it in the spring, Honza brings the little dog home half drowned. His mother tells him that he should have tied a string around the dog's head and led it home. Later, his aunt gives Honza a loaf of bread. He ties a string around it and drags it home.[41]

A few of the Czech national legends, about semi-historical, semi-mystical characters, were preserved in Texas. The best known tales concern King Václav (The Good King Wenceslas of the English Christmas carol), who is asleep with his knights inside Blaník Mountain, waiting for the day when his nation will need him most. At that time, he will ride forth and bring victory and peace to the suffering people. Various connected tales describe the adventures of characters who find their way into the mountain and see the sleeping king. Other folktales are described in Appendix B.

The Texas Czechs are traditionally fond of all sorts of ghost stories and tales of the supernatural. Many of these stories concern manifestations of the "ethnic" supernatural creatures discussed in this chapter,

[40] The concept of the "wise fool" is central to Czech folklore and literature. Perhaps the figure best known to modern readers is Jaroslav Hašek's Dobrý Voják Švejk (Good Soldier Švejk), the anti-hero of the novel by the same name (1920-1923).

while other stories about ghosts and demons are not substantially different from those told by members of other ethnic groups. Most of these stories are, of course, primarily intended to entertain children and even adults, although some stories about unexplained events, manifestations of extrasensory perception, and even some ghost stories may be taken at least half seriously. On the other hand, Texas Czechs delight in practical jokes designed to hoodwink someone into thinking he had "seen a ghost."[42]

Proverbs are often thought of as expressions of the "popular wisdom of the people" or "folk wisdom." Borrowings from the Bible and classical and medieval literature turn up in comparative studies, however, so that it is impossible to locate a purely folk wisdom. At any rate, the Czechs had, from time immemorial, shown a great respect for the proverb and considered it to be integral to the language and to both oral and written literature. The Czechs in Texas maintained the oral tradition to a great extent. As in the case of fairy tales, some are undoubtedly "international" proverbs. A few of the hundreds of proverbs current among the Texas Czechs are listed below.[43] Others are found in Appendix B.

Ani slepice zadarmo nehrabe.
Even a chicken does not scratch for nothing.

Bez peněz, k muzice nelez.
Without money do not go to the music.

Desetkrát měř, jednou řež.
Measure ten times; cut once.

Dobrá hospodyňka má pro pírko přes plot skočit.
A good housekeeper should jump across a fence for a feather.

Každá liška svůj ocas chválí.
Every fox praises its own tail.

Koho Pánbůh miluje, křížkem ho navštěvuje.
Whomever God loves he visits with a cross.

Laskavé slovo lepší než měkký koláč.
A loving word is better than a soft *koláč* (tart).

[42] I can recall hearing several (perhaps apocryphal) variants of stories of such incidents from my father. Generally, the victim (sometimes inebriated) is walking or riding a horse home after visiting a friend or attending a dance and must pass a graveyard, etc. (CM)

[43] Pazdral, 72-83.

Rád ho poslouchám když mlčí.
I like to listen to him when he is silent.

Sliby se slibují, blázni se radují.
When promises are promised, fools rejoice.

Sytí lačnému nevěří.
The satiated one does not believe the hungry one.

Ve víně je pravda.
In wine there is truth.

There is evidence that at least a few of the proverbs originated in the American South:

První pán — a potom černoch.
First the gentleman — then the Negro.

Some of the proverbs illustrate the earthy, scatological humor of the Czechs:

Paráda na ulici, hovno v truhlici.
A parade in the street, shit in the coffer.[44]

A *truhlice*, for most Texas Czechs, was a large wooden box in which provisions such as flour, sugar, tea, and other dry foods and spices were stored. The meaning of the proverb is that those who "show off" or "parade" themselves (in fine clothes, etc.) probably do so at the expense of more essential needs. It also illustrates the typical Czech ridicule of pretension and ostentaciousness, while implying the values of *hospodářství*.

Texas Czech adult humor is often coarse although seldom truly obscene. The following joke illustrates the typical rural setting and the eternal husband-wife conflict.

"A man was being driven crazy by his wife because she hadn't said a word to him in three days. 'I've got to get her to speak to me,' he thought, and went to a neighbor for advice. On the fourth day of her silence he put the neighbor's plan into effect. At high noon, he silently dressed himself in hat, coat, and high-top rubber boots. Then he lit a kerosene lantern and carried it with him to the smokehouse, where he began to rummage around, making a lot of noise. [The smokehouse was often used as a storehouse for tools and other goods when not being used to cure meat.] The wife listened and watched

---

[44] This one was current in my mother's family. (CM) See the discussion of *hospodářství* in Chapter 3.

from her kitchen window until she could stand it no more. She ran across the yard, stuck her head into the door of the smokehouse, and shouted, 'Are you crazy, old man?' He just kept rummaging around. 'What in the hell are you looking for, any way?' At that, the man set down his lantern and exclaimed, 'I've been looking for your damned tongue for three days, woman, and I hadn't found it until now!' " [45]

MUSIC

Music is the most important art form among the Texas Czechs. When aged informants are questioned about the cultural activities of early Czech families and communities in Texas, they almost always emphasize the songs and dances. [46] The love of music, like the love of good food and drink with their attendant social rituals, is not restricted by religious or other affiliation among the Czechs. They brought with them a strong musical tradition from their homeland. It seems that almost every family had at least one musically-inclined member, perhaps even with some formal training, and other families were "musical" as a whole and founded family bands.

The well-known Czech classical musical tradition, which is associated with America primarily through the composer Antonín Dvořák (1841-1904), obviously did not have the opportunity to develop in rural Texas, although it continued to be nourished by Czechs in the large urban centers of the North. Even in Texas, when opera stars such as Jaromila Novotná or Czech orchestras toured the cities, Czechs turned out in great numbers to see them. [47] For the most part, however, the Texas Czechs remained spectators rather than participants in this tradition. One exception is the organization of a tamburash orchestra by Josef Drozda in Houston in 1932. The tamburash is a lute-like instrument which is said to have been invented by the Czechs four centuries ago.

Czech folk music, on the other hand, was of tremendous importance and nurtured by the Texas Czechs from the beginning. After language, folk music is the most important indicator of Czech identity

[45] The source for the joke is an interview with Betty Beran Marek; Bryan, Texas; March 21, 1975.

[46] It is uncommon for an informant to remember a single *pohadka* (fairy tale) but common to perfectly recall, and be willing to sing *a capella*, dozens of folk songs.

[47] In the early twentieth century, many Texas Czechs were familiar with a few Czech national operas. The best known was Smetena's *Prodaná nevěsta* ("The Bartered Bride").

in the state. It is important to understand that folk music is, among the Czechs, as it is among certain other nationalities, not merely a popular tradition to be preserved in artificial way by enthusiasts and scholars, but a living force among the people. In fact, the major Czech classical composers — Dvořák, Bedřich Smetana (1824-1884), Leoš Janáček (1854-1928) — rely heavily on folk themes and motifs, so that there is a very close relationship between folk culture and "high" culture. Folk music was one of the most important expressions of national identity in the Austrian-dominated Czech lands where political forms of expression were difficult or impossible.[48] Later, the surviving widows of Lidice sang folk songs in Nazi prison camps.[49] Czech literature, particularly of the National Revival period in the nineteenth century, glorifies folk singing as an almost mystical force for goodwill and unity among the people, and by all accounts, folk singing really was an important part of the daily life of the Czech peasant as well as an activity for festivals and celebrations. Workers sang in the fields; the mother sang her child to sleep; old people whispered the words of songs to themselves; young people sang at informal gatherings.[50]

While it would seem that life in America is not conducive to this kind of traditional musicality, folk singing did continue to be a vital force in the Texas Czech community. Many Czechs would carry little leatherbound, wallet-like song sheets with them for ready reference when visiting friends. Family gatherings, neighborly visits, fraternal lodge meetings — all were occasions for singing. On Saturday night there was likely to be a dance, featuring orchestra arrangements of folk songs. And then on Sunday, there was singing of Czech hymns,[51] some of which could probably be classified as folk songs, too. Weekend outdoor band concerts featuring arrangements of folk songs were joined in the 1920s by the radio "polka shows," by far the most popular radio entertainment among the Czechs.[52]

[48] See Marie Z. Němcová, "Preface" to Marjorie Crane Geary's *Folk Dances of Czechoslovakia* (1927).

[49] The widows continue to sing the same folk songs that they had sung in the prison camps at the annual commemorative gathering in Lidice.

[50] See F. Bartoš, "Národní Pisně," in *Česká čitanka* (Praha, 1912).

[51] Among the most important religious music preserved in Texas are the Czech Brethren Christmas hymns *"Narodil se Kristus Pan"* (1522) and *"Syn Boži se nam narodil"* (1636).

[52] As late as 1949, Robert L. Skrabanek wrote of the Texas Czech community of Snook: "The most popular radio program on the air, so far as the inhabitants are concerned, is Czech music. This program is preferred by all three generations in the community, but its popularity decreases with each succeed-

Literally hundreds of Czech folk songs survived in Texas throughout the period we studied here, and many of them are familiar to thousands of Texas Czechs even today. Many of the songs, such as the popular *"A já sám"* ("I Alone") are melancholy or wistful; however, even these sad lyrics are matched with a brisk melody, either a waltz, or in this case, a polka, suitable for lively dancing. Others are outright, rollicking drinking songs, such as *"Nemelem, nemelem"* ("We Are Not Milling"), also a polka.

As might be expected, the songs are full of earthy, rural imagery: fields, streams, crops, animals. Also unsurprisingly, the most popular theme is the love between a young man and woman in all its joyful and tragic manifestations. Even in English translation, many of these songs communicate something of their poetic charm and beauty. Below are the lyrics to *"Louka zelená"* ("Green Meadow"), probably the most popular Czech waltz in Texas, with the English translation.

Louka zelená, neposekaná,	Green meadow, unmowed,
Roste na ní kvítí.	Flowers grow on it.
Kdo chce holku mít	He who wants to have a girl
Musí za ní jít	Must go to her
Když měsíček svítí.	When the moon is shining.
Já jsem holku měl,	I had a girl,
Já jsem za ní šel	I visited her
Když měsíček svítil.	When the moon was shining.
Ona nespala,	She was not sleeping,
Na mě čekala	She was waiting for me
Když jsem za ní přišel.	When I came to her.

Other typical love songs which rely heavily on a rural setting and nature imagery are *"Okolo Libice,"* ("Around Libice"), *"Na Bílej Hoře"* ("On White Mountain"), *"Borovičky borový"* ("The Pines of Borovice"), *"Na tej louce"* ("On the Meadow"), *"Měsíček svítí,"* ("The Moon Is Shining"), *"Pod dubem, za dubem"* ("Over the Oak, Under the Oak"), and *"Co ten ptáček povídá"* ("What That Bird Says").

Another fairly prominent category of Czech folk song concerns the plight of the young recruit into the Austrian Army, who must leave his loved ones in order to serve a government he hates and perhaps to die in battle. Examples are *"Mý zlatý rodiče"* ("My Dear Parents") and *"Na tu svatú Kateřinku"* ("To Saint Catherine").

The songs sung by the Texas Czechs are divided about equally be-

ing generation." "Social Life in a Czech-American Rural community," *Rural Sociology*, vol xv, no. 3 (December, 1949), 221-231.

tween those of Moravian and Bohemian origin, although a few Slovak songs, such as *"Tancuj, tancuj"* ("Dance, Dance") were also popular, a testimony to cultural overlap.

Certain other popular songs cannot be technically termed "folk" because their composers are known, but they were so completely absorbed into the repertories of the bands—and into the consciousness of the people—along with the true folk songs that little distinction is made between the two groups. Well-known examples are *"Škoda lásky"* ("The Sorrow of Love") by J. Vejvoda (known to Anglo-Americans as "The Beer Barrel Polka") and the *pochody* or marches by František Kmoch, such as *"Koline, koline"* (the name of a Czech town). The marches were inspired by the Austrian military music which was typically played by Czech musicians. Also preserved in Texas were a few patriotic songs about recent national heroes. The best example is *"Spi, Havlíčku"* ("Sleep, Havlíček"), dedicated to Karel Havlíček. The term "folk music" as used here, includes these exceptions, but the vast majority of the songs were true folk songs, of ancient but indeterminate origin.

In a sense, the folk song tradition was stationary in Texas, just as it was in the homeland; the age of true folk song composition must pass with the age of the old peasant society. However, new polkas and waltzes continued to be composed in this country, and in musical style and tone, they fit well into the basic folk song repertories. The Czech folk song tradition remained vital and central to the immigrants' lives because there was no sharp distinction between folk and popular music. To a large extent, folk music *was* popular music, not for preservation so much as for participation. Probably even more important than the fact that the people sang folk songs is that they danced to them. Most of the popular songs existed in dance band arrangements, either polkas (a dance form of Czech origin) or waltzes. Texas Czech polka bands began to proliferate toward the end of the nineteenth century, and by the 1920s and 1930s there were probably as many as one hundred Texas Czech bands in existence at any one time and scores of dances held at the various fraternal halls all over the state on a typical Saturday night.

Although most Texas Czech orchestras were native to this country, some of them had a musical background in the homeland. A few started with the members of musical families who had emigrated to Texas. In some cases the orchestral composition, musical rhythms and arrangements can be identified with the region of Moravia or Bohemia from which they came. This is true to some extent of the Bača family, the most famous of the Texas Czech musical families.

The Bača Band ca. 1935. John Bača, band master, is standing fourth from the left.

—*Photo from Naše dejiny.*

When Josef Bača settled on a farm near Fayetteville in 1860, he named the place Bordovice after his native Moravian village.[53] Although the Bačas had had a reputation as a "musical family" back home, the exigencies of the Civil War, the Reconstruction period, and a hard pioneer life retarded the composition of a formal Bača musical unit until 1892, when Josef's son Frank J., who had been playing trombone and writing music for a Fayetteville city band, formed the Bača Family Band. And all thirteen of his children participated! As time went on, non-related talented musicians from around Fayette County joined the band, but it retained the family image. One of Frank's sons, Joe O., rose to prominence over the years, winning local and national solo contests with his cornet. Joe became band leader after his father's death, and under his leadership, the band's reputation began to grow. According to some accounts, when Antonín Dvořák, grandson of the famous Czech composer, emigrated to Texas in 1912, he was playing in the Bača band only two days after his arrival in Galveston.[54] The band was always in demand for festivals and special occasions in the Central Texas area. One of the most memorable was a gigantic celebration at the Fayetteville SPJST hall at the end of World War I.

After Joe's death in 1920, brother John R. Bača took over the leadership of the band. Under John, the band played for the first time on radio, in 1926 on KPRC Houston, and recorded phonograph records on the OKAY, Columbia and Brunswick labels in the 1930s. By 1937 there were three Bača bands: besides John R.'s, there was the L. B. Bača Band and Ray Bača's "New Deal" Band, all doing well in different parts of the state.

The Bača family tradition is a particularly notable one, connected with all sorts of stories and legends which imply an almost mystical relationship between men and music; for example, several band members requested that they be buried in their band uniforms. However, the Bačas were by no means an isolated phenomenon. There were at least 85 other "musical families" among the Texas Czech, from Adamčík to Zdrůbek.[55]

[53] The following history of the Bača band is based primarily on Cleo R. Baca, *Baca's Musical History: 1860-1968* (La Grange, Tex., 1968).

[54] *The Houston Post*, April 30, 1967.

[55] Series of interviews and conversations with members of the Bača, Pavlas, and Slováček families. Calvin C. Chervenka, in *The Czechs of Texas* (Unpublished Manuscript for Southwest Educational Development Laboratory, Austin, 1975), compiled the list of 85 Texas Czech family names traditionally associated with music and the formation of bands and orchestras. Among the

One particularly interesting aspect of the early Bača bands was their use of the *cymbál*, a type of Czech dulcimer. This many-stringed instrument, which is played with wooden mallets, is native to Moravia and may be of Gypsy origin. Reportedly the first *cymbál* in Texas was made by Joe O. Bača's uncle Ignác Křenek. It had 120 strings and 2½ octaves. Although a few other homemade *cymbály* appeared in Texas among the Moravian settlers, the instrument remained a relative curiosity. In fact the most distinctive kind of Moravian instrumentation for folk melodies, which accentuated string instruments such as the *cymbál* and various kinds of violins, and can still be heard today in festivals like the one in Strážnice, Moravia, never materialized in Texas.[56] Instead, a hybrid sound of violins, accordions and Anglo-American instruments such as the guitar and banjo gave way to the kind of instrumentation variously called "brass," "military," "picnic" or "German," that is more characteristic of the traditional Bohemian sound. At any rate, little of the wild "Gypsy flavor" of Moravian music crossed the Atlantic with these settlers.

A typical "brass" band would consist of two or more clarinets and/or saxophones, two or more trumpets and/or cornets, and an accordian and possibly even a dulcimer up front; a trombone, baritone, alto, and/or French horn in the second row; drums, bass horn and possibly a piano in the rear. The band would perform for a public concern at a picnic or on the city square, playing marches, polkas, and waltzes, possibly along with laendlers and overtures. For the dance at night, whether it was held on an open platform or in the dance hall, they would generally drop some of the brass instruments and strive for a less martial-sounding and more danceable music. The "band" then would be considered an "orchestra." For the most part, the orchestra would stick to the standard repertory of "old-time favorite" polkas and waltzes, most of which were arrangements of the Czech folk songs.

best known are Adamčík, Adamek, Bača, Beseda, Boháč, Černý, Červenka, Diviš, Drozd, Dušek, Dybala, Haisler, Honza, Janečka, Ježek, Kohut, Kostohryz, Kovář, Křenek, Kubala, Kubin, Kučera, Maca, Majek, Marek, Matocha, Matuš, Menšík, Mikula, Milan, Motl, Němec, Paták, Patek, Pavlas, Pavelka, Pokladník, Ripl, Shiller, Šimek, Slováček, Sodek, Vaněk, Vražel, Vrla, Vytopil, Zbranek, and Zrůbek.

[56] For example, listen to SUPRAPHON Mono O 17 1764 G (1975), *Strážnička brana se otevírá*, which includes selected musical performances, 1947-1972, representative of the most authentic Moravian folk music. Strážnice is located in an area from which many of the Texas settlers came. The absence in Texas of this kind of music, along with that of the potent plum brandy *slivovice*, remains a mystery.

Jazz and the "big band" sound influenced the music of the Czech bands in the 1930s and 1940s, but, generally speaking, the basic folk music repertory remained intact. More serious were the inroads made by Country and Western music in the 1950s and 1960s and which continue to erode the old-time repertory of the Czech bands.

One other curious "musical instrument" should be mentioned. A kind of sophisticated grinder organ called a *flašinet* was an early import from the Czech lands. The *flašinet* ranged in size from that of an accordian to that of a modern-day jukebox. The player turned a crank which caused air to blow past vibrating reeds. In order to work properly, the crank had to be turned, very consistently, at the proper speed. Several communities owned these Czech imports; they provided music for house dances, parties, and picnics when no band was available.

Choral clubs for the singing of folk songs existed at one time or another in most of the Texas Czech communities. Nevertheless, Habenicht, in 1904, reported that the choral club, like the Sokol, was relatively underdeveloped in Texas compared to Czech population centers in other states.[57] Čapek reports the choral club to be an almost ubiquitous feature of Czech-American communities.[58]

Because the polka is a native Czech dance form, the "polka dances" as they evolved in Texas (and other states) can be considered folk dances. During the first three decades or so of the Texas Czech community, dances were held almost exclusively in private homes. During a family visit, chairs would be cleared out of one of the rooms and one or more individuals would provide the music on a violin or accordion. A birthday or wedding might be the occasion for a multifamily party with music and dancing, and more than one room might be needed.

As the fraternal organizations grew in membership, and more and more lodge halls began to be built toward the end of the nineteenth century, larger-scale community dances began to be a more frequent Saturday night event. The lodge halls would also be used for parties and dances on special occasions, especially weddings and anniversaries.[59] There was usually one continuous bench or a row of

[57] Jan Habenicht, *Dějiny čechů amerických* (St. Louis, 1910).

[58] Tomáš Čapek, *The Čechs (Bohemians) in America* (Boston and New York, 1920).

[59] Before these halls were available, large community dances were sometimes held on a large wooden-plank platform built especially for the occasion. These were called, appropriately enough, "platform dances." Interview with Lee Pavlas, Sr.; Caldwell, Texas; May 22, 1975.

benches lining the inside wall. The women, children and young ladies would sit on the benches, waiting to be asked to dance or simply watching.

On the other hand, the men were usually divided between the dance hall and outside, talking and drinking. Beer was usually not allowed inside the hall. Inside, eligible young bachelors stood in a group at the center of the dance floor that was sometimes called the "bull ring," until they got enough courage to ask the young ladies to dance. If a young lady refused a request to dance, this was called *dávají mu koš*, "giving him the basket." If the young lady wanted to be asked by others in the future, however, she had to be careful not to "give too many baskets."

Other folk dances not usually associated with ballroom dancing were also preserved in Texas. Groups or societies dedicated to both folk singing and dancing began to be more and more popular with the rise of the Sokol and the fraternals. These folk dances are usually performed at special events, celebrations and festivals. Probably the most notable of these dances is the *beseda*. The literal meaning of the word is "social gathering." The *beseda*, as it developed in the Czech lands, was actually a composite of various folk dance forms that were native to different provinces; in fact, the *beseda* developed into three related but distinct variants — the Czech, the Moravian, and the Slovak. All three survived in Texas.[60]

The *beseda* shares certain movements with American square dancing. The dance steps known as the "star," the "chain" or "grand right and left" and the "heel and toe polka" are examples. Also, the dance step called *"valašský-šatečkový"* in the Moravian *beseda* is similar to the "dishrag" in American folk dancing. The man and woman who form a couple hold two kerchiefs between them. They alternately turn toward each other and away from each other three or four times out of the circle and then turn back into the circle. The *beseda* and the square dance have the same "home" formation. It is a circle with couples one and three as the lead couples and couples three and four as the side couples. The Slovak *beseda* has both the chain or grand right and left and a star formation. The star formation

---

[60] The descriptions of the *beseda* are based on those of Calvin C. Chervenka in *The Czechs of Texas*.

also appears in the Czech *beseda* and in this case closely resembles the "wagon wheel" of square dancing. The "heel and toe" or "double" polka is used in the Czech *beseda* and in many other Czech folk dances. The polka and waltz steps are the most frequently used steps in the *beseda*, and they are often alternated. Two rules peculiar to the *beseda* are that the number one couple always faces the music in forming the circle with couple number two on their right. Hands are kept on the hips when not being used in a dance step.

Many other of the folk dances are done by children: the Czech *holka modrooká* (blue-eyed girl), the Moravian *řezničká* (butcher), and the Slovak *tancůj, tancůj* (dance, dance).

Toward the end of the period covered by this book, an important new outlet for Texas Czech music was opened. The radio "polka" shows that began in the late 1920s quickly gained a wide popularity.[61] Although the John R. Bača orchestra played on KPRC Houston as early as 1926, it was not until the 1930s that this became a widespread practice. In the early 1930s the Májek orchestra could be heard on a Cameron station and the Joe Merlick orchestra on KFJZ Fort Worth. Then in the years 1935-1940 the polka program "Adolph and the Boys" could be heard each weekend morning from 8:30 to 9:00 a.m. over the Texas Quality Network (TQN). The stations in TQN included WBAP Fort Worth, WFAA Dallas, WOAI San Antonio, and KPRC Houston. The program was sponsored by Gold Chain Flour and was broadcast live from studios in Schulenburg. Because of this exposure, Adolph and the Boys became so popular during this time that there was "standing room only" at many of their dance performances.

One of the earliest was also the longest running show, and it is still being broadcast today: the Czech Melody Hour on KTEM Temple. Like most of the other shows, it was broadcast on Sunday afternoons. The first performance was by the I. J. Bača orchestra on November 29, 1936. Besides many performances by this group in the early years, the Diviš, the Kostohryz, and the Májek orchestras were also frequent guests.

The Texas Czech polka shows were an early example of "ethnic programming" in Texas radio. The ordinary format was very simple. In the early days, the performances were live. The announcer, speaking in Czech, would introduce the orchestra and each song, read the commercials, and announce upcoming events of interest to the audience. The most common occasion for a "dedication" was a wedding

---

[61] *The Czechs of Texas*, 113-116.

anniversary. Loyal fans of the show kept up a stream of correspondence, making requests and indicating their interest. In the early 1940s, as recording by the polka bands became widespread, the live performances began to give way to disc jockey programs, with, however, a similar format.

By the end of the 1930s, with dozens of Czech polka dances across the state each week and numerous polka shows on the radio, Czech ethnic folk music was in its golden age. The music, like Czech ethnicity in general, was shattered by World War II, which broke up most of the polka bands as it disrupted the relative isolation and tranquility of the Texas Czech communities.

Map 5
Dialects of Bohemia and Moravia

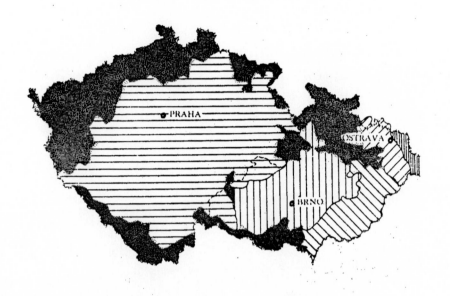

	České
	Hanácké
	Moravsklovenské
	Lašské

From Jaromir Bělič, *Naštin české dialektologie* (Praha, 1972)

Front page of the newspaper *Svoboda,* August 20, 1892.
— Photo courtesy of Barker Texas History Collection,
University of Texas at Austin.

CHAPTER 6

Czech, Language, Journalism, and Literature

Co štítem jediným nás v boji těžkém krylo?
Naše řeč.
(What has protected us like a shield in battle?
Our language.)
—from *"Naše řeč"* by Svatopluk Čech,
Czech Poet (1846-1908)

LANGUAGE

Perhaps the most important piece of cultural baggage which every Czech immigrant brought with him was his language. At least four distinguishing characteristics of the language spoken by him and his descendants led to linguistic diversity among Czech speakers in Texas. Most basic was the native dialect of the immigrant, and the influence of literary Czech was second in importance. Other important influences were those of German and English.

Czechs came to Texas speaking the various dialects of Bohemia and Moravia.[1] These dialects were, of course, mutually intelligible. Map 5 shows four different regional dialects in the two areas. *Český* dialect is spoken in Bohemia; here it will simply be called Czech. *Hanacký* is spoken in southern Moravia and will be called Hanak dialect. *Lašský* is spoken in an area called Lašsko and will be called Lašsko dialect. Moravskoslovenský dialect is spoken in an area named Moravian-Slovakia and will be so called. Literary Czech the standard dialect

---

[1] For a more complete description of Texas Czech dialects see James W. Mendl, *Texas Czech: Historical Czech Dialects in the New World.* Masters Thesis (1976), The University of Texas at Austin.

used in most published books and in journalism, is similar to Czech dialect except where noted in the examples below. Speakers of each of these dialects moved to Texas and, therefore, all of them have been heard in many Texas Czech communities. However, in Texas, alone among the United States, the Moravian dialects predominate in the spoken language. For this reason, Czech speakers from other sections of the country may be confused when they encounter Texas Czech for the first time. The major differences among the dialects can be briefly summarized.

First, they can be distinguished by phonemic differences, or differences in individual sounds within words. For example, the word meaning "to lie" is pronounced in Czech, Hanák, and Lašsko dialects *ležet*. But in Moravian-Slovak dialect it is *ležat*.[2] The 'e' has become an 'a'. This same difference is seen in other words, such as *sázet* (to plant) and *běžet* (to run).

Another 'a' and 'e' difference occurs at the end of a word. For example in Czech dialect one hears *duše* for "soul," but in all the Moravian dialects the word is pronounced *duša*. This vowel shift also affected the grammar of the dialects in that the Czech dialects contain a class of feminine nouns that end in "e".[3] In the Moravian dialects however, there is no such class. Examples are "shirt," *košula* (Moravian), *košile* (Czech); "monkey," *opica* (Moravian), *opice* (Czech).

Another difference between Moravian and Czech dialects is "u" to "i." In Czech dialect "shirt" is *košile*, but all Moravian dialects have *košula*. Also, the Accusative Singular of feminine nouns was affected by this shift. In Czech, "soul" is *duši*, but in all Moravian dialects, *dušu*.

A sound change also affected the adjectival endings. The masculine adjectival ending in Czech dialect is "ej," for example in *dobrej kluk* ("good boy"). But in Hanák dialect "good boy" is *dobré kluk*, with a long "e." In Lašsko and Moravian-Slovak however, it is *dobrý kluk*. In literary Czech the form is also *dobrý kluk*.

The differences involving the dipthong "ou" are also important. In Czech dialect and literary Czech one hears words with the dipthong like *mouka* (flour) and *louka* (meadow). But in Hanak dialect the words are pronounced with a long o, as in *móka* and *lóka*. In Lašsko

---

[2] Only a few representative examples which illustrate the most general features are given here.

[3] The Moravian is actually the more ancient form. The Czech dialect underwent the vowel shift from "a" to "e".

and Moravian-Slovak, however, the sound is a long u, as in *múka* and *lúka*.

A similar difference in the dialects can be noted in the command form of some verbs. In Czech dialect and literary Czech one hears *přidej* and *dej* ("sell" and "give"), a dipthong of "e" and "j." In Hanak, though, the dipthong has become a long "e," as in *prodé* and *dé*. But in Lašsko and Moravian-Slovak one hears the dipthong "aj," as in *prodaj* and *daj*.

The Czech and Moravian dialects were distinguishable by lexical items, too. For example, the phrase "Where are you going?" in Czech is *"Kam jdeš?"*. Most often heard in Texas however is *"Kde jdeš?"*. The Czech word *kam* ("whither") does not exist in Texas Moravian. *Kde* is used for both "where" and "whither."

Other typically Moravian words which are commonly heard in Texas are *včil* for "now" instead of *ted'*, *lože* for "bed" instead of *postel*, *stařenka* and *stařiček* for *babička* and *dědeček* ("grandmother" and "grandfather"). There are many more.

L. W. Dongres, a prominent Czech-American journalist, best described the pervasiveness of the Moravian dialects — and the Moravian people — in Texas in an article which appeared in the 1924 *Amerikán národní kalendář:*

> In schools in the old country we learned that the West Slavs were called the Czechoslovaks and were comprised of the Czechs in Bohemia, the Moravians in Moravia, and the Silesians in Silesia. But that the difference between them was only enthographic and that all were in fact Bohemian.
>
> That theory would serve a person very badly in Texas. I recognized that immediately in 1893 when Jan Rosicky, the editor of *Hospodář* and my boss, sent me to Texas to do a story on farming in the South. As I was riding in Fayette Co. one day, I hailed several women working in a field whom I suspected were Czech. I said in Czech, "Good morning, mother! Could you be so kind as to tell me if any Czechs live around here?" "Good morning," came the reply. "Only Moravians live around here, but about four miles down the road from us, on a bend in the river, live some Czechs who came down from the North." I continued, "And where is your husband, mother?" "In the field, *'Sazija s ogary kobzole.'"* Anxious to add to my technical expertise about farming, I got off my horse and followed her husband in the row trying to find out what this new plant *"kobzole"* was and how one plants *"s ogary."* Upon closer inspection I found that "kobzole" were potatoes and that the father was planting them "s ogary"; "along with the boys."

Our countrymen from Moravia comprise about 80% of our immigrants in Texas and the majority of them come from eastern and northern Moravia on the Silesian border. They have rejected and to this day reject the term "Czech."[4] They refer to themselves as Moravians.

Also, the local dialects have been preserved. A Hanák and his children who were born here speak Hanák dialect, the Valachs, Valach, and so on.

Our people in Texas, even in the second and third generation, "čne" [read] and *pše* [write] Moravian. They take Moravian newspapers, go to Moravian churches where they have Moravian priests and Moravian sermons. In their organizations they happily sing *"Kde domov můj"* [Czech National Anthem, "Where is my Home"] but full of enthusiasm, strength and love for their homeland, they sing the [extra] verse, "I am Moravian, that is my pride" *(Jsem Moravan, toť chlouba má)*.

Czechs who settle in Texas begin using words like *"tož"* (well) and *"včil"* (now) after only a short time. Their children even begin to speak Moravian. Not long ago my daughter asked me, "How is it that the *okurky* [cucumbers] that we eat at home are exactly like the *charky* [Moravian for cucumbers] that we eat at grandfather's?" [She also used the Moravian word for grandfather, *stařeček*, rather than the Czech *dědeček.*]"

Dongres concludes his description of Texas Moravians with this observation:

In the future in Czechoslovakia when the children study the divisions of the Czech people they will say, "The Czechs live in Bohemia, Moravians in Moravia, Slovaks in Slovakia. In North America there once lived Czechs who became Czech-Americans. In Texas lived Texas Moravians who were the last to become extinct.[5]

The second influence on the Czech spoken in Texas was modern literary Czech. By 1853, when the first groups of Czechs came to Texas, Czech nationalism was highly developed. The nationalistic movement described briefly in Chapter 1 was more cultural than political.

[4] Dongres, who registers his surprise at the distinctiveness of the Texans' Moravian identity, probably exaggerates his point. Many of the Texans undoubtedly would have rejected the term "Czech" in its narrow meaning of "Bohemian" but at the same time acknowledged a common "Czech" heritage with the Bohemians. See the discussion of these key terms in the "Introduction."

[5] L. W. Dongres, *Amerikán národní kalendář* (1924), 269-70.

In 1809 Josef Dobrovský published a Czech grammar entitled *Ausfürliches Lehrgebäude der bömischen Sprache* (in German because many educated Czechs read only German at that time) which set some laws of Czech grammar and orthography and attempted to substitute many Czech words for German words. He and his students went so far as to borrow words from other Slavic languages such as Russian and Polish and to substitute Czech equivalents of these words in their Czech dictionaries. One of his best-known students, Josef Jungmann, published a German-Czech dictionary in 1835. With Jan Gebauer's grammar of Czech in 1895, the foundation of modern literary Czech was complete.

These developments in Bohemia and Moravia profoundly affected the Texas Czechs. Most of them firmly believed in education and especially in the preservation of their language.

Of course, Czech was the medium of instruction in most of the early schools and was taught along with English after 1853. Many of the teachers, especially before 1900, came directly from Europe and were educated in the latest Czech grammars. Later, an increasing number of Czech teachers were native to Texas, but the language they all taught was literary Czech. As a result, many Texas Czech school children learned it in school, and later used it in their careers. Newspaper editors like Augustin Haidušek published newspapers in literary Czech. Many religious leaders, priests and ministers were taught literary Czech and used religious literature which came from Europe or from Czech printing presses in the northern states printed in literary Czech. This is not to say, however, that the Czech in Texas periodicals was pure literary Czech. It was not exactly like that used in Prague,[6] and it showed the influence of the Moravian dialects and the new linguistic environment. However, there has always been a suspicion among many Czech speakers in Texas that they don't speak "good" Czech: they are conscious of a difference between what they read and what they speak. This tension arises from the difference between the spoken "Texas Czech" and the literary Czech of even Texas publications.

The German language also influenced Texas Czech. As mentioned earlier, the Czech peasant during the 17th and 18th centuries was the guardian of the Czech language. Many German words, how-

---

[6] Jan Perkowski takes a look at this phenomenon in "Some Notes on a Literary Text in Texas Czech," *The Czechs in Texas: A Symposium,* ed. Clinton Machann (College Station, Tex., 1979) 142-47.

ever, did creep into the language he used and become an integral part of the vernacular. In addition, this tendency was reinforced by contact with the Germans in Texas. Examples are words such as *špek* (bacon) instead of *slanina*, *luft* (air) instead of *vzduch* (which was borrowed from Russian by Jungmann), *blavjas* (pencil) instead of tužka, *fusakle* (socks) instead of *ponožky*.

The influence of English on Texas Czech has, of course, been great. Although the language of the first generation of Czechs in Texas was a more or less pure dialect of Czech, they had to develop a vocabulary to describe unfamiliar animals, objects, experiences. For instance, the word "polkat" was used to describe a skunk; such common animals as "horse," "cow," and "chicken" continued to be called by their Czech names — *kůn*, *kráva*, and *slepice* (*slepica* in the Moravian dialects).

In a 1967 study of the "Letters to the Editor" of *Nový domov*, Margaret Kutač found borrowed English words at several levels.[7] She observed that some words were borrowed without any change whatsoever: "black widow," "best man," "bedroom," "barn," "boyfriend."[8] These words added neither features of Czech grammar nor orthography.

Some words, however, were altered according to Czech grammatical rules. Therefore, a phrase such as "big shot" in the plural became *"big šoti* (with "i" being the nominative masculine plural marker, which corresponds to "s" in English).[9]

Some verbs were borrowed from English and given Czech suffixes; for instance, "adopt" became *adoptovat,* to "combine" (wheat) became *kombajnovat,* to "win" (or "beat") became *bitovat.* These words were then conjugated accordingly: *adoptoval* (third person past), *kombajnujou* (third person plural, present), and *Který bude bitovat?* (third person singular, future).[10] Some nouns acquired

---

[7] Margaret Mary Kutac, *English Loan Words in the Czech Literary Language of Texas,* Masters Thesis at The University of Texas at Austin (1967). Kutac drew all of her examples from a single periodical *(Nový domov)* in the period 1963-65, but her generalizations seem to be applicable to Texas Czech of the early twentieth century, based on examples encountered by the authors in their research. Texas Czech surely did not remain static for a century, but no systematic study of its development exists.

[8] Kutac, 61-66.
[9] Kutac, 68.
[10] Kutac, 75.

from English took regular Czech diminutive endings, for example *box* ("box"), *boxík* ("small box"), *boxička* ("very small box").[11] Some adjective noun combinations were mixed: *braunový svět* ("the brown race"), *pinkové housenky* ("pink worms"), and *Krismusový zvon* ("Christmas bell").[12] Some interesting borrowings combine an English noun with a Czech nominal suffix: *džinář* ("ginner"—owner of a cotton gin), *renčák* ("rancher"), and *stewardka* ("stewardess.").[13]

The nature of borrowed words is revealing. Many, indeed most, of the words borrowed were things for which the immigrants had no Czech words; for instance, "cultivator" is *kolovetra*, "can" is *ken*, "combine" is *kombajn*, and "barbecue" is *barbekue*. Another set of borrowings are those for which there is a term in Czech that is not quite equivalent to the English words; this includes many words for measurement, such as *akr* for "acre" and *bušl* for "bushel."

Some words, however, were borrowed and used quite extensively all across the state, even though there were Czech or Moravian equivalents. The reason for borrowings for such words as *trubl* ("trouble"), *boket* ("bucket"), *bogy* ("buggy"), and *Krismus* ("Christmas") is not clear. It can best be explained by the overpowering nature of the Anglo cultural environment.[14]

The hardiness of the Czech language in Texas has been as remarkable as its richness. The sheer number of Czech-language newspapers produced by the Texas Czech press through the years indicates the high rate of fluency among the people. Of course, more Texans speak than read the language. As pointed out in Chapter 2, the U.S. Census counted about 50,000 "foreign white stock" speakers of Czech in 1920,[15] and 62,680 people whose first language was Czech in 1940.[16]

[11] Kutac, 67.

[12] Kutac, 76.

[13] Kutac, 75.

[14] English has also begun to influence the Czech spoken in Czechoslovakia, however, just as it has influenced numerous other European languages, and the influences are often similar to those discussed above. For example, Czech Texans use verbs such as *fixovat* for "to fix." But *fixovat* is actually an entry in Poldauf's Czech-English Dictionary published in Prague in 1965!

[15] United States Department of Commerce, Bureau of the Census, *Thirteenth Census of the United States: 1920*, Volume II, General Report and Analytical Tables, Table 10, 1001.

[16] United States Department of Commerce, Bureau of the Census, *Sixteenth Census of the United States: 1940*. Nativity and Parentage of the White Population. Mother Tongue by Nativity, Parentage, Country of Origin and Age for States and Large Cities, Table 2, 20.

About 84% of the individuals included in the 1940 figure lived in rural areas.[17] The concentration of Czech speakers in relatively isolated, rural communities has had a major impact on the longevity of the Czech language in Texas.

In the rural communities, the language was pervasive. In 1893, L. W. Dongres arrived in Fayetteville by train. He was met by a black porter who informed him, *"Já ti tu tašku ponesu"* ("I'll carry your bags for you"). When Dongres looked at him with a surprised expression, the porter explained, *"Já su černý Moravec."* ("I am a black Moravian.") Dongress learned that there were several black families whose children spoke better Moravian than they did English.[18] Undoubtedly, this situation was not unique in sections of the state heavily populated by Czechs before and after 1900. The Moravian dialect spoken by the majority of Texas Czechs was naturally acquired by some of the Anglos, Mexicans, and Blacks closely associated with the Czechs.

The early Czech immigrants and their descendants always held two ideals after those of farm and home — education and *mateřština* (the "mother tongue"). The earliest Czech schools were almost invariably conducted in Czech by Czech teachers, many of whom came from Europe. Rev. Josef Bergman probably taught in both Czech and German at Cat Spring. Josef Mašik, the first formal Czech teacher in the United States, began his school in 1859 at Wesley, Texas. In 1864, Anna Holub started a Czech school in the home of Valentin Haidušek in High Hill.

Czech schools were also established in Lavaca County and other areas where Czechs settled, sometimes along with other linguistic groups such as the Germans and Anglos. This association in Lavaca County literally created a burning issue. In 1875, Mr. Skřehot, a Czech, was chosen as teacher; Mr. Hauschild, a German, was supposed to teach the next year. After one year, however, the school house suddenly burned — or was burned — to the ground. It was rumored that some members of the community did not approve of a German school teacher. Local citizens later met (under a tree — no one seemed to want to offer his home as a meeting place) to select a new teacher for the

---

[17] United States Department of Commerce, Bureau of the Census, *Sixteenth Census of the United States: 1940*. Nativity and Parentage of the White Population. Mother Tongue by Nativity, Parentage, Country of Origin and Age for States and Large Cities, Table 3, 31.

[18] *Amerikán národní kalendář* (1924), 274.

proposed new school building. This time, Mr. Skřehot was rehired.

Despite a few such incidents, the Czechs, alone or in cooperation with other groups, did establish public schools. These schools received state support after the legislature provided for it in 1853.[19] In schools that were located in completely Czech areas, the medium of instruction was Czech. This situation brought about a crisis in the Texas Czech community after 1871, when the state required all teachers in public schools to pass an examination in English. An ensuing controversy, involving Judge Augustin Haidušek's enforcement of this law in Fayette county, will be discussed in Chapter 7.

The Czech Texans did not rely on the public school system to propagate their language or culture, although they were fiercely loyal to them. Many had been deeply affected by the Czech Revival in Europe. They passed a deep emotional tie to the language on to their children. But just as in the old country, the repository for the language was not in such public institutions as the educational system or the government, but the people themselves. (An old Czech proverb, popular in Texas, says, "He who is ashamed of his own language deserves the scorn of all.") This was true in the darkest days of Hapsburg oppression and it was also true in Texas. Czech Texans, in the main, did not interpret Haidušek's philosophy as an attempt to do away with the Czech language, which it was not, but, instead, as a sensible adaptation to a new environment. In this environment, Czech children would have to compete in an economic and political system in which the rules, written and unwritten, were formulated in English.

Both Czech Protestants and Catholics emphasized the preservation of the language, as noted in Chapter 4. It was necessary for a Czech priest, just as for a Brethren pastor or Sunday school teacher, to know how to perform his religious services in Czech. The Brethren Hus School was taught entirely in Czech until 1948. *Naše dějiny* mentions several communities where Catholics quit attending church because their confessions could not be heard in Czech.[20] Catholic institutions such as Our Lady of the Lake College in San Antonio and St. Edward's University in Austin offered Czech language courses, and Czech was taught in St. Mary's Catholic Seminary in La Porte, beginning in

[19] T. H. Leslie, *The History of Lavaca County Schools*, Masters Thesis, The University of Texas at Austin (1935), 207.

[20] Národní svaz českých katolíků v Texasu, *Naše dějiny*, (Granger, Tex., 1939).

1906. Other private or religious institutions such as Southwestern University in Georgetown, also offered Czech studies.[21]

As increasing numbers of Texas-born Czechs worked their way through the rough country schools and into public colleges and universities, sentiment grew for the establishment of Czech courses at those institutions as well. The main goal was to create a Czech program at the University of Texas in Austin. Such a program at the largest and most prestigious state-supported university would not only enable young Texas Czechs to pursue the study of their ancestral language on higher academic levels but would signal a new status for, a new recognition of, the ethnic group as a whole.

In 1914, members of "Čechie," a Czech student club at the university, petitioned the University of Texas Board of Regents for this purpose. The document was signed not only by club officers Karel Knížek and Karel Z. Chval, but by students of Czech descent from Baylor University, Trinity University, San Marcos Normal, and Denton Normal, as well.[22] The petition itself is still interesting today because it is a strong statement of ethnic pride. It contains rather extravagant claims for the Czech language: "In richness and expressiveness of words, variety and subtlety of structure . . . it has the advantage over Latin and other languages . . . Czech is the most advanced of all Slavic tongues." The students claimed about 100,000 "countrymen" in Texas, and pointed out that some other American universities located in states with small Czech populations offered courses in Czech.[23]

The Board of Regents did not institute the desired courses; however, the Texas Legislature did, when it passed the Wagstaff Bill of 1915, "the greatest step . . . made to promote study of the Czech language, history, literature, and culture in Texas."[24] As the *Daily Texan* (university student newspaper) of May 25, 1915, reported:

> The Czech language is to be taught in the University of Texas next year. The House of Representatives yesterday afternoon in passing upon the first three sub-divisions of the Wagstaff education appropriation bill voted $1800 annually for two years to provide for a chair in this language. The passage of this feature of the bill is the success-

[21] As early as 1907, Southwestern University offered courses in Czech language and history, taught by Rev. Václav Cejnar.

[22] The signers were E. Mikeška of Baylor University, I. Schiller of Trinity University, J. Migl of San Marcos Normal, and H. Hošek of Denton Normal.

[23] Quoted in Estelle Hudson and Henry R. Maresh, *Czech Pioneers of the Southwest* (Dallas, 1934), 190-92.

[24] Eduard Miček, *Duch americké vychovy*, 50.

ful termination of active work of former residents from Bohemia who have sought the passage of the bill for several years past.[25]

Senator Myron Blalock was largely responsible for the legislative action. Blalock, also a university student, roomed with Henry Maresh, a young Czech student who was applying for entrance to the university's medical school in Galveston. Maresh asked to take the required foreign language examination in Czech, a language he had learned as a child. Dr. Battle, the acting President of the University, decided that would be impossible since the university did not teach Czech. Maresh told his troubles to his roommate, who took up the matter with several Senate colleagues. Meanwhile, Blalock's friend Frank G. Burmeister helped convince House members who said they had never heard of the Czech language. Burmeister said that he could show them tons of literature written in Czech. The proposal to offer Czech classes at the university picked up support as the legislators began to see the issue as a way to court Czech voters.[26]

The first Czech teacher at the University of Texas was Karel Knížek, born in 1888 in Chvalovice, Bohemia. After coming to Texas, he attended Southwestern University, and he graduated from the Preparatory Department with honors. He attended Polytechnic College in Fort Worth and then became a graduate student and President of Čechie at the University of Texas. Knížek taught Czech and Russian until 1923, when Czech was discontinued due to lack of students. The Čechie club also died in 1923, but, due to a new influx of Czech students, was revived in 1925. Although seventeen students wanted to take Czech, in that year, the University could not find a teacher. The students carried out their own search, and recommended Dr. Eduard Míček, who was hired in 1926.

Míček came from Frýdek, Moravia, and had been educated at Charles University in Prague, King's College at the University of London, and the University of Chicago. He went to Chicago in 1924 and arrived in Texas in 1926. Míček's program grew from 14 students in

[25] The Daily Texan (University of Texas student newspaper) May 25, 1915.

[26] See Hudson and Maresh, 298-300. A slightly different version of the story appears in William Philip Hewitt, *The Czechs in Texas: A Study of the Immigration and the Development of Czech Ethnicity, 1850-1920*. PhD Dissertation, The University of Texas at Austin (1978). Maresh, who went on to become a physician, collaborated in the writing of *Czech Pioneers of the Southwest*.

1926 to 91 in 1938. During World War II the Nazis closed all Czechoslovak institutions of higher learning, and Míček's classes at the University of Texas were among the very few Czech courses at the university level offered in the world. He also wrote two books, *Duch americké výchovy* (The Spirit of American Education) and *Amerika se učí* (America is Learning). He was active in the Czech intellectual community and wrote various articles for and about Czechs.

JOURNALISM

Czech-language journalism was central to Czech culture in Texas. The highly literate Czechs naturally craved current reading matter in their own language from the beginning, especially since few of them could read English when they arrived in Texas. In a broad sense, the Czech-language press helped perpetuate ethnic culture and a communal spirit. The success of Czech-language newspapers served as a measure of the health of the Czech language and thus, indirectly, of the Czech-American community itself. On the other hand, it helped to intermediate between the Czech and American cultures and gradually lead to assimilation and the establishment of a distinctive Czech-Texan culture. Perhaps it eased the trauma of assimilation, by dealing with American concerns in the Czech language. Interpretations of laws and customs, as well as coverage of national news, were common fare.[27] In a narrower sense, various religious, political, and fraternal groups within the Czech community sought their own voices through journalism as the Czech population, and thus a Czech-reading audience, continued to grow in Texas.

However we interpret the cultural dynamics of Czech journalism in Texas, its importance is obvious. The popular reading clubs, which began to be formed in the sixties, featured newspapers. In some cases, newspapers substituted for textbooks in early Czech-language schools. Newspaper reading is repeatedly mentioned in the memoirs of early Czech settlers in Texas as a popular leisure-time activity. The most colorful, as well as the most influential, intellectuals and political leaders among the Texas Czechs are associated with journalism. For example, Augustin Haidušek, probably the most important political and secular cultural leader in Texas Czech history, was the founder and editor of the La Grange *Svoboda*.

[27] See virtually any issue of *Svoboda,* for example.

Texas journalism, however, was part of the national milieu. Czech-language journalism flourished in all the major areas of Czech-American settlement in the late nineteenth and early twentieth centuries and is well documented by the writer-historian Tomáš Čapek.[28] Here it is helpful to give at least a short overview of Czech-American journalism before turning to a more specific discussion of Texas Czech developments. The well-known Czech intellectual and traveler Vojta Naprstek laid plans for a Czech-American newspaper as early as 1857, but the plans fell through when he returned to Europe. Three years later, František Kořízek launched the *Slovan amerikanský* in Racine, Wisconsin, which was followed shortly by the St. Louis *Národní noviny*. In the next year, 1861, the two merged to form the Racine *Slavie*, which was able to build up a substantial readership and, from that point, Czech-American newspapers began to proliferate. According to Čapek, 326 Czech journals were introduced in the period stretching from January 1860 to the spring of 1911.[29]

Although many of them were short-lived, others were quite successful. Eighty-five were being published in 1920; among them, the *Hlasatel* (Herald) of Chicago claimed a circulation of 25,000, while the Omaha *Hospodář* (Husbandman) claimed 30,000. In 1875, the first daily, *Svornost*, was issued in Chicago. By 1920, Chicago had four Czech-language dailies.[30]

The Czech-American press represented many shades of public opinion. Socialists and anarchists, in addition to freethinkers, Catholics, Protestants, Democrats, and Republicans, all had their say. The *Slavie*, under Karel Jonáš, was staunchly Democratic, while Jan Rosický's *Pokrok zapadů* in Omaha was ardently Republican. The *Hlas* (Voice), *Katolík* (Catholic), and *Národ* (Nation) were Catholic journals, but anti-clerical journals such as *Pokrok* (Progress), *Svornost* (Unity), and *Šotek* (Imp) had larger circulations and were more influential. Overall, the press reflected a bias toward rationalism, women's rights, and even socialism: a "liberal" and "progressive" slant that had its own Czech origins rather than primarily a reflection of American values.[31] The rhetoric of the press was not ordinarily what we

[28], See Tomáš Čapek's *Padesát let českého tisku v Americe* (New York, 1911) as well as the ample chapters devoted to journalism and literature in his books *The Čechs (Bohemians) in America* (Boston and New York, 1920) and *Naše amerika* (Praha, 1926).

[29], Čapek, *The Čechs*, 171.

[30] Čapek, *The Čechs*, 171.

[31] See Čapek's chapters on "Rationalism" and "Socialism and Radicalism" in *The Čechs*, 119-54.

would call "objective," however. Jan Habenicht, writing in the introduction to his *Dějiny čechů amerických* (1910), deplored the contentiousness among the journalists, especially the religious arguments that "set the Czech people one against the other."[32] A few well-known editors such as Karel Jonáš and Václav Šnajdr maintained a reputation for restraint and fairness. More often than not, however, newspapers contained vitriolic editorials attacking the editor's or publisher's ideological (or personal) opponents, in addition to news, advertisements, fiction, humor, recipes, English language lessons, and the travel and biographical accounts of Czech settlers which were evidently much favored by the readers.

In describing the power and influence of the Czech newspaper editor, Čapek writes that "he was invariably picked out to umpire quarrels, many of which . . . were of his own making. He was chosen as orator to address meetings and conventions; played leading roles at amateur theatricals; taught the local Čech language school; helped to organize new lodges; was called upon to write funeral orations, political speeches, and banquet toasts.[33] Nevertheless, the Czech-American press was also characterized by aspiring but unsuccessful editors whose journals failed one after the other and itinerant journalists who lived in poverty for most of their lives. Even many relatively successful journalists and editors traveled widely and lived adventurous, colorful lives. Some of those who are associated with Texas will be discussed later in this chapter.

In journalism as in other institutions, Czech Texas developed its own, independent course. The Texas Czech's religious, political, and social views were generally more conservative than those of the Northern and Midwest Czech press, and of course, he wanted to read local and regional news. Nevertheless, there are important ties between Texas and this more nationally-oriented Czech press.[34] One important reason is that Texas did not have its own Czech-language press until 1879, and no Czech Catholic press until 1895.

Any estimate of the number of Texas subscribers to out-of-state

[32] Jan Habenicht, *Dějiny čechů amerických* (St. Louis, 1910).

[33] Čapek, *The Čechs*, 173-74.

[34] The Chicago *Amerikán národní kalendář* in particular continued to be an important outlet for nonfiction and fiction by and about Texas Czechs. Many valuable biographies and autobiographies of Texas Czech pioneers are preserved in this publication.

journals in the fifties and sixties is conjectural (and the number of readers per newspaper was relatively large, at any rate), but references to these newspapers, including their use in the schoolroom and in reading clubs, are numerous. One particularly interesting incident concerning the *Národní noviny* occurred on the eve of the Civil War in 1861. Texas Czechs shared with their Northern countrymen a strong opposition to slavery, and for this reason were held in suspicion by Texas slave owners and supporters of the Southern cause. Josef Lešikar, one of the early Czech pioneers in Texas and then a resident of New Ulm, was a particular target. He had been one of the founders and stockholders of the St. Louis paper and was the local correspondent and distributor. Local pro-slavery vigilantes (correctly) suspected *Národní noviny*, which they could not read, of strongly supporting the abolitionists and Republicans and Abraham Lincoln's candidacy for President of the United States. Lešikar was threatened with hanging and forced to send an entire shipment of the paper back to St. Louis.[35]

Experienced editors from the Midwest and North tried their luck with newspapers in Texas later in the century, with varying degrees of success. In addition, as late as the 1920s, at least two popular veteran free-lance contributors to the liberal Czech-American press lived in Texas: the socialist Josef Buňata and L. W. Dongres.

About thirty Czech-language newspapers, journals, and newspaper supplements were published in Texas before World War II.[36] In some cases, the publications were so ephemeral that no known issues have survived. Others have played prominent roles in the development of Texas Czech culture, and a few are still being published today.

The first Czech-language newspaper in Texas appeared in La Grange in February, 1879. The publisher of the weekly *Texan* was František J. Glueckmann and the editor was L. L. Hausild. The *Texan* survived only until July, 1890, when it was bought by František Lidiak and renamed *Slovan* (Slav).

The *Slovan*, which remained in La Grange, was published by Lidiak until 1885, when it was purchased by Josef S. Čada. Under Čada, the paper developed a supplement entitled *Česko-slovenský rolník v Texasu* (The Czecho-Slovak Farmer in Texas), which began a long tradition of Texas Czech journalism devoted to agricultural news. The *Česko-slovenský rolník* became an independent publication in 1887 and survived until 1889.

[35] See Čapek, *Padesát let českého tisku v Americe*, 26.
[36] See list of Texas Czech Periodicals and Newspapers in Appendix D.

By the fall of 1886, Čada had become embroiled in a controversy which ultimately forced him to leave La Grange. Augustin Haidušek had begun to publish a rival Czech newspaper, *Svoboda* (Freedom). As will be seen later, Haidušek and Čada were violently opposed on the issue of English-language instruction in public schools dominated by Czechs: Haidušek for it, Čada against. The men became bitter enemies. Haidušek saw his chance to discredit Čada when a *Slovan* article appeared which praised Czech women and, in the process, compared them favorably with (native) American women.[37] Unlike Czech women, American women were described as lazy: poor widows would prefer to do without food rather than condescend to work, or, in extreme cases, they would turn to a life of sin and shame. Haidušek translated the article into English and made it available to the local English-language press. Needless to say, the translated article, when published, led to an uproar in the Anglo-American community. An angry mob of Anglos gave Čada three days to get out of town before they would resort to force. Although most of the area Czechs sided with Haidušek on the ethnic issues, they resented this show of force, and popular sentiment caused Čada to defy the ultimatum. Because of the scandal caused by this incident, however, he finally moved his press in May of 1886 to Bryan, where he continued to publish *Slovan* until later that year, when he sold it to Edward A. Krall. The Haidušek-Čada feud is reminiscent of controversies in the Czech press of the Northern and Midwestern cities; it is not really typical of Czech journalism in Texas. In a sense it represents the purge of Northern elements from the Texas press. (Most of the big-city Czech papers supported Čada in his attacks on Haidušek.) Although big-city journalists would continue to be involved in the Texas press, it was increasingly clear that another Texas Czech institution, with its independent interests and direction, was evolving.

Krall's *Slovan* was edited first by Hugo Chotek and then by Josef Buňata, until the paper ceased publication at the end of 1889. In the relatively short history of *Slovan*, at least two publishers and four editors involved before and after with Northern and Midwest Czech journalism were associated with it: publishers Čada and Krall; editors Buňata, Chotek, J. E. Kroupa, and Antonín Hradečný. Another notable Czech-American journalist, the socialist František Škarda, although he did not edit a Texas paper, lived the last years of his life (until 1900) in La Grange, poor and obscure.[38] Škarda, whose name is

---

[37] This account is based on Habenicht, 99-100.
[38] See Habenicht, 100.

linked to the Cleveland *Dělnické listy* and other big-city Czech news-papers, illustrates the stormy and tragic life led by many Czech-American journalists.

In the meantime, Čada's La Grange rival, Augustin Haidušek, was doing well with *Svoboda*, which first appeared in December of 1885 and outlived its creator, surviving as a supplement of the *El Campo News* even into the 1960s. Haidušek's co-editor until July, 1886 was Jaroslav Chudoba; after that, Haidušek alone edited *Svoboda* until the 1920s.

Čapek's generalization about the wide-ranging influence of the Czech newspaper editor can be aptly applied to the editor of *Svoboda*. Haidušek, who emigrated with his family to Texas at the age of eleven, became an authentic voice of the Texas Czechs and a powerful and influential community leader. He tended to de-emphasize international and national news and, instead, concentrate on local and state matters. In his newspaper editorials, he dealt with many issues, but his support for English-language instruction in the Czech-majority public schools was the most controversial, and it will be discussed in Chapter 7. The polemical stance of *Svoboda* was decidedly Democratic, and Haidušek constantly urged his readers toward increased political consciousness and involvement in local and state government. One of the first Czech-Americans to obtain a law degree, he served as Mayor of La Grange, two terms as State Representative, and as Fayette County Judge.[39]

In his analysis of *Svoboda* editorials, Josef N. Roštinský finds a philosophy of individuality and self-culture, which he contrasts to the more communally-oriented bias of the Catholic newspaper *Nový domov*.[40] Shortly before his appointment as bishop of San Antonio in 1895, Father John A. Forrest, a Frenchman who had served as pastor to Texas Czech Catholics for over thirty years, urged the founding of a Catholic newspaper.[41] František Jakubík, a former school superintendent, store owner, and farmer, bought a press which had been pub-

[39] The most complete account of Haidušek's life is given in Jesse Johec, *The Life and Career of Augustin Haidušek*, Masters Thesis, The University of Texas at Austin (1940).

[40]. Josef N. Roštinský, "Two Functional Aspects of Czech Journalism in Texas," in *The Czechs in Texas: A Symposium*, 69-71.

[41] See Rev. Alois J. Moŕkovský, "The Church and the Czechs in Texas," in *The Czechs in Texas: A Symposium*. 80.

lishing the journal *Obzor* in Hallettsville since 1891. *Nový domov* of Hallettsville was the result, and this officially-recognized Catholic newspaper survived until the 1960s. Jakubík published *Nový domov* until his death in 1904, when his wife took over.[42] This newspaper was joined by the Catholic weekly *Našinec* of Granger in 1914. *Našinec*, supported by the Czech Catholic fraternal organization KJT, was successful in building up a relatively large circulation, concentrating primarily on news within the Texas Czech community but offering national and international news as well. It is still being published today.

Bratrské listy (Brethren Journal) was first published in Brenham in 1902 and became the official organ of the Evangelical Unity of the Brethren in North America. Under the influence of its first editor, the indefatigable Rev. Adolf Chlumský, *Bratrské listy* developed a strong ethnic, as well as Protestant religious, orientation. It was later moved to Temple, and finally to Austin, where it is still published today (although in the English language). Another Protestant newspaper, *Buditel evangelický methodistický* (The Evangelical Methodist Revival) was founded in 1908 by Rev. Václav Cejnar. Records of its existence are sketchy, however, and it apparently did not long exist.

The SPJST began a bi-monthly publication called *Slovanská jednota* (Slavic Unity) in September, 1897, the first year of the fraternal organization's existence. The publisher, František Lidiak of La Grange, gave up the project as unprofitable after only ten months, however. The SPJST officials subsequently contracted František Fabián, who was still publishing *Obzor* (at that time called *Obzor hospodářský*) in Hallettsville.[43] *Obzor* then served as the official organ of the SPJST until 1912, when an independent bi-monthly fraternal newspaper named *Věstník* (Herald) was established in Hallettsville under Fabián's direction. Later in the same year, *Věstník* was moved to La Grange, where it was printed in the office of *Svoboda*. After another brief move to Hallettsville following a disastrous flood in La Grange, *Věstník* was moved to Fayetteville. Fabián followed the paper and served as publisher and editor until 1916. Fabián was a freethinker, but unlike more radical freethinking Czech editors in the North and Midwest, he maintained a moderate editorial stance and did not engage in controversial political issues. Even Habenicht describes him favorably as a "sincere Czech."[44]

Fabián was succeeded by Joseph Ťápal, who edited the *Věstník* un-

---

[42] *Nový domov* was sold to Joseph Kopecký in 1906; he sold it to Josef and Vladimir Malec in 1931.

[43] For a history of the SPJST publications, see *Věstník;* June 20, 1956.

[44] Habenicht, 103.

til 1932, when it was moved to West, where it was edited by Frank Moučka and published by the Czechoslovak Publishing Co., under the direction of August J. Morris. Because of the large SPJST membership, the *Věstník* came to be probably the most important Texas Czech publication. In addition to its function of recording official SPJST business, it served to promote a sense of cohesiveness within the ethnic community by reporting the various social events that were intertwined with business and advocating the preservation of the Czech cultural heritage.

From time to time, English-language newspapers which served areas heavily populated by Czechs offered Czech-language sections. During the period 1906-1909, František Jakubík edited such a section for the Taylor *Journal.* The West *News* contained a section entitled *Westské noviny* from 1908 to 1920. The first editor was Dr. J. S. Zvesper, who was followed by John Vašíček, and, finally, August Morris.

Czech-language journalism was central to the Texas Czech experience. This fact is attested to by the large number of journals published in the state, by the extensive influence that certain journals such as *Svoboda, Vestník,* and *Našinec* had in the Czech community, and by the frequent references to newspapers and newspaper reading found in first-hand accounts of life in the Czech community.[45] At the peak of its success, *Svoboda* had about 4,000 subscribers, and the average number of readers per newspaper was undoubtedly very high, since newspapers were often distributed through formal or informal reading clubs, reading aloud to family members, and so forth. Major journals with institutional connections, such as *Věstník, Našinec,* and *Bratrské listy,* would be guaranteed a fairly large readership. In 1940, the SPJST had 16,604 policies in force. The evidence suggests that prior to World War I, Texas Czechs depended primarily on Czech-language journalism for their news. Even in the twenties and thirties, large numbers of mostly first-generation Czech Texans still could not comfortably read the English language. And even for those who could, the Czech periodicals contained news about Czech organizations and from the relatively isolated Czech rural communities that would not be available in the English-language press in any event. Today, correspondents from these communities continue to report on local farming conditions, social events and others news.

Texas, with its small Slovak population, never supported an im-

---

[45] A good example is Henry R. Maresh's account of how he learned to read Czech as a child. Both his father and mother were in the habit of reading aloud serial stories from *Svoboda.* In his impatience, the boy would peek at the text over the shoulder of the reader. Hudson and Maresh, 238.

August J. Morris
— Photo copied from
Památník Čechoslováků.

Dr. Henry Maresh
— Photo copied from
Czech Pioneers of the Southwest.

portant Slovak-language press; however, two Slovak papers were founded in Rosenberg during the 1890s. One of them, *Kazatel'na,* apparently survived for about six years.[46]

LITERATURE

Any discussion of Czech-American literature must take into account the close relationship between journalism and literature. It was principally through periodicals that Czech-Americans maintained contact with Czech-language literature of all types. In addition to containing a smattering of poetry and an occasional serialized novel, virtually all Czech-language periodicals included the kind of non-fiction which was overwhelmingly favored by its readers: autobiography, biography, and travel literature. Most popular were relatively short *paměti* (memoirs) and longer *vlastní životopisy* (autobiographies) in which Czech settlers described their experiences in a new homeland. Often these accounts would appear in a letter-to-the-editor format. Sometimes journalists would interview individuals and write short biographies.

[46] See the list of Texas Slovak Periodicals and Newspapers in Appendix E.

The historian Karel Bicha has made a useful, if pessimistic, analysis of Czech-American literature. He points out that the 7,600 entries in Esther Jerabek's bibliography of the *Czechs and Slovaks in North America,* the majority of which relate to Czechs, include much material that is no longer extant and otherwise largely consist of cookbooks, devotional literature, grammars and dictionaries, translations of American political propaganda and mere news, and other works of little literary value.[47] He goes on to characterize the "distinctive residue," the biographical and autobiographical accounts of the Czech ethnic experience in America, as having a "flat, skeletal, vital statistics kind of orientation."[48] He compares typically "flat" examples with the sensitive and probing reflections of a Norwegian immigrant. Bicha also refers to the "exaggeration and partisanship" which skews the Czech-American historical record and to the fact that many valuable historical and literary sources have been corrupted, damaged, or completely lost.[49]

Only a tiny fraction of Czech-American book publishing was done in Texas, by the newspaper presses, while New York City had at one time or another five Czech-language publishing houses, Chicago had three, and Cleveland, Milwaukee, and Omaha had one each. Most important, however, was August Geringer's publishing house in Chicago, which produced a great many books in addition to the daily *Svornost,* the weekly *Amerikán,* and the *Amerikán národní kalendář.* Czech Texas relied on the Northern and Midwest press, then, for its Czech-American publications. It is impossible to accurately estimate the number of books among the Czech population of Texas, but current collections, such as the SPJST library in Temple, Texas, made up mainly of donations from Texans, suggest a variety of Czech literature of American origin as well as the more numerous book collections brought over, or ordered, from Europe.[50] Religious literature predominated, as might be expected: the Protestant Kralice Bible, Czech missals, and Czech Protestant and Catholic prayer books and devotional readings.

Because relatively little literature was published in Texas, the problems relating to provenance referred to by Bicha are of lesser moment

[47] Karel D. Bicha, "Researching the History of the Czechs in America," a paper delivered at the 9th World Congress of the Czechoslovak Society of Arts and Sciences in America, Cleveland, 1978. Unpublished manuscript, 2-3.

[48] Bicha, 4.

[49] Bicha, 7.

[50] Based on lists obtained from Otto Hanuš, Librarian, SPJST Library, Temple, Tex.

Eduard Míček
— Photo copied from
Czech Pioneers of the Southwest.

Charles Knížek
— Photo copied from *Naše dějiny.*

here, although in several notable cases, valuable archives of documents, diaries, original transcripts of interviews, and other irreplaceable materials have been carelessly lost or senselessly destroyed. The newspaper archives are in fairly good condition; however, no known copies of some of the less successful periodicals have been preserved, and the archives of some of the more important ones are in some disorder.[51] As for the exaggerated polemical nature of much of Czech-American literature, this characteristic is generally less pronounced in Texas Czech publications, due to the special characteristics of the Texas immigrants and the nature of their social institutions, as discussed elsewhere in this study.

The highpoint of Czech ethnic publishing in Texas came with two seminal books in the 1930s: *Czech Pioneers of the Southwest* (1934), by Estelle Hudson and Henry R. Maresh, and *Naše dějiny* (Our History, 1939), compiled by the National Union of Czech Catholics in Texas *(Národní svaz českých katolíků v Texas)*. The former was published by South-West Press of Dallas, a regional publishing house which specialized in Texana, and the latter by the publisher of *Našinec* in Granger. Both of these works came toward the end of the historical period surveyed in this book, a time of rising Czech ethnic consciousness due to the formation of Czechoslovakia after World War I, but also a time of fervent American (and Texan) nationalism.

Czech Pioneers is by far the most important English-language source for Texas Czech history; nothing before or after has approached its comprehensiveness. Čapek had naturally included information about Texas in his landmark Czech-American studies of the 1920s, but because he concentrated on Northeastern and Midwestern Czechs, one must go back to the chapter on Texas in Jan Habenicht's Czech-language *Dějiny čechů amerických* (1910) to find an equally valuable source. Like most studies of Czech-Americans, it is an "ethnic" work and therefore appropriate to this discussion. Maresh (Mareš), who had figured in the institution of a Czech language program at the University of Texas, was a prominent Houston physician with family connections to many of the "pioneers." In spite of its title, it is exclusively concerned with the state of Texas. Its organization is sometimes awkward, and its narrative technique is inconsistent. It is, however, an extremely valuable document, particularly because it records many accounts of the early life of Texas Czechs by first-generation and second-

---

[51] The most complete collections are in the SPJST Library, Temple, Tex., and the Barker Collection, The University of Texas at Austin.

generation individuals, and it attempts to deal with all religious, fraternal, and other factions among the Czechs. Much of the most interesting material is given as direct quotation.[52] For example, the important Schiller family history in Texas is reconstructed in first-person accounts by Josef H. Shiller (who emigrated in 1853) and his niece, Mrs. Alvin Matějka, daughter of Vincenc and Frances Schiller, who was born in Texas during the Civil War. Without the book, much information would be unavailable to us today. *Czech Pioneers* is also interesting as an expression of Texas values and attitudes at the time it was written: ethnic identity married to American patriotism and faith in material progress.

Naše dějiny is the most valuable source book for Czech Catholics in Texas. It is clearly a work assembled by committee. Officers of the National Union of Czech Catholics listed on the title page are Father Pavel P. Kašpar (President); Monsignors Josef Pelnář and L. P. Netardus; priests Josef C. Kunc, Jan Vaniček, Alois W. Nesvadba, and Ignác J. Valenta; State Senator L. J. Šulák, Prof. Eduard Míček of the University of Texas, and other laymen Antonin Stibořík, C. H. Cmajdalka, Stanislav Novotný, Vladimír Malec, Josef Viktorín, Mrs. Josefa Habarta, Alois J. Kallus, Jan L. Svrček, and Mrs. Marie Yurek. *Naše dějiny* contains biographical sketches of noteworthy Czech Catholic pioneer priests and ecclesiastical officials, short histories of virtually every Catholic center in Texas, and reports on the Czech Catholic fraternal orders, among other information. It is truly a substantial book, over 700 pages of heavy paper, copiously illustrated with photographs of people and church buildings. Like *Czech Pioneers,* it is also an expression of ethnic (as well as religious) pride and Texan-American identity.

As Bicha suggests, however, the most distinctive and abundant examples of literary expression among the Czechs are the short biographies which appeared in periodicals and were incorporated into works like *Czech Pioneers.* In general, his criticism of the "flat, skeletal" nature of these accounts holds true for those written by Texas Czechs, and the same characteristics might be applied to most biographical and historical accounts as well. The individual is usually careful to note certain vital facts: the date and place of his birth, the names of his parents, the date of his emigration, his occupational history, the date of his marriage, number of children, and so forth. Often isolated economic facts such as the cost of coffee in 1880 or the price obtained for

---

[52] Some of the original sources are lost, as Maresh's notes were apparently destroyed after his death.

cotton in 1890 will be included. Similarly, relatively brief historical accounts will often contain details such as the precise cost of a new church building or parsonage. Of course, the overwhelming majority of these people were small farmers and businessmen, not far removed from a peasant past, with a sprinkling of professional and religious men, and one should not expect literary diaries from them. Still, they were a highly literate group, and Bicha is probably correct in noticing a "vital statistics kind of orientation" in their personal accounts, as compared to those of, say, Scandinavian immigrant groups.[53] To a certain extent, this characteristic can be attributed to the ideal of *hospodářství* discussed in Chapter 3; however, it would be a mistake to conclude that the Czech settlers in Texas were fiercely materialistic or unconcerned with the quality of life or human emotions. The matter-of-fact tone of the following account by John Havlík, Jr. describing childhood experiences during the Civil War is typical:

> In 1861, father contracted to haul cotton to Mexico for the government. This arrangement left mother and we three children at home to shift for ourselves, as it took father several months to make one trip. In 1863, while he was away on one of these trips, mother passed away at childbirth.
>
> Well do I remember the day, for after the burial only we three children, the oldest a girl of eight, were left. Soldiers came often to the house, looking for father, or any other men that might be found, to take them for service in the war. They would ransack our home, eating up what little food we had. Parched corn was used for coffee and cornmeal for bread. There was no flour, sugar, or coffee.[54]

Frances Chalupník, daughter of Anton Dvořák, describes her family's experiences when they are caught at night by an unexpected "norther" in the 1890s before they could build a shelter:

[53] An outstanding example of the "vital statistics . . . orientation" is found in the case of F. W. Pustějovský, a successful farmer who lived near West in McLennan County. For forty years, beginning in 1892, Pustějovský kept a careful, complete record of his cotton production and the price received. (The highest price was 40 cents per pound for two bales on January 31, 1920; the lowest was 4.45 cents per pound for three bales on November 11, 1894). "This forty-year record relating to the cotton crop on one farm is believed to be without precedent, and the credit is due this one of the Texas-Czech citizens for the thought and the method and accuracy with which the record was kept." (Hudson and Maresh, 159.)

[54] Quoted in Hudson and Maresh, 141.

There we were in the middle of the prairie with nothing but a few boards propped against the wagon to break the force of the wind. Inside the wagon, mother tried to bake some bread, but the little cookstove produced more smoke than heat. We children cried from hunger and cold. The suffering of that night cannot be described. In the morning the three-months-old baby was dead. Father made a box for a coffin and buried the child in the cemetery on Holub's farm.[55]

Just as little attempt is made to describe the physical suffering and mental anguish of the pioneer experience, positive experiences such as romantic love are given short shrift in even the most interesting and full accounts. For example, Josef Holík, Jr. says of his future wife: "I always got the same peculiar feeling when I took hold of her hand."[56] This is the farthest extent of such descriptions.

And yet these accounts do not convey a cold lack of emotion, but rather a stoic acceptance of life that has its own peculiar charm. While we would like to know more about the thought processes of these people — especially regarding the wrenching dilemmas so often involved in immigrant experiences — we must accept the fact that intense introspection and the literary conventions of psychological realism, which serve both fiction and nonfiction in modern American culture, are not part of their cultural heritage. Perhaps related to the lack of these conventions, which presuppose a high degree of conscious individual autonomy, is the very vital and coherent folk traditions which the Czech immigrants brought with them and successfully transplanted in Texas. The genuine poetic feeling of the folksongs is the primary example. Again, however, we must guard against seeing the early Texas Czechs as too unconscious and thus "primitive," since their political and historical consciousness was relatively well developed, as were their craving for formal education and their technological abilities.

The autobiographical writings of Anthony M. Dignowity stand out from all the rest and are far from the usual kind of reminiscences. *Bohemia Under Austrian Despotism* (1859) is his best-known work.[57] Dignowity was the first Czech-born writer to publish in America, but he wrote in English. Although he traveled through and lived briefly in more than twenty states, he settled down and made his fortune in San

---

[55] Quoted in Hudson and Maresh, 161.

[56] Quoted in Hudson and Maresh, 111.

[57] Dignowity apparently wrote two book-length sequels: *American Despotism* and *Crimes and Cruelties Committed by the So-Called Courts of Justice on the Sacred Rights of Individuals*. See advertisement on the page facing 236 in *Bohemia Under Austrian Despotism* (New York, 1859); also see account of Dignowity's writing in Hudson and Maresh, 50.

Antonio, Texas. He was highly visible in public affairs there and he owned mines and real estate in addition to practicing medicine. A friend of Sam Houston, Dignowity was discussed even by Anglo-Texan writers at the turn of the century and appears in John Henry Brown's *Indian Wars and Pioneers of Texas* (1904).

Dignowity lived an exciting, colorful life by any standards, but he was a man of the world—not a professional writer. However, although *Bohemia* is characterized by an arbitrary organization and an occasional bitter tone due to his sense of persecution when he wrote the book, it is worthwhile reading even today. Its portrayal of Dignowity's early years and treatment of political and religious issues of the day are revealing. The son of a Kutná Hora miner, Dignowity suffered from poverty in his childhood, but his descriptions of family life and vignettes of the Bohemian countryside convey a genuine sense of affection. Like many other Czechs who eventually emigrated to the United States, Dignowity fled the Austrian conscription laws, and his adventures included a brief sojourn in the Polish Revolutionary Army in its struggle against the Russian Czar in 1830. Besides his experiences as fugitive and rebel soldier, his boyhood occupations such as pretzel vendor and birdcatcher, his stay in the Catholic Charity Hospital of Prague and his conversion of a Hamburg prostitute to respectability, among others, make engaging reading.

He sailed from Hamburg for New York in 1832 and never visited Europe again. After his rise as a successful San Antonio doctor and businessman, Dignowity's troubles began as the Civil War approached. He wrote *Bohemia* to "clear his name" in 1859 after he had been convicted of a real estate swindle, briefly imprisoned until pardoned by Governor Houston, and then charged with another swindle. In the book, Dignowity rails against the "tyranny" of American "public opinion," which he compares to that of the Austrian government, and criticizes the "injustice" of the American legal system, particularly the grand jury.[58] Dignowity was undoubtedly correct in his claims of persecution. He had made no secret of his ardent Unionist and abolitionist sympathies, unpopular at the time, to say the least. In fact, two years after publishing *Bohemia,* in 1861, Dignowity narrowly escaped public hanging at the San Antonio Plaza, and traveled by horseback to Washington, D.C., where he was employed by the Federal Government. His property was confiscated and two of his sons were conscripted into the Confederate Army, but they later escaped to Mexico and then joined the Union Army. After the war, Dignowity returned

[58] See *Bohemia,* 45-57 for a typical example of this rhetoric. Dignowity goes so far as to compare his persecution with that of John Hus.

to Texas, but he was a sick man then and was never able to rebuild his fortune. During the Reconstruction period, he appealed to the Republican Congress for moderation on behalf of the "loyal residents" of the South.[59] He died in 1875.

A few other volumes of biography and autobiography exist, most of them privately printed, but much more significant is the material printed in the Czech periodicals in Texas and in the important series of autobiographies and biographies printed in the *Amerikán národní kalendář* from 1874 on. Short accounts from such Texas personalities as journalists Josef Buňata, L. W. Dongres, Hugo Chotek and settlers such as early pioneers Vincenc Lešikar, Anton Lesovský of Cameron, Antonín Štupl of Industry, Ignác Křenek of Ellinger, Martin Ermis of Buckholts, and many others, tell us a great deal about the Texas Czechs.[60]

It is not surprising that belles lettres did not flourish in a frontier area such as Texas. Even in urban centers such as Chicago and New York, not a great deal of serious literature was written, although essays, poems, satires, and "popular" fiction written in America competed with the "imported" Czech literature of Božena Němcová, Alois Jirásek, Karel Rais, and others.

By far the most talented and most prolific poet among the Texas Czechs was Marie Nováková. Born Marie Kunčarová in the village of Havřice, near Uherský Brod, Moravia, in 1892, she came with her family to Texas in 1911. Although she had had little formal education, one of her teachers had recognized her poetic talent and encouraged her. Her earliest surviving poems date from the time of immigration. This sensitive girl responded to the uprooting of her family in Moravia, the discovery of a beautiful but frightening new homeland, her courtship and marriage within a year of her arrival in Texas, and the beginning of a new life on a small Austin County farm, with verses recording her emotional experiences.

Later she published poems in the Texas Czech Catholic newspapers *Nový domov* and *Našinec*, and the national (St. Louis) Czech Catholic newspapers *Hlas* (Voice) and *České Ženy* (Czech Women). Two of her poems also appear in *Naše dějiny*, but, most importantly, her collected works were published in 1934 under the title *Pod texaským*

[59] See Dignowity's pamphlet *Reconstruction!* (Washington?, 1865).

[60] See Esther Jerabek, *Czechs and Slovaks in North America* (New York and Chicago, 1976), 47-58 for a listing of the hundreds of biographical articles and sketches, many of them concerning Texans, published in the *Amerikán národní kalendář*.

Marie Nováková
— Photo copied from *Naše dějiny*.

nebem (Under the Texas Sky). Two hundred and thirty-six poems are included.

The book can be seen as part of the renaissance in Texas Czech literature that was taking place in the thirties. In the same spirit that was to emerge in the Czech Catholic *Naše dějiny* five years later, *Pod texaským nebem* celebrates the Czech-Moravian heritage and, to some extent, the new homeland of Texas, in addition to expressing a strong religious faith. To say only this is to ignore the poetry as the genuine artistic expression of a talented individual, however. Although Nováková is usually remembered today as a devotional poet and although she is closely associated with Catholic publications, a genuine lyric strain runs through her poetry that is not always tied to religious subjects. Besides the occasional verses (on Mother's Day, on KJZT conventions, etc.) and those poems dedicated to Jesus Christ and the Virgin Mary are many lyrics about love, sorrow, and death that rise above the merely conventional and sentimental. Poems about her mother, the death of her father, the Czech "immigrant experience," and the paradoxes of Czech culture in Texas are particularly striking, and show a degree of insight lacking in mere versifiers. Nováková is always the Texas Czech farm wife, though, and images such as the one in which she compares rows of corn in the field to lines of her verse on the page have a rustic charm.[61] She is a unique artist, closely tied to time and circumstances, and yet an authentic, individual voice. Her Czech prosody is simple, yet well suited to her purpose.

Other religious and topical verse is found in the pages of the Texas Czech journals. *Naše dějiny* includes verse that can be described as at once nationalistic and religious. Josef Buňata's *Památník Čechoslováků* (1918) includes rousing patriotic poems by E. Bažant, who had worked in a spinning mill near Beroun, Bohemia for twenty years (where he was persecuted by the Austrian government due to his involvement in political activities among the workers) before he emigrated to Texas and settled down to farming near West.[62]

One of the great Czech poets, Josef Václav Sládek (1845-1912), spent the years 1868-70, travelling in America, and Texas was one of the states he visited. He spent all of March 1869 "wandering alone,

---

[61] The image referred to appears in a poem entitled "Kukuřičný klas" ("Ear of Corn"), *Pod texaským nebem* (East Bernard, Tex., 1934), 33.

[62] See Josef Buňata, *Památník Čechoslováků* (Rosenberg, Tex., 1920), 19.

with a rifle on his back, from Houston to San Antonio." [63] In San Antonio, Sládek spent six months with the Polish priest Wincenty Barzinski and became his good friend. He later wrote several short stories set in the Texas Polish settlements. From San Antonio, he wandered all the way to St. Louis, a trip through woods and prairies that took him about five weeks. He described this experience in his essay "On a Czech Farm in Texas." [64]

Over thirty years before, the "wild frontier" of Texas had attracted the attention of another Czech, the Moravian Karel Postl, one of the most enigmatic figures in American literature. [65] Born in 1793, Postl was the son of a vinter in the village of Popice. The last family member to see him was his brother Josef, who visited him in Prague in 1823, where Karel lived as an ordained priest at a monastery. Evidently suffering from a crisis of faith as well as an intense dissatisfaction with the Hapsburg regime, Postl simply disappeared shortly afterwards. He apparently made his way to Switzerland and then on to New Orleans, Louisiana, travelling under the assumed name H. Sidons. In America, Monsieur Sidons adopted the name Charles Sealsfield, and thereafter identified himself as a citizen of the United States. Postl traveled widely in both the United States and Europe, living for a time in Pennsylvania, a time in Switzerland, but it was his travels in Louisiana and Texas that most excited his imagination, and he celebrated these regions in his tales, which, after his first two tries in English, he wrote in German. Probably because of the literary language he chose, Postl is not well known to English-language readers today, but his works were enormously popular in their day and are studied by German-language critics even today. They resemble early Mark Twain and Bret Harte in their glorification of the libertarian frontier ethic. No writer in English has been more closely identified with a staunch republicanism and galloping Americanism

[63] Rudolph Sturm, "Czech Literature in America," in *Ethnic Literatures Since 1776: The Many Voices of America*, Part I. (Lubbock, Tex., 1978), 168. Also see Sturm's "America in the Life and Work of the Czech Poet Josef Sládek," *Harvard Slavic Studies*, v. 2. 1954, 287-96, and *Sojourn of the Czech Poet Josef Sládek in the United States and the American Influence in His Writings*, PhD Dissertation at Harvard University (1956).

[64] See Sturm, "Czech Literature," 168. Also see Josef Václav Sládek, "Z cesty do Texas," *Slavie*, May 19, 1869.

[65] During his early career as a writer, Postl was not widely known even by his pseudonym of Charles Sealsfield. Instead, he was known as *Der Unbekannte* (The Unknown). Some readers assumed that he was a German-American. See Bernhard Alexander Uhlendorf, *Charles Sealsfield: Ethnic Elements and National Problems in his Works*. PhD Dissertation, University of Illinois (1920), 7.

than Postl. Of the several tales set in Texas, perhaps the most interesting is "On Fields Unshorn," which freely adapts several incidents from the Texas War of Independence from Mexico, and develops three striking characters: the narrator Col. Morse, a young adventurer-settler from Maryland; the Alcalde, a sort of Texas patriarch; and Bob Rock, who is at once crazed murderer and Texas hero.[66]

Postl's true identity was revealed only when his will, which left his substantial estate to his brothers and their families, was opened following his death in 1864. Despite the fact of his origin and the fact that he reportedly spoke both English and German with a heavy accent all of his life, Postl's Czech identity has been largely ignored by his German critics.

More significant for this study, however, are the Czech-Americans who wrote about Texas in Czech for a Czech-American audience. Like Sládek and Postl, other Czechs in America were fascinated by the frontier, cowboy, and "Wild West" images of Texas, just as English-speaking Americans were. The fact that Texas had been an important area of Czech settlement since the 1850's was an additional factor. *Povídky* (novelettes or short stories) concerning the adventures of Czech settlers in this "wild land" were fairly common fare in the big-city periodicals, in particular Chicago's *Amerikán národní kalendář*, which was by far the most important vehicle for Czech-American "popular fiction" as well as certain kinds of nonfiction. Among the authors who set their stories in Texas were Václav Petrželka, O. B. Pokorný, J. B. Zahradecký, and Hugo Chotek.

Hugo Chotek published at least thirteen pieces of fiction in the *Amerikán národní kalendář* in the late 1800s and the early 1900s, as well as biographical and travel stories for several Czech-American journals. In some of his best stories, he deals with life among the Moravian immigrants of Texas, where he had lived for some years and edited the newspaper *Slovan*.[67] Chotek can be considered a representative writer, and two of his *Amerikán povídky*, will be examined here: *"Z dob utrpení"* ("From the Time of Suffering"), published in 1900, and *Zahuba města*

---

[66] Charles Sealsfield [Karel Postl], *The Making of an American,* ed. and adapted by Ulrich S. Carrington, (Dallas, 1974), 21-126. See another version of the story, called "Adventures in Texas," in *Scenes and Adventures in Central America,* edited and adapted by Frederick Hardman (London, 1852), 57-214.

[67] Chotek, who, like many of the Czech-American journalists and writers, led an itinerant and adventurous life, died in Cleveland in 1911. His biography can be found in *Amerikán národní kalendář* (1912), 270-72.

Galvestonu'' (''Destruction of the City of Galveston''), published in
1906.[68] Although these stories cannot be called great literature, they illustrate the complex and ambiguous significance of culture contact and
interaction in their treatment of the ''immigrant experience.''

Both *povídky* could be classified as historical fiction with some melodramatic qualities. The works are fast-moving, suspenseful, and representative of a relatively high level of popular fiction. However, the narrative outlines of the stories are the primary concern here. Popular fiction provides an aesthetic structure to satisfy the psychic needs of its audience. ''Suffering'' and ''Galveston'' provide the Czech-American
reader with two paradigms for reconciling typical ambiguities and contradictions.

''Galveston'' demonstrates Chotek's characteristic method. He
places his immigrant protagonists in the midst of an historical disaster in
1900, the nearly complete destruction by hurricane of the island city of
Galveston, the port by which the great majority of the Czech immigrants had entered Texas.

The main plot concerns the misfortunes of a Moravian immigrant
named Veronika Holeček, a naive but haughty orphan girl who arrives
in Galveston with an inheritance of $1500.00. A ring of criminals who
specialize in exploiting the newly-arrived Czechs attempts not only to
swindle her out of her money but to lure her into prostitution at its
''secret villa'' outside of town. Veronika rejects the help of the well-
meaning Ignác Rusek,[69] a friendly Texas Czech who acts as a guide and
counselor to the immigrants, and loses her money, but Rusek and Jindřich Kaufman, son of the Austrian ambassador, rescue her unharmed
from the villa. (The criminals escape the law but are killed by the hurricane.) After surviving the storm, Veronika marries a suitor who has followed her from home. A year later, the couple moves back to Moravia.

Chotek's treatment of the immigrant's story in ''Galveston'' is in
some ways quite conventional, despite the extraordinary setting. The
novelette shares with much Czech-American fiction of the time a para-
digm for the interpretation of the immigrant experience: there is finally
no reconciliation between Czech ethnicity and American identity for the
principal characters. The fiction as a whole tends to be pessimistic in this
regard. Immigrants are often left with a life-long *angst* associated with a

---

[68] Hugo Chotek, ''Z dob utrpení,'' *Amerikán národní kalendář* (1900),
33-77; *''Zahuba města Galvestonu,''* *Amerikán národní kalendář* (1906),
33-89.

[69] Rusek, a real person, is discussed in Chapter 1.

failure to satisfactorily accommodate themselves to their new cultural environment and a yearning, however vaguely defined, for their homeland. Many readers will recall Mr. Shimerda's quiet suicide in Willa Cather's *My Ántonia*. Although it is not from a Czech ethnic novel, this incident illustrates the pattern well.

Unlike the majority of such stories, however, "Galveston" offers an escape from failure to adapt to the new country: Veronika and Miroslav' are able to return home. The essential conflicts are resolved simply by retreat to the homeland.

It is significant that this young couple is part of the turn-of-the-century immigration and caught up in the evils of the American *city*. Early in the story, the narrator contrasts the pioneer immigrants of the fifties, such as the Ruseks, who had depended only upon themselves for survival but had succeeded due to physical and moral courage, with the later "softer" and more dependent groups of immigrants. The implication seems to be that the later immigrants were not as strong as their earlier countrymen because they did not expect to have to fight so hard to survive and endure. Also, the narrator makes several references to the solid, rural-based way of life and contrasts it unfavorably with the superficial allurements of city life.

The Texan community in this case does not finally re-establish a satisfactory moral or legal order. Despite the romantic reuniting of the young lovers and despite the help of (Anglo) friends in establishing economic and social stability for their new family, escape is the final solution. Certainly the impractical or seemingly impossible dream of returning to the homeland must have functioned as a powerful fantasy among the first-generation Czech-Americans of the time.

Another of Chotek's novelettes also deals with the complexities of the immigrant experience, but in a different and an ultimately more positive way than does the essentially "escapist" "Galveston." In "From the Time of Suffering," written in 1900, six years before "Galveston," Chotek had portrayed the lives of the immigrants of the 1850s, positively represented by the Rusek family in the later work.

The action of "Suffering" takes place on the Podhajský farm in central Texas and in the Matagorda Bay area of southeast Texas, just prior to and during the Civil War. The Podhajský's farm is supposed to be "typical," and details of farm life are plentiful.

The Podhajský family is made up of old father Josef, his wife, two sons in their early twenties, a younger son in his early teens, and two teenage daughters. They are described as fairly prosperous farmers, who keep livestock and raise cotton as a cash crop. Life on the farm demands long days of hard work, but it is tranquil, and the countryside is beautiful. As the story opens, however, the father is vaguely aware that something unusual is going on in the area. Groups of riders have been visiting the neighboring Thompson farm at odd hours.

Billy Thompson is an unsavory character and his two sons are no better. He has a reputation among the farmers as a vengeful man, and Podhajský's wife remarks that "he thinks he is better than the Moravians." In fact, he is lazy and shiftless, periodically borrowing supplies and sums of money from Podhajský, whom he usually neglects to repay. Once, when a group of riders visits Thompson, little Rudolf Podhajský is sent as a "spy" and overhears a conversation which he can only partially comprehend. The men discuss the upcoming presidential election and the possibility of the secession of the Southern states if Lincoln is elected.

Subsequently, the Podhajskýs and other Czech families are caught up in events they little understand. None of them are slaveholders, of course. Because they are "foreign" and because some of them subscribe to "Yankee" journals (Czech journals from the northern United States), they are distrusted and harassed. Chotek includes a reference to the real-life Lešikar incident, described earlier in this chapter. The secessionist movement in Texas gains strength after the fateful election and the secession of other Southern states. Despite the opposition of Sam Houston and a few other leaders, the movement is enormously popular and wins the day.

Against this background, the romance of Lidunka, Podhajský's daughter, and Jeník Zapaláček, son of an immigrant farmer from a neighboring county, is played out. It is complicated by the fact that Jack, son of Billy Thompson, although he despises Czechs in general, is also attracted to Lidunka. He tries to force himself upon her in an isolated cotton field, but Jeník rescues the girl. Jack swears revenge.

Podhajský gives Jeník permission to marry his daughter but insists that the couple wait until the cotton crop is sold in Houston, so that they can have a properly grand wedding. Jeník stays behind with the Podhajsky family while the old man and a group of neighboring Czech farmers carry their crop to market in a caravan of wagons.

When the farmers do not return as soon as expected, Jeník and other young men form a search party. However, they are intercepted by a group of rebel soldiers under the command of Billy Thompson, and Jeník, Rudolf Podhajský, and a friend are forcibly recruited to the Confederate Army.

Podhajský complains to the local sheriff and marshall, but they are unsympathetic and, in fact, insist that at least one other member of the family must join the army. Twenty-two-year-old Josef Podhajský volunteers, and, subsequently, the law officers are more sympathetic to the Podhajský and other Czech families. Letters sent from young Jeník and Rudolf to their families recount horrible experiences, but confirm the fact that they are still alive and stationed in San Antonio. Another letter sent to Lidunka is more ominous, however. Jack Thompson commands her to meet him at Matagorda on a specific date. If she does not, he will take her by force.

Neighbors offer to help the Podhajskýs protect the girl but, after weeks of anticipation but no action, they all let down their guard, only to awaken one night to a burning home and gunfire. During the bloody skirmish which follows, Jack and his followers (part of a rebel force under his command) succeed in kidnapping Lidunka.

This time, however, the law officers are sympathetic to Podhajský and his friends when they ask for help. Jack is seen as a criminal who embarrasses the noble Southern cause, and a warrant is posted for his arrest.

Meanwhile, Jack, his men, and his hostage board the ship owned by Cohort (a character with a symbolic name that is no doubt less obtrusive from a Czech point of view), a wealthy slave trader, at Matagorda and sail for Galveston, from whence they expect to set out for the West Indies. They are intercepted, however, by a Confederate warship, and the outlaw crew is arrested. Jack, the ringleader, is court-martialed and executed.

Jeník and the other Czech youths are able to return home, and he and Lidunka are wed.

Like "Galveston," "Suffering" could be classified as a "local color" story and as "historical fiction." These novelettes are similar to much English-language popular fiction of the time and their plots are to some degree melodramatic. No doubt the most obvious function of such literature is to provide entertainment and "escape" from the real world, and some aspects of the plot seem contrived.

Nevertheless, Chotek makes claims for the realism of his stories. In a footnote to "Suffering," he claims that the characters and their way of life are drawn from close observation and that historical events and dates are corroborated by standard historical sources. The claim of realism may itself be a convention, but Chotek's descriptions of the appearance, behavior, and language of his immigrant protagonists is often subtle and convincing, probably drawn in fact from his personal observation and experience. Furthermore, not only the better-known historical details, such as the popular hero Sam Houston's opposition to the secessionist movement in Texas, are accurate: others, which would have been of primary interest to the Czech community in Texas, such as the *Národní noviny* incident and the intimidation of Josef Lešikar, are also modeled after real events.

In a larger sense, the Civil War brought a traumatic conflict of cultures. The war was "the external agent that forced the Czechs in Texas to recognize and clearly define the differences between 'Us' . . . and 'Them'."[70] From a sociological point of view, Chotek's treatment of the attitudes and behavior of the Czech ethnic community is realistic, and this aspect of the work in turn leads us to a consideration of its function on a *mythic* level to reconcile basic contradictions or oppositions in the cultural environment of the ethnic community. The basic oppositions are associated with ethnic identity and assimilation.

The (Anglo) Americans are seen in an ambiguous way. On the one hand, the Texans are crude, dishonest, drunken, violent men who defend the inhuman (and incomprehensible) institution of slavery. The Thompsons and their associates are stereotypical villains with virtually no redeeming moral qualities. In addition to the portrayal of their more obvious faults, however, there is a deeper, more subtle, criticism of their way of life. It is obvious from the description of the Thompson house and farm that the Thompsons, in stark contrast to the Podhajskýs, do not value hard work, do not love the earth, do not look upon the upkeep of their home and farm as an important duty. It is significant that the Thompson household is all male. Like their farmland, the Thompson family is barren and unfulfilled, especially in contrast to the vital Podhajský family unit, founded on the stability and life of the home, carefully balanced between masculine and feminine values.

One particularly interesting aspect of the rejection of Anglo-American values in this and other Czech-American fiction is the absence of the "cowboy" or a similarly idealized hero whose ethic, after all, is that of the adolescent boy's gang.[71] Jeník, who at one point saves the girl, does demonstrate his prowess in besting the villain Jack Thompson in a physical confrontation, but in his description there is no trace of the exaggerated self-reliance or the rootlessness of the Anglo-American hero. Of course, the idealized cowboy, who is traditionally associated with the rangeland rather than the farm, would be out of place in a narrative which affirms the positive values of the fam-

[70] William Philip Hewitt, "Czech Immigration and Community, 1850-1900," in *The Czechs in Texas: A Symposium*, 47.

[71] See Brion Davis, "Ten Gallon Hero," *American Quarterly*, 6, 2 (Summer, 1954), 123-25. In a literal sense, a few Texas Czechs did become cowboys who worked on ranches and participated in rodeos.

ily home and close-knit community life above all others. Jeník is a typical Czech-American protagonist in that he settles down with the girl once he gets her rather than "moving on."

On the other hand, the Americans' system of law and justice eventually functions to re-establish the ethical order that has been disturbed by the villains, despite the fact that the villains are Confederate soldiers, potential war heroes. The local sheriff and marshall initially ignore the complaints of Podhajský and his friends, but after Czech youths begin to serve in the Confederate forces, these civilian authorities are more sympathetic, and, with cooperation from Confederate military authorities, they eventually bring the villains to justice and save the girl.

The wedding and general celebration at the end of the story serve to reaffirm the ethnic identity of the Czech community. Jack Thompson, the potential Anglo-American mate of the Czech girl, has been exposed as completely evil. However, the Czech boys, although forced to serve in the Confederate Army, fight bravely. After their return home, they are at one point referred to, jokingly but approvingly, as "true Texans," because of their hardiness, by their fathers.

Historical forces have partially shattered the isolation of the Czech community, with frightening but not altogether unfavorable results. Podhajský resists involvement with the social and political world outside his restricted family and ethnic community, but he and his neighbors have no choice. The Czechs in the story have undergone a "time of suffering," associated with partial assimilation and partial affirmation of ethnic identity in the continuation of the traditional, agriculturally based, family unit, in order that their descendents may enjoy the good life. A postscript tells the reader that after thirty-five years (that is, about 1900) the old immigrants like Podhajský are dead, while their descendents have moved to other parts of the country and other states. We are not told where Lidunka and Jeník, now grandparents, live, only that they live *v lásce a štěstí* — in love and happiness.

Literature of this kind, which has been nearly forgotten, can tell us much about the culture of the people who wrote it and read it. The mere fact that it existed in America is significant.

CHAPTER 7

Ethnic Identity
And Assimilation

No parish school, no church congregation, no
foreign-language community can long withstand
the *force majeure* of Americanization.
Tomáš Čapek, *The Czechs in America*
(1920)

An American ethnic culture, as opposed to a "special interest
group," can appear monolithic only from the outside. From the inside, it is full of antitheses, oppositions, and ambiguities, which are
part of the dynamic structure of any vital culture. The Texas Czechs, as
has been seen, had their share of internal divisive and complicating
forces. Most serious was the religious question, of course, but the other
side of the extreme socialization inherent in the myriad of clubs and
organizations was a complex factionalism characterized by chronic dis-
agreements and misunderstandings among individuals, families, and
various groups. Then, too, an individual, subgroup, or the ethnic
group as a whole can simultaneously hold various contradictory or conflicting beliefs and opinions. Nevertheless, the Texas Czechs developed
a highly successful, coherent ethnic culture that was an especially powerful and important force in the state until about the time of World
War II. By readily assimilating selected aspects of Anglo-Texan
culture, while rejecting others, this group made compromises that led
to a unique culture well suited to its time and place and yet, like so
many other American ethnic cultures, doomed by its very success in at-
taining its divergent goals.

Obviously the culture of the Texas Czechs did not remain static
from the 1850s up until World War II, but it did develop along certain
definable lines, and it remained recognizably Czech. In order to de-

fine the unique ethnicity of the Texas Czech, this chapter will first compare it with that of other Czech-Americans, then briefly discuss interaction between the Texas Czechs and other Texas minority ethnic groups, and, finally, examine the subjects of assimilation and pluralism in some detail. In the process, many of the generalizations made during the course of this study will be extended and analyzed.

CZECHS IN TEXAS AND ELSEWHERE IN THE U.S.A.

The first major groups of Czech settlers in Texas from northeastern Bohemia were the first from that region to emigrate to America. Later, the great majority of immigrants came from rural villages in Moravia. Neither group was entirely typical of Czech immigrants in the United States. Among many of the eastern Bohemians and some of the Moravians, the legacy of the Czech Protestants was particularly strong, so that they and their descendants were able to establish a Czech ethnic Protestant denomination in Texas. On the other hand, the Moravian Catholics, by Czech-American standards, were highly loyal to the Church. The Czechs in Texas, then, were relatively congenial to organized religion. Their religious outlook was related to a conservative political and social orientation and a rural way of life.

It would be misleading, however, to assume that the conservative or even reactionary political outlook of the Texas Czech community in the context of today's American politics was characteristic of the early settlers: they were conservative only in comparison to their countrymen who settled in other states. Early pioneers such as Josef K. Lešikar and Jan Reymershoffer were politically active and familiar with the progressive ideas of the Czech freethinker and national hero Karel Havlíček.[1] Although there was a smaller percentage of socialists and atheists among them, their politics were "liberal" by American standards of the day, Czech nationalism was strong among them, and they frequently cited political oppression as an important factor in their decision to emigrate to America. Although Protestants complained of a double-edged political/religious persecution under the hated Austrian Hapsburgs, Catholic sentiments toward the monarchy were very similar. For example, the statement made by Valentin Haidušek, quoted in Chapter 1, gained the status of a proverb among the Texas Czechs: "I would rather live in this cabin as a free citizen than to live in a palace and be subject to the ruler of Austria."

[1] Lešikar's and Reymershoffer's political activity is referred to by Jan Habenicht, *Dějiny čechů amerických* (St. Louis, 1910), 79-82.

As already seen, close ties to the Midwestern Czechs were maintained, especially in the nineteenth century. Czechs from the large urban centers provided a great deal of journalistic, literary, and social (fraternal) leadership during those early years, and their influence never completely died away. Most important was the influence of the Czech-American urban press; the Czechs, unlike some less fortunate ethnic groups in America, had a standard literary language which literate members from any province of the Czech lands could understand. Nevertheless, the observations of L. W. Dongres quoted in Chapter 6 are evidence of the distinctively Moravian identity of the majority of the Texas population, an identity most closely linked with the Moravian dialects. Also, toward the end of the nineteenth century, the Czechs in Texas were developing a strong regional press which drastically decreased the influence of the northern journals. Even more significantly, Texas fraternal orders, both religious and non-denominational, were rapidly displacing the national ones. Although this split-up was part of a growing rift between eastern and western sectors of the national ethnic community, no single state other than Texas developed its own independent Czech institutions to such an extent. Texas had its own freethinking and Catholic fraternal organizations, its own Czech Protestant Church, and its own Czech-language press, all of them initiated either just before or just after the turn of the century, all of them successful. These institutions not only contributed to a growing Texas Czech identity, but in each case served to ameliorate the tensions that were causing Czech-American culture to come apart at the seams in some other parts of the nation. The freethinking SPJST did not take an anti-clerical stance, and instead refused to become identified with either religious or political controversy. The pacifist Unity of the Brethren muted anti-Catholic sentiment, and at the same time managed to preserve important aspects of Czech ethnoreligion. The most influential newspaper, *Svoboda,* published and edited by a nominal Catholic, did not remain aloof from political and social issues but eschewed religious controversy.

The relatively homogeneous Texas population, which had been almost directly transplanted from the rural homeland into Texas farm country,[2] felt it could and should go its own way. Although part of its

[2] There were, of course, exceptions to the typical Texas Czech as described in this chapter and elsewhere in the book. A few of the Texas settlers had come from Prague, or another Czech urban, rather than a rural, center. Some had initially settled in the Midwest, or elsewhere in the United States, before moving to Texas. A notable example is Václav F. Herold, who was born in Beroun, Bohemia, in 1845, and spent his early life in Prague, where he learned to be a

regional orientation consisted of adopting aspects of the Anglo-American culture in Texas, in retrospect the Czechs in Texas were generally more successful in maintaining their ethnic identity than those who settled in other areas and maintained a more nationally-based orientation. This is ironic when one considers the Czech nationalist opposition aroused in the big-city Czech press when Judge Haidušek and the Texans opted for English-language instruction in their public schools. But the Texans not only clung to their language with the help of their own ethnic institutions; they were further removed from the social forces that undermine relations between parents and children, between men and women, and thus undermine family, and finally community, solidarity. Although the Texas Czechs lacked the custom-supporting characteristics of illiteracy and a strong social heirarchy, and although they espoused public education and a philosophy of progress, they maintained a strong family life in a rural setting.

The Texas Czechs were more rurally oriented in their Northeast Bohemian and Moravian homeland, more rurally oriented in America, less "Germanized," less susceptible to the disrupting forces of mass transportation, mass communication, technological advances, and others usually associated with urban environments. Conversely, small rural communities in a "frontier" area afforded the opportunity of relative isolation. One other important factor set the Texas Czechs apart from their countrymen in America. While relatively isolated from some aspects of the Texas Anglo culture, the Texas Czechs gradually learned to closely identify not only with the United States but with Texas; this Texas "nationalism" was a powerful, romantic, regional identity that was uncharacteristic of most other Czech-Americans.

INTERACTION WITH GERMANS

Despite some internal factionalism, then, the Czechs settling in Texas were relatively cohesive. And they settled in somewhat isolated rural communities. Not only was farming to them an attractive way of

butcher. After immigrating to America, he had a long and successful career as a butcher in Cleveland and Chicago before retiring in Corpus Christi, Texas. (See K. V. Styblo, "Václav F. Herold," *Amerikán národní kalendář*, 1921.) A small number of the Czech immigrants were Jewish. An example is Moritz Kopperl, a Moravian Jew who became a successful trader and importer, and a leading citizen of Galveston, in the late 1800s. A number of Slovaks also settled in Texas. (See the "Introduction" for a discussion of the problematic relationship between Czechs and Slovaks.) A Slovak-language journal was published in Rosenberg, Texas, for several years in the late 1800s. (See Appendix E.)

life — to a certain extent, they intentionally isolated themselves from the larger society. But the larger society, the region that they most heavily settled, was the most heterogeneous one in Texas.[3] Central Texas, like other regions of the state, was dominated by Anglo-Americans, many of Scotch-Irish stock, who had emigrated principally from the Old South. That is, states like Virginia, the Carolinas, Alabama, and Mississippi contributed more of them than did the neighboring states of Louisiana and Arkansas. However, Central Texas differed from East Texas and the Coastal Plains, where they clearly established small-farm-squatter and plantation cultures analogous to those of the Deep South; differed from West Texas where Anglos established a ranching culture based on the raising of livestock; differed from South Texas, where Anglos displaced the old hidalgo leaders in a highly stratified Anglo and Hispanic hierarchy. The nucleus of Central Texas was the old Austin Colony, the birthplace of Anglo Texas; nevertheless, in addition to Anglos, Hispanics, and Negroes, Central Texas, by the time of the first mass migrations of Czechs, had sizeable populations of other European groups. By 1845, the German town of New Braunfels already had a population of about 1500. By the 1860s, Catholic and Lutheran Germans constituted perhaps a quarter of the population in this region. Along with the Czechs came other, smaller, groups as well — Sorbians (Wends), Silesian Poles, Scandinavians. The very fact that these groups tended to found their own communities and keep to themselves made the Czechs something less than unique in this most pluralistic of Texas regions.

Although Texas had a lower percentage of European immigration in the nineteenth century than did the Great Plains states to the north, by 1900 it was home for nearly 160,000 first- and second-generation Germans. At the same time, over 620,000 Blacks lived in Texas,[4] and although data for the total number of Mexican-Americans living in Texas at the time are not available, the number of native Spanish speakers in the state was over 234,000 in 1910.[5] The Germans were by far the largest European minority, however, and had begun to immigrate into Texas about twenty years before the first groups of Czechs.

[3] See Donald W. Meinig, *Imperial Texas* (Austin, 1969), 50-55, on ethnic groups in Central Texas.

[4] United States Department of Commerce, Bureau of the Census, Abstract of the Twelfth Census of the United States: 1900, Table 39, 40.

[5] United States Department of Commerce, Bureau of the Census, *Thirteenth Census of the United States: 1910*, Volume I, General Report and Analytical Tables, Table 15, 980.

The relationship between the Czechs and the Germans is both important and problematic. In his autobiography, Anthony M. Dignowity wrote of the Germans: "Their lust for political power is so great, that we cannot wonder that secret combinations were formed even in this country [the United States] in opposition to foreign influence" and "When I reflect who are the greatest tyrants and greatest opponents to all political freedom and all democratic institutions, the conviction forces itself on me, that they are the Germans—the combinations of princes."[6] But at another point, he wrote, "I always did respect them [the Germans], and would have in my younger days, if opportunity offered, spilled my blood to assist them in regaining their liberty."[7]

Dignowity's ambiguity is not simply a personal matter. The Czechs in general saw German nationalism and even the German language as a symbol of oppression. Political and religious persecution by the Hapsburg Germans since 1620 was the most immediate cause of the hostility, but some of the suspicion extended to the Germans from Oldenburg, Westphalia, Nassau, and Hessen who colonized Texas. In fact, hostilities between Slav and German had existed from the dawn of history and extended to the period of Nazi hegemony in Europe, when nationalistic German "Bund" groups in Texas allegedly planned the redistribution of property according to ethnic identity.[8] While there was only occasional open hostility between the two ethnic groups — perhaps it was most often expressed by children on the playground[9]—there was a common fear that the Germans would "swallow up" the Czechs, to deny them their separate ethnic identity. Clearly, this was an Old World view transported to America; however, it was exacerbated by the majority Anglo-American tendency to think of Czechs as "Germans." The fact that the less numerous Sorbian population in Texas, which held the Lutheran faith, actually became so

[6] Anthony M. Dignowity, *Bohemia under Austrian Despotism* (New York, 1859), 21. Dignowity held many enlightened views on politics and social issues (he was ardently in favor of women's rights, for example) but, like many thinkers of his time, believed in phrenology, which, he thought, showed that the "Germans as a body cannot compare with the Slavic race of Bohemia," 14.

[7] Dignowity, 56.

[8] Whether true or not, some Texas Czechs claim that this "plot" was a real fear among some of them during the war.

[9] H. A. Parma of Ennis is quoted on the harassment of Czech, by German, children at school in Estelle Hudson and Henry R. Maresh, *Czech Pioneers of the Southwest* (Dallas, 1934), 158.

thoroughly "Germanized" that its Slavic heritage was almost completely lost suggests that the fear was not entirely without foundation. Even today a German critic can refer to Karel Postl's native Moravia as the "most medieval" of the "Austrian provinces,"[10] and a celebratory history of Cat Spring can ignore the fact that this "German settlement" was one of the most important early Czech settlements and the most important "jumping off place" for the Czech settlers in the nineteenth century.[11]

Ernest Raba, a talented San Antonio photographer who was active during the period 1890-1951, was perhaps the only Texan with a Czech surname to actually identify himself as an "Austro-Hungarian."[12] A few Texans with Czech surnames identified themselves as German — perhaps due to mixed parentage, perhaps due to the Old World sense of upward mobility, educational advancement and cultural superiority associated with things German. On the other hand, many surnames apparently German — Šiller (Schiller) and Haisler, for example — belonged to thoroughly Czech families. In general, there was much less overlap between German and Czech ethnic identity than Anglo-Americans might assume, and the great majority of Czech-speaking immigrants from Bohemia and Moravia did not consider themselves to be German at all. As Dignowity put it, "There is more difference between the Bohemians and the Germans than there is between the English and the French; in language still more."[13]

In spite of all this, the Czechs felt a certain cultural affinity with the Germans. Most important was the fact that while very few Czechs had even a rudimentary knowledge of the English language upon arriving in Texas, many (but by no means all) of them were fluent in

[10] See Ulrich S. Carrington, *The Making of an American* (Dallas, 1974), 4, 6.

[11] Cat Spring Agricultural Society, *The Cat Spring Story* (San Antonio, 1956).

[12] See Glen Lich, "The Raba Question," in *The Czechs in Texas: A Symposium* ed. Clinton Machann (College Station, Tex., 1979), 165-72. Lich probably exaggerates the extent to which the ethnic boundaries between Czech and German were blurred, however.

[13] Dignowity, 10.

German. Generally, a Czech's knowledge of German would be dependent upon the extent of his formal education and his socio-political and economic status in the homeland, since German was the language of literature, commerce, and politics. (For these reasons, a man would be more likely to speak German than would his wife.) Moreover, the Czechs were much more like the Germans than like the Anglos in their family structure, farming ethic, and general way of life.[14] It is true that by 1880, more than half of the Texas Germans lived in town, while the great majority of Texas Czechs remained on the farm. Still, a substantial number of Germans continued to strive for a small-farm self-sufficiency that was very similar to the typical Moravian ideal. Most of the Germans had begun their life in America in a state of poverty, just as most of the Czechs had. The German consensus, like that of the Czechs, was anti-slavery, and German and Czech alike were persecuted during the Civil War years for their half-hearted support of the Southern cause. Finally, there were religious affinities, which will be discussed below. All in all, Czechs would have a much better chance of "fitting into" a German-American rather than an Anglo-American environment. For this reason, they tended to settle in areas that already had a significant German population.

Some of the early ties between Czechs and Germans in Texas have already been alluded to. Father Bohumir Menzl, the first Czech Catholic priest in Texas, ministered to the German settlers at New Braunfels. Most significantly, Rev. Josef Bergman, and to some extent his colleague Rev. Josef J. Zvolanek, both pastors in the German Evangelical Church, enticed Czech settlers not only to come to Texas but to pass through the village of Cat Spring, the German-Czech settlement through which they were funneled into Fayette County and beyond. Bergman not only serves as a good example of an ethnic Czech with a German name but also reminds us of the close connection between Czech and German Protestantism. Because native Czech Protestantism was outlawed, even after the 1781 Edict of Toleration, Czechs looked to German Protestants (among others) for missionaries to preach in the Czech lands, for sanctuary across the border when religious exiles required it, for Protestant theological schools for young Czechs, and for the printing of Czech Protestant religious material (hence the Gothic script of many old Czech Protestant texts).

It must be remembered, however, that when the Czech-Moravian Brethren finally were able to organize in Texas, they explicitly turned

---

[14] On German small-farm and anti-slavery attitudes, see Curt E. Schmidt, *Opa & Oma* (New Braunfels, 1975), 22-32.

down the opportunity to merge with the German Evangelicals (fore-runners of the United Churches of Christ) and instead decided to reas-sert the separate identity of the Hus-Chelčický tradition. Furthermore, their official journal periodically through the years expresses a fear and resentment of German Protestant encroachment.[15] Although Czech Protestants were probably more amenable to socialization and cooper-ation with both Anglo and German Protestant churches than were Czech Catholics with other Catholics, the Brethren in Texas main-tained a consesus to remain an *ethnic* religion until the issue of ecum-enicalism exploded in the 1960s and resulted in schism.[16]

At any rate, it was common for Czechs and Germans, both Prot-estant and Catholic, to co-exist in many communities, particularly in Fayette, Austin, and Washington counties, but in many others, too.[17] For example, the majority of Ellinger's five hundred inhabitants in 1859 were German. The first Catholic church in the area was built mainly by Germans in 1859, and a parsonage and school were added in the following years. By the 1880s, however, Moravian Catholics in the area outnumbered the Germans. Fayetteville and Industry are other "German" centers that became "Czech" as well. It was not un-common for even second-generation Texas Czechs to be fluent in Czech, German, and English. As the young J. J. Holík discovered, flu-ency in all three languages was a real asset for Central Texas merchants in the nineteenth century.[18]

RELATIONS WITH OTHER ETHNIC GROUPS

Because very few of the Czechs ever owned slaves in Texas, the legacy of guilt and hatred associated with White-Black relations that is so important to Southern culture had much less meaning among the

[15] See Richard Machalek, "The Ambivalence of Ethnoreligion," in *The Czechs in Texas: A Symposium,* 104, for example.

[16] Machalek traces the history of the Texas Brethren in "The Ambivalence of Ethnoreligion" and, more completely, in his 1972 Masters Thesis at The University of Texas at Austin, entitled *Intra-Organizational Conflicts and Sch-ism in an Ethnic Minority Church: The Case of the Unity of the Brethren in Texas.*

[17] The examples are based on Habenicht, 89-90.

[18] See Holík's memoirs in Hudson and Maresh, 107-12. Holík was a busi-nessman and farmer who became the second President of the SPJST (1899-1902). Among several interesting aspects of this account is a reference to Rev. Zdrůbek, who served as parish schoolteacher, as well as minister, at Wesley (109).

Czechs. Not only was slavery irrelevant to their social structure and farming methods, as discussed in Chapter 3, but they were also opposed to it on principle. Only a few were outspoken abolitionists before the war as Dignowity was. Unlike that San Antonio doctor, most of them had immigrated more recently, were far from being securely established in Texas, were frightened and confused, and feared persecution, with good reason. Their opposition was more passive; they simply didn't want to have anything to do with the institution of slavery. In Central Europe, the memory of serfdom was still strong, and, in fact, even in the mid-nineteenth century, the Czech word *otroctví* (slavery) was widely used to characterize the subservient relationship of the people to the landowning aristocrats.[19]

After the war, Czechs, particularly Catholics, and other "foreign" elements were occasionally persecuted by the Ku Klux Klan and other terrorist groups committed to a "pure" white American society, although to be sure, their persecution was not nearly so severe as that of the Blacks. At any rate, the Czechs had many reasons to be sympathetic with the plight of the Blacks both before and after the Civil War. It should not be assumed that the Czechs were without racial prejudice, however., Many of them, upon seeing Black people for the first time, were startled and frightened. It is not likely that a people characterized by a tightly structured, enclosed family and community life and suspicion of those who are "different" would be quick to break down racial barriers. Miscegenation would be not so much sinful as simply unthinkable. Expressions of racial prejudice can occasionally be found in nineteenth-century Czech-American journalism and literature.[20] Nevertheless, this prejudice remained for the most part passive rather than active. In many areas, Snook and Tunis, for example, Czech and Free Black communities peacefully co-existed in close proximity. Perhaps there was even some linguistic influence. The Texas Czech English accent has some affinities with Black dialect.[21]

There was some, but not a great deal, of interaction with Hispanic

[19] For the European background of "slavery" connotations, see Jerome Blum, *Noble Landowners and Agriculture in Austria, 1815-1848* (Baltimore, 1948), 52-53.

[20] For example, Hugo Chotek's story *Zahuba města Galvestonu*, discussed in Chapter 6, contains rather unflattering descriptions of Black Americans.

[21] When shown a transcript of typical Texas Czech (English) speech in 1975, Prof. Ian F. Hancock of the English Department, University of Texas at Austin, noted several points of correspondence with Southern Black dialect. Prof. Hancock is a specialist in the fields of English dialects and creoles.

Texans in the early years.[22] In particular, some mixed communities with a significant Czech population such as Caldwell had Catholic churches with mixed Hispanic and Czech congregations. (As in the case of German-Czech or Anglo-Czech parishes, the cemetery was usually divided along ethnic lines.) Although the two ethnic groups to a large measure "kept to themselves," co-operation in various parish activities would lead to some group interaction. There was no large migration of Czechs to South Texas, where contact with Hispanic Texans would have been much greater, although a few Czech farmers and businessmen were active in the area. The Mexican-American border culture does have one interesting affinity with Czech (as well as Polish and German) culture — the love of polka dancing.

Josef J. Barton's comparison of Czech and Mexican immigrants in Nueces County during the period 1880-1930 is one of the few studies of its kind. The Czechs allied themselves in families of three generations, with very strong kinship ties. The Mexicans, on the other hand, showed strong lateral kinship ties. Using their reserve of family labor, most of the Czechs secured farming land, while the great majority of the Mexicans remained agricultural laborers and developed working-class organizations and loyalties.[23]

Another European immigrant group should be mentioned here. The first mass migration of Poles to America came with the Poles from Prussian Silesia, who began to enter Texas in the period 1854-56, about the same time that Czechs began settling in large numbers.[24] The Poles initially settled in colonies at Panna Maria, Bandera, San Antonio, and Martinez. Despite affinities of race, language, and culture between the two Slavic groups, there was not a great deal of interaction between them. As pointed out in Chapter 4, the Polish Catholic priest, Tom Moczygemba, was one of several who served Czechs when Czech-speaking priests were unavailable. Nearly all the Poles were Catholic, and, naturally, contact with Czech Catholics was much greater than that with Czech Protestants. In general, however, the Polish communities were perhaps even more insular than the Czech ones, and the Poles did not seek to establish ties with the Czechs.

[22] Ignác J. Gallia, first President of the SPJST (1897-1899; 1902-1905), was one of the few Czech Texans who tried his hand at farming in the Rio Grande Valley. See his memoirs in *Věstník*, vol. 46, no. 25 (June 1956) 7-8; 46.

[23] Josef J. Barton, *Land, Labor, and Community in Nueces: Czech Farmers and Mexican Laborers in South Texas, 1880-1930* in *Ethnicity on the Great Plains*, ed. Frederick C. Luebke (Lincoln, Neb., 1980), 190-209.

[24] The Poles in Texas are well documented in T. Lindsay Baker, *The First Polish Americans* (College Station, Tex., 1979).

THE CZECHS AND THE AMERICANS

For the early Czech settlers, of course, "American" meant Anglo-American, but the boisterous culture which had wrested control of Texas from the hands of Mexico less than two decades after the first major colonization, while unquestionably American, had already created something of a separate identity for itself. After all, Texas had existed as an independent republic for nine years, during which time it had had its own nationalistic, even imperialistic, ambitions. Now as part of the United States and, furthermore, as part of the South, the Lone Star State was still something special, with its own unique history, its own myths. In choosing to settle in Central Texas, the Czechs may have chosen the most pluralistic region, but it was also the heartland of Anglo-Texas, the region settled by Stephen F. Austin himself.

The Czechs, from the beginning, found Anglo Texas fascinating, and many characteristics of its culture highly desirable. Karel Postl wrote of its early history with almost unalloyed admiration. The myth of the rugged, fearless, free-spirited Texan was a very popular one. The Czech settlers, with their intense craving for a political liberty they had never known, found this myth almost as appealing as the promise of cheap, abundant farm land. Despite the very serious clashes with both the everyday way of life of the Anglo Texans and some of their ideals, the basic appeal of the Texas myth never died among the Czechs.

In one way, the first Czech group migrations to Texas came at an inopportune time. Often, there was only a short interval between the shock of landing in a foreign land after a terrifying journey and confrontation with war. The conflict between North and South was considered not only unfortunate but almost incomprehensible to many of the Czechs. The fact that "brother was fighting brother," the defense of the institution of Black slavery and other aspects of Southern culture that were unattractive or hard to understand: it was horrible and confusing. The situation was made all the more traumatic because many of them, beginning with Dignowity himself, were literally fleeing the severe Austrian conscription laws — now they found themselves in a situation in which they were expected to fight and perhaps die for a cause they could not understand or identify with.[25] Added to these considerations was the fact that those immigrants who identified with the Unity of the Brethren tended to be pacifists on principle.

The friction caused by northern Czech journals in Texas has already been alluded to in Chapter 6. In addition to the *Národní noviny*, the Racine newspaper *Slavie* proved to be very controversial. This

[25] This dilemma is illustrated by some of the cases discussed in Chapter 1.

journal attracted a great deal of attention because the Anglos thought that its name meant "Slave." When the newspaper's anti-slavery stance was discovered, several subscribers were threatened with hanging. One of the better known immigrants so threatened was Jan Reymershoffer, who was then living in the Alleyton community of Colorado county. In order to save himself, Reymershoffer actually purchased a slave for nine hundred dollars.[26]

In some cases, renegade rebel bands of soldiers harassed and even looted Czech communities. The most serious problem, however, was the reluctance of Czech men to serve in the Confederate forces, as noted in Chapter 1. The case of Josef Holík and his family, who settled at a farm near New Elm shortly after their arrival in Texas in 1859, is representative.[27] Rather than face conscription into the army, Holík hid in the woods while his wife and children ran the farm as best they could. He was captured by Southern soldiers when he tried to visit his family upon hearing a false rumor that the war was over, but he escaped and remained in hiding for the duration of the war. There were many such "draft dodgers" among the Czechs, and they were not considered to be cowards by their countrymen. A few Czech, as well as German, young men were killed while resisting conscription.

Many Czech men avoided actual military service by engaging in an activity that was almost as vital to the survival of the Confederacy: the cotton trade with Mexico.[28] Cotton was one of the South's most valuable assets, but the Federal blockade effectively prevented its export by any major route except the overland one to the Mexican port of Matamoros. The Confederate cotton (much of it confiscated) was hauled in convoys of from three to fifteen wagons. Most of these convoys originated in Fayette county; three months was allowed for a round trip. The journey was arduous and dangerous, but it served not

[26] On the *Slavie* and Reymershoffer's slave, see Ferdinand F. Dubrava, "Experiences of a Bohemian Emigrant Family," in *Wisconsin Magazine of History*, viii (1925), 406. Alleyton, where the Reymershoffers then lived, was a stronghold of secessionist and pro-slavery sentiment. The Alleytown precinct voted for secession 113-2 on February 23, 1861. The vote was closer in some other Colorado County precincts: 201-93 in Columbus, for example, and Frelsburg, Harbey's Creek, and Dunlavy voted against. See Leonie Hand and Houston Wade, *An Early History of Fayette County* (La Grange, Tex., 1936), 244-45n.

[27] Josef Holík (Sr.) is the father of J. J. Holík (Josef, Jr.). The elder Holík's adventures during the Civil War are told in Hudson and Maresh, 105-107.

[28] The discussion of Czech teamsters during the war is in Chapter 1.

only as a relatively desirable substitute for service in the army but as a means of making money as well. However, the Confederate authorities tried to limit this teamster service to the young and infirm.

Some Czechs did volunteer for the Confederate Army, of course, and others were conscripted. Some of them, including the brother of Augustin Haidušek, died on the battlefield.[29] In spite of the Czech resistance to the Southern cause, the war years were a time in which the young Texas Czech population was compelled to come to grips with its American identity. Hugo Chotek's short story, "From the Time of Suffering," discussed in Chapter 6, dramatizes this social reality very well. The story ends with the reuniting and affirmation of the Podhajský family and the ethnic community, as the war apparently rages on. However, the Confederate-American system of justice ultimately prevails in helping to resolve the basic conflicts of the story. The outcome of the war, the Unionist victory, is not emphasized. The impetus for the story is the dynamics of culture contact, not the war itself. "Suffering" provides an aesthetic and mythic model for successful, if painful, assimilation. The common Czech culture is preserved but has partially adapted itself to American (and Texan) culture. Surely the Civil War is the first great milestone on the road to assimilation.

The end of the war did not, of course, mean an end to ethnic strife. Czechs who settled the community of Moravia in the seventies were robbed by bands of outlaws and harassed by "Irish" pranksters.[30] In other communities, bands of Anglo youths would occasionally "shoot up" a Czech celebration or dance. This kind of physical violence was comparatively rare, however. More common was a subtler kind of ethnic conflict that often led to ill will between Czech and Anglo communities. For example, in 1885, the *Flatonia Argus* reported on a Czech school at Praha. The apparently well-intentioned reporter noted that the students were carrying out their studies in three languages: Czech, German, and English. He went on to remark that "It was gratifying to us to know that a class of foreigners, whom our people are disposed to look down upon as a race too inferior to associate

[29] See Haidušek's reference to his brother's death in *House Journal,* Seventeenth Legislature, State of Texas, 152-53, quoted in Jesse Jochec, *The Life and Career of Augustin Haidušek,* Masters Thesis, The University of Texas at Austin (1940), 98. Also see the discussion of the war years in Chapter 1.

[30] Thadious Polášek cites examples of this kind of harassment in "Early Life in Moravia, Texas," in *The Czechs in Texas: A Symposium,* 64-66. Other examples are found in Mollie E. Stasney, *The Czechs in Texas,* Masters Thesis, The University of Texas at Austin (1938), 33.

with, were manifesting sufficient interest in their progeny to have them educated in the language of their adopted country.'' The condescending tone of this article caused a furor among Czech residents in the area.[31]

In nineteenth-century accounts or memoirs by Czech immigrants and their children, however, instances of conflict with the *Američani* are about equally balanced by examples of "neighborliness."[32] In many cases, established American families provided food and medical assistance to suffering Czech pioneers.

For the most part, the Texas Czechs were ignored by the majority population rather than harassed. A few characteristics of the Czechs were widely accepted, however. They were supposed to be "clannish" but fun-loving, light-hearted people who loved to dance, sing, and eat their ethnic food (especially the ubiquitous koláče). It was also generally acknowledged that they were industrious and excellent farmers. One journal article credited them with being able to turn what an American would use for a hog pasture into a profitable farm.[33]

The pattern of settlement in many areas worked to keep the Czechs isolated from their Anglo neighbors. The Czechs tended to live in small rural communities, even in the areas of their greatest concentration. For example, both Anglos and Germans outnumbered Czechs in La Grange, the county seat of Fayette County, while the Czechs were predominant in most of the surrounding countryside. Some rural communities, such as Snook, were nearly 100% Czech. In other communities, especially the larger ones, the Czechs constituted a minority of the population. Although the Czechs did not necessarily physically cluster together in such situations, their tightly-knit social structure in effect often created a Czech enclave.[34] The city of West offers an interesting example of the relationship between Czech and Anglo factions in a population center.

Several small farming communities were formed in northeastern

[31] The *Flatonia Argus*, April 22, 1880 is quoted in Stasney, 41.

[32] See Stasney, 36, for typical examples of neighborliness. Out of their ignorance, Czech pioneers in Texas sometimes ignored potentially helpful advice from the Anglo farmers concerning the cultivation of cotton and corn (unfamiliar "American" crops).

[33] This article appeared in the *Galveston Daily News*, October 28, 1907.

[34] Intermarriage with "Americans" was generally frowned upon by Czech parents. One of several popular injunctions was aimed at young Czech men: Don't marry an *Amerikanka* or *budeš jest biskety* (you'll eat bisquits). Interview with Al Vrana, March 20, 1980. Evidently Czechs did not enjoy this part of the traditional American cuisine.

McLennan County during the 1870s. One of these was a Czech Catholic village named Tours, after the famous cathedral town in France. During the following twenty years, however, the town of West developed into the dominant commercial center in the area.[35] This railway-centered community was incorporated in 1892. At this time, the town had a population of about 1,000, and it resembled other Texas towns settled and developed by Anglo Protestants. Although there were a few Czech and German residents, the non-Anglos were in a decided minority and had very little civic power or prestige. West continued to boom, and, by the turn of the century, had doubled in population. Anglo Protestants were still the dominant ethnic group, but the situation had begun to change. The railroad that had helped West to grow also made it accessible to more and more immigrants. The pattern of Czech settlement changed, and increasing numbers of Czech Catholics and Protestants alike moved into the commercial center of West rather than remaining in outlying agricultural areas. Meanwhile, the Anglo Protestant population remained stable, not keeping up with the Czech growth. During the nineties, local Czech businesses such as the now-legendary Němeček meat market and Joseph Janek's saloon indicated the growing commercial activity of the Czechs. In 1892, Reverend Adolf Chlumský founded a Brethren church in West. Also in 1892, a Czech Catholic church was built in the city, and Reverend Chromčík became pastor in 1893. By the early 1900s, Reverend Václav Pazdral was delivering sermons in Czech in a local Presbyterian church. Meanwhile, successful Czech farmers in the area such as John Stanislav were instrumental in opening up a dialogue and commercial interchange between Czech Catholics and Anglo Protestants. In 1900, he purchased $3,000 worth of stock in the West Cotton Mill. This transaction was considered a breakthrough in Czech-Anglo commercial relations.

By 1910, the Czechs had founded several clubs and organizations in West, including chapters of the Sokol and the SPJST which held its state convention there in 1909. Also in 1909, J. S. Zvesper began publishing a Czech language supplement to the *West News*. As discussed in Chapter 6, the Czechoslovak Publishing Company, responsible for the SPJST journal *Věstník*, was established in West in 1920.

Method Pazdral, a Czech Protestant, served as West city attorney from 1905 to 1915. Rudolph Marak was the first Czech elected to the West City Commission and became mayor pro-tem in 1919. In the next year, a Czech named Paul S. Škrabánek became president of the

---

[35] The short history of West given here is based primarily on Henry M. Apperson, *A History of West, 1836-1920* (Waco, Tex., 1969).

West Bank, the bank that had been founded thirty-five years earlier by the Anglo-Protestant pioneer T. M. West himself. It was generally conceded by this time that West had become a predominantly Czech city, and it remains so today.

Several points about the evolution of West from Anglo to Czech community are of special interest. The Czechs left their isolated, self-sufficient farming villages to come to live in, and eventually dominate, the city of West. Once securely established in the city, however, the Czechs, at least according to the prevailing Anglo view, reverted back to their isolationist ideals and in fact retarded the growth of West, which became a "self-contained" community that would never grow beyond its size at the peak of the "boom" years: a population of about 3,000. During the time of the Czech "intrusion" into the city's population and power structure, Anglos frequently voiced resentment over the Czechs' "clannishness" and the typical large families that contributed, along with increased immigration, to the rapid growth of Czech population in the area. The Czech element included Catholics, Brethren, and Czech Presbyterians, but ethnic identity was clearly dominant over religious identity. Nevertheless, the Czech Presbyterians were credited by the Anglos for leading the way in the "Americanization" of the Czechs. The Catholics, on the other hand, were considered to be the most clannish and least progressive group, because they shied away even from American Catholics and they were the group most often blamed for the cultural shift taking place in West. Despite some resentment, however, the Anglos admired the thrifty and hard-working nature of the Czechs.

ASSIMILATIONIST IDEALS

The goal of a fuller participation in American community life, through increased business and political activity, was prominent among the Czechs who moved into West during the final decades of the nineteenth century, and it was becoming increasingly characteristic of all Texas Czechs during this time. The man who most clearly articulated the desire for increasing involvement in American life and who was personally most responsible for bringing it about was the legendary Augustin Haidušek. Haidušek's name has already been mentioned at various points in this study, particularly in the Journalism section of Chapter 6. Because of his central role in the development of Texas Czech ideals of assimilation, however, it is appropriate that his life and influence be examined in more detail in this chapter.[36]

Haidušek was born in 1845 in Missi, a Moravian village located between the towns of Frenštát and Příbor. Valentin, the father, was a comparatively well-to-do farmer who decided to emigrate primarily for political reasons. Augustin was known as a studious youth in his Moravian school. In 1856, after arriving in the area of Fayette County which his father named "Dubina" ("Oak Grove"), he avidly studied in both Czech and English with his father and an old Anglo teacher at the country school which was later known as "Světlo." At the age of sixteen, he left school to enlist in the Confederate Army, Company F, Bates's Regiment, stationed at Velasco. Even during his military service, he continued his education by reading and rereading the English Bible.

After the war, he returned to his Fayette County home. By day he worked as a farm laborer; by night, he continued his reading, now under the direction of the Polish Catholic priest Josef Bitovský. Following brief stints as a public school teacher and store clerk, he was accepted by the firm of Jarmon & Cross in La Grange to study law in 1868. By the end of 1870, he had passed his state bar examination and become one of the first Czechs to practice law in the United States. In order to enhance his La Grange law practice, he studied and mastered the German language in addition to his continuing readings in Czech and English. In the early years of his practice he supplemented his income by teaching in the public school at Ross Prairie, and he married a girl from that community, Anna Bečková, in 1872.

Haidušek's law practice — and his prestige in the community — grew quickly. He was elected chairman of the Fayette County Democratic Executive Committee in 1874. In the following year he was elected mayor of La Grange, apparently the first American of Czech descent to hold such an office. He was re-elected in 1877. He suffered a temporary setback when he unsuccessfully tried to unseat J. C. Stiehl as Judge of Fayette County in 1878, but, after returning to his law practice in partnership with R. A. Phelps at La Grange, he made a successful bid for the State Legislature in 1880, representing Lee and Fayette Counties, and served two terms. As the first Czech-American to be elected to a state legislature, Haidušek was very active, if not always effective. One of the bills he introduced was enacted: each county was allowed to hire out its

[36] Haidušek's life is discussed in many sources. Perhaps the fullest account is given by Jochec in his 1940 Masters Thesis. Also see H. J. Schovajsa, "August Haidušek and His Influence on Czech Culture in Texas" in *The Czechs in Texas: A Symposium,* 83-87.

Judge Augustin Haidušek.
— Photo copied from
Czech Pioneers of the Southwest.

criminals who were serving out their jail sentences, at fifty cents per day per person, but only within the boundaries of the county. He unsuccessfully opposed the poll tax amendment to the state constitution and proposed two unsuccessful amendments of his own: the authorization of a state agency to promote foreign immigration to Texas and the authorization to invest the permanent school fund in county bonds and similar securities. He also introduced eight bills, none of which was enacted, a resolution to specifically define the crime of "sodomy" in the state penal code, and a resolution to condemn the assassination of the Russian Czar Alexander and offer sympathy to his bereaved nation. Neither of the resolutions passed. In spite of the fact that his arguments did not always win the day, Haidušek was respected by his colleagues, and he gained widespread publicity for some of his causes—especially the attraction of more European immigrants to Texas.

He ran again for the Fayette County judgeship in 1884, and this time he won. He was re-elected in 1886 and 1888. As County Judge, Haidušek was an activist and took many controversial positions. He exerted the decisive support for the purchase and maintenance of the first toll-free bridge spanning the Colorado River in Fayette County and the building of a new courthouse. He also advocated the use of convict labor in county road work, taking advantage of the recent legislation which he had himself introduced. It was another policy concerning the county roads that led to the defeat of Haidušek—as well as all the county road commissioners—in the election of 1890. Under Haidušek's leadership, the practice of thoroughly repairing one road at a time rather than piecemeal repairs all over the county was introduced. This approach led to more economical, permanent road maintenance in the long run, but, in the meantime, residents served by the unrepaired roads grew dissatisfied and threw their support behind the candidate W. S. Robson.

When he was first elected County Judge in 1884, Haidušek found that he was consistently criticized by Josef Čada's *Slovan,* the only Czech-language newspaper in the county. As will be seen, the chief quarrel between Haidušek and Čada was over an "ethnic" issue. He was determined to counteract Čada's influence, and with about fifty friends, formed a joint stock company to launch the competitive Czech journal *Svoboda.* Not only was Haidušek successful in his feud against Čada, as related in Chapter 6, but he made *Svoboda* the most successful and influential Czech newspaper in the state. The circulation of the weekly paper had climbed from 345 in 1887 to 1534 in 1890, when Haidušek took over as sole owner and editor, positions he maintained until the paper ceased publication in 1927. By 1895, after intense efforts to bolster circulation, the paper had about 3,000 subscribers, although Haidušek complained of difficulty in collecting subscription fees.[37]

Although he was sorely tempted to go back to a more lucrative law practice and pressured to resume his political career, Haidušek was determined to establish a new role for himself. In fact, his overall influence as publisher and molder of public opinion among the Czechs was probably much greater than as a public official. His paper was open to social and political—but not religious—controversy. The most important ethnically-oriented controversy in which he became involved came near the beginning.

As County Judge, Haidušek was also ex officio superintendent of public schools, under the state law of the time. During his first term of office, a tour of county schools convinced him that the study of the English language was being neglected in many of the Czech schools. He issued the following proclamation in Čada's *Slovan* in 1886:

> I hereby notify my fellow countrymen that after the current year the English language must be taught in the public schools. To be sure, other languages may be taught, but English must be used by all

[37] See Jochec, 76.

teachers and must occupy the most important place in the program, whereas the other languages may occupy second place. I am advising you, my countrymen, to elect teachers who are thoroughly capable of speaking and teaching the English language.[38]

In fact, Haidušek was merely applying the letter of the state law which required English as the principal medium of instruction in the classroom, but his approval of the law's principle was evident from his energy in enforcing it. Čada immediately began attacking Haidušek's position in his editorials, arguing that he was attempting to deny Czech students the right to their own language. Čada's view was widely supported by the Czech-American press around the nation, which took up the issue. F. B. Zdrůbek himself wrote one of the most virulent attacks. It was entitled "Crimes of a Czech Renegade, Judge Haidušek in Texas."[39]

This controversy was, of course, the main impetus behind Haidušek's decision to found *Svoboda*. Although a number of Texas Czechs initially supported Čada's position, and a few even wrote threatening letters to Haidušek, it became obvious over the next year or two that the majority supported the Judge. Haidušek developed his stand on language into a more comprehensive position on Americanism, which he expressed in a series of editorials. Two of them became especially well known. The first appeared in *Svoboda* in January, 1889.

> We left the country of our birth with the intention of making America our permanent home. We did this of our own free will; no one forced us into it. We selected the United States as our mother country; therefore, our interests are identical to those of the other citizens here. . . . Anything that is beneficial to them cannot be harmful to us. Whoever recognizes this must recognize that our sacred duty is to become American citizens. . . . When we do this we are obliged to support the American institutions not only because the law requires it, but because it is our moral obligation. If we do not like some of the institutions, we have a right to point out their faults and make efforts to have them corrected. Our nationality is well suited for American citizenship. We love liberty; we are honest, industrious, economical, and law abiding. These are the essentials of a good citizen. . . . An American citizen must possess certain knowledge, but this we do not have. Every sensible person understands that the most important part of a democracy is its educated citizens. . . . In a de-

[38] *Slovan*, May 6, 1886. The translation is by Stasney, 79.
[39] See Stasney, 79-80.

mocracy, the people attend to their affairs through their representatives. In order to get this work done well, the citizens themselves must understand it. That which we do not understand well we are incompetent to manage. The idea that a person who does not know the English language can be as useful an American citizen as one who knows it is truly ridiculous. The people who do not understand are incapable of indulging in politics.[40]

In an editorial later the same year, Haidušek wrote,

We came here as strangers but were received kindly. We came in contact with people who speak a different language and who support a different form of government from the one in our native country. These people were here long before we came. They are proud of their forefathers and customs and like no one who wishes to change them; therefore, when a foreigner comes here he should support all of their institutions.[41]

These statements of an assimilationist ethic have been frequently quoted with approval by Texas Czech leaders since they were written by Haidušek.

Over the following years, Haidušek continued to reinforce his position as the most prominent Czech in the state of Texas. He was elected to the board of directors of the First State Bank of La Grange in 1896 and was given credit for rescuing it from mismanagement. In 1905, Governor Lanbaum appointed him to the Texas A&M College Board of Directors, creating yet another "first" for persons of Czech descent. His support was routinely sought by Democratic political candidates in Central Texas because of his great influence. Only once did he support a Republican candidate—R. B. Hawley for the Tenth Congressional District against Haidušek's old enemy W. B. Robson in 1898. Hawley won. The *Austin Statesman* wrote articles praising Haidušek's integrity. All along, Haidušek kept his ties with both Czech ethnic and Anglo-American civic organizations. A speech by Judge Haidušek (as he was invariably called) was the highpoint of many Czech celebrations.

Unfortunately for Haidušek, both his influence and his personal fortune were severely damaged in his old age. In 1916, he supported the candidacy of W. P. Hobby and opposed the re-election of James E. Ferguson for State Governor. This stand was so unpopular that *Svoboda* subsequently lost almost 2,000 of its subscribers — more than

---

[40] *Svoboda*, January 14, 1889. The translation is by Stasney, 71-72.
[41] *Svoboda*, October 31, 1889. The translation is by Stasney, 72.

half.[42] Neither the man nor the newspaper ever fully recovered from this blow.

Haidušek, however, had created a legend among the Texas Czechs that only continued to grow after his real personal political influence had waned, and after his death in 1926. Again and again in Czech biographical sketches he is compared to Abraham Lincoln: the image of the pioneer Czech boy studying by firelight so that he may someday lead his people is irresistible.[43] His editorials in *Svoboda* and public speeches made him the most-quoted Texas Czech by far. His breakthroughs in the law profession and in the holding of public office were of inestimable value to the younger Texas Czechs who were to follow him.

He was a small man with a "boney" frame but a big personality who inspired respect from the Anglo Texan press and public for his zeal in defending controversial positions which he believed to be right. Also, although he could be merciless to his political antagonists, he was known for his fairmindedness in judicial decisions and for his profound knowledge of constitutional law. He appealed to a wide constituency: even at the beginning of his career when he defeated his non-Czech opponents in the La Grange mayorial elections, most of the voters were non-Czech.[44]

Although he became something of a patriarchical figure, his Czech audience did not necessarily accept his word on all issues. His assimilationist views obviously struck sympathetic chords. Acquisition of the English language and assimilation would surely have taken place had Haidušek never lived, but it is revealing to examine his formulation of the issues which helped to define the pace and the modes that assimilation would take. No doubt Haidušek was correct in seeing language as the key to assimilation. Language not only opened up the crucial understanding of American laws but also the opportunity for economic and social advancement. There was already a kind of reverence for education in Czech culture, despite the counterweight of rural anti-intellectual tendencies, to which Haidušek could appeal. The Czechs had a saying that "he who is born under a bench should not rise above it," and in general did not seek great wealth or prestige; however, they also exhibited a certain stubborn persistence in gradual-

[42] See Jochec on Haidušek's stand in the election of 1916 and its consequences, 102-103.

[43] Jochec does this, for example. See p. 6.

[44] At the time, Czechs probably constituted a majority of the county voters but were heavily outnumbered in La Grange, the county seat.

ly bettering their lot; they sought a steady economic advancement toward financial security and social respect within the Texas community. They were, on the whole, quite willing for their children to learn the English language and American ways in order to succeed. Painful sacrifices were necessary, of course. The "generation gap" between the old settlers and their children would be widened, as the young became more Americanized, but this, up to a point, was an acceptable price to pay. The American political and economic systems had always been seen as ideal. Some of the old European customs were quite dispensable. Still, there was an indispensable ethnic core to be preserved. Strong family and ethnic social ties would be maintained. A strong folk culture, along with the intertwined institutions of church and fraternal organization would remain strong. Children would still speak Czech at home and on special social occasions, if not at school. They would continue to eat Czech food and perform and listen to Czech music. The American "melting pot" still allowed for a degree of pluralism. Perhaps a degree of "clannishness" could be retained, and young Czech men and women would continue to marry each other. They would be immune to extreme individualism, decadence, and big-city values because they had been brought up in the right way. At the same time, they would do well in the world and share a piece of the American pie.

The above is probably a fairly accurate statement of the Texas Czech majority opinion at the turn of the century. Of course, some individuals and even families, because they felt ashamed of their "lowly peasant," foreign origins, or because they were caught up in an historical vision of American reality, were ready to leave their Czech identity behind altogether. However, the extraordinary survival of Czech culture and social institutions up to the time of the Second World War is evidence that the great majority of Texas Czechs did not adopt this attitude. In a sense, the "underground" nature of the Czech culture within the Austrian state had provided a model for the maintenance of separate Czech institutions within a dominant society. Few, if any, Texas Czechs analyzed the situation as it is presented here, but, nevertheless, the behavior of the ethnic group as a whole manifested this attitude. It is especially important to avoid misinterpreting the attitude of the Texas Czechs at the turn of the century in terms of activist ethnic movements within the U.S.A. during the second half of the twentieth century. The complex of attitudes described here was a "given," largely unconscious received pattern and not aimed against or consciously opposed to, what they perceived to be American idealism.

A curious fact is that Czech nationalism actually *grew* after the time of Haidušek. Haidušek, although he consistently maintained a pride in the Czech language and his own ethnic identity, tended to downplay Czech nationalism in *Svoboda,* and he had very little interest in reporting European news or news about Czechs from around the United States.[45] In this, he was consistent with the prevalent tendency of his time. Haidušek was formulating his ideas about the same time that Czech fraternal and religious organizations were splitting away from the national groups and going their own separate ways.

This regional or state split was irreversible; however, the first three decades of the twentieth century saw a steadily increasing national consciousness among the Czechs that paralleled the planning, realization, and development of Czechoslovakia. Tomáš Masaryk said that the Czechoslovak state could never have been realized without the help of Czech-Americans that helped to bankroll the cause in Europe. But, along with the outpouring of money, and, indeed, the reason for it, was Czech-American sympathy and identification with the new country. The Czech and Slovak peoples, so long among the oppressed minorities of Europe, were now proudly fighting for their freedom.

It is true that Czechs felt some pressure from the general xenophobic reaction following the United States' entrance into World War I. In 1917 any professor at The University of Texas who was a citizen of an enemy country was fired.[46] The Panola County Council of Defense proposed "an act of Congress declaring the German language extinct" and that "the teaching of all foreign languages except Greek and Latin should be abolished."[47] The Czechs, perceived by the "Americans" as being a "foreign element," came in for special treatment as well. In 1918 the State Council of Defense, which had been organized by Governor James Ferguson, enacted its Americanization Bureau. One of the aims of this group was "to help immigrants from Slavonic countries and to assist them in their efforts to become good American citizens."[48] The bulletin published by the council added, "Thus through our endeavor to educate them we shall render a patriotic service to our country and enhance civic improvement and beautification of the American nation."[49]

The council need not have been concerned about Czech loyalty to

[45] See Jochec, 80-82.
[46] See Hewitt, 310.
[47] Quoted in Hewitt, 312.
[48] Quoted in Hewitt, 313.
[49] Quoted in Hewitt, 313.

the Allies, for it was deepseated in them. The Czechs in Texas, indeed Czechs all across America, were united in their opposition to the Austro-Hungarian Empire. In the war they saw the "window of history" opening to allow the freedom sought by so many of their forebears since 1620, when the Czechs lost their independence at the Battle of White Mountain. The great majority of Czechs in Texas, without reservation, identified with the struggle to "return the affairs of the Czech people to themselves."

Overall, Americans did see the Czechs in a sympathetic light. Favorable public opinion in the United States toward the Czechs at this time probably helps to explain the ready support for a Czech language program at the University of Texas, as explained in Chapter 6. The Liberty County *Daytonite* argued in a 1915 editorial that an increased American knowledge of the Slavic languages would help to secure the trade of the Slavic countries (at the expense of Germany) after the war.[50]

During the war, both Czech-Americans and exiled Czech leaders criss-crossed America, delivering speeches at rallies and collecting money to support the "Czech War of Liberation." Masaryk himself visited America twice and became very popular with the American people, not only the Czech-Americans. After some initial difficulties, even the Catholic-Freethought rift was overlooked for a time, as Czech-Americans displayed a solidarity they had never felt before. The *České národní sdružení* (The Czech National Alliance) was formed to co-ordinate the national effort and to a certain extent worked in partnership with the Slovak League.[51] Czech individuals, fraternal organizations, and church groups in Texas were, of course, caught up in the national enthusiasm. Women's *Včelky* ("Bee" groups) turned out sweaters and comfort kits for Free Czech soldiers serving in France, Italy, and Russia. Local groups held bazaars in Czech communities all over the state which collected thousands of dollars from farmers and working people of mostly low and moderate incomes. A comparison of the nations most successful bazaars of this type will indicate the extent of the Texas effort. A bazaar in New York City yielded $22,250. Subsequent bazaars in Cleveland and Cedar Rapids, Iowa each yielded about $25,000. About the same time, the bazaar at Taylor, Texas, described in Chapter 2, collected well over $50,000. Only Omaha sponsored a more successful event prior to the 1918 nation-wide Thanksgiv-

[50] Reported in *The Daily Texan*; May 25, 1915.
[51] See the discussion of the Czech National Alliance in Chapter 2.

ing rally, which yielded about $320,000.[52] The pictorial history of the Czech National Alliance activities in Texas entitled *Pamatník Čechoslováků* (1918), also described in Chapter 2, is a remarkable statement of Czech — as well as American — nationalism.

On July 15, 1919, 1104 Czech Legionnaires passed through Houston on their way from Siberia to Czechoslovakia.[53] They were part of the corps of Czech volunteers who had fought in Russia after deserting from the Austrian forces during the war. They received a tumultuous reception as war heroes by a large crowd of Texas Czechs at the train station. Bands played as a woman's group distributed 10,000 *koláče* and various other gifts. The local lodge of the SPJST, Pokrok Houston, had borrowed $1200 to distribute to the soldiers, and the banner of the local branch of the Czech National Alliance was presented to the men, who did not possess a flag of the new republic. The flag was adorned with a red and white ribbon inscribed *"Našim Legionářum — Čechoslováci v Houstonu"* (To our legionnaires — the Czechoslovaks of Houston). Judge C. H. Chernosky translated the speech of the commander, Major Jirsa, into English, and the bands played *Kde domov můj* — the Czech national anthem.

This occasion perhaps marked the highpoint of Czech nationalism in Texas, which remained very strong, however, until the ascension of the Czech Communists in the years following World War II. During the time of World War I, there seemed to be no conflict at all between American patriotism and enthusiastic support of Czech nationalism. The liberation of the Czechs and other subjugated peoples was, after all, what America was fighting for. As might be expected, there was little opposition to either World War I or World War II from Czechs in America. The Czechs in Texas were proud of the fact that the first Texan to die for the cause in World War I was Dominik Naplava, a young immigrant who had been born in Zadovice, Moravia, and he is remembered as a hero to this day.[54]

Because of these historical circumstances, then, Americanism, which for the Texas Czechs always had a distinctly Texas coloring, and Czech ethnic pride, grew side by side. Both forces are enthusiastically expressed in two important Texas Czech publications of the 1930s:

[52] The figures for the bazaars are taken from Tomáš Čapek *The Čechs (Bohemians) in America*. (Boston and New York, 1920), 269.

[53] An account of the Czech Legionnaires' visit to Houston is given in Hudson and Maresh, 358-61.

[54] A chapter is devoted to Naplava in Hudson and Maresh, 351-57.

Naše dějiný (1939) and *Czech Pioneers of the Southwest* (1934). The works have already been discussed in Chapter 6, but now they can be put into the context of the Texas Czech between-the-wars culture as analyzed here.

The National Czech Catholic Union in Texas, which compiled and published *Naše dějiny*, was the Texas division of a national group organized during the war years to support the cause of Czech liberation. It was made up of prominent Texas Czech clergymen and lay leaders, most of them associated with the Catholic fraternal orders. The title, "Our History" in English, refers to the history of the Czech *Catholics* in Texas, not of the ethnic group as a whole, although by implication, it includes all Czech Texans in some of its generalizations. Some notable characteristics of the book are relevant to the present discussion. First, several inspirational poems interweave the attitudes of a) faith in and thanksgiving to God, b) pride in the Czech heritage, and c) a celebration of the freedom and material progress available in the Lone Star State, into a total ethno-religious vision of history.[55] The poems as well as the historical sketches of parishes and fraternal organizations have an optimistic tone and stress the great progress made since the Czech pioneers struggled through the first hard years. Obviously inspired by the Texas Centennial celebration of 1936, the book includes a chapter describing the Czech exhibit at the Dallas exhibitions of that year.[56]

Similar values are expressed in a more vigorous tone by *Czech Pioneers of the Southwest*, published two years before the Centennial. Henry R. Maresh, the co-author, was a well-known Houston physician and "spokesman" for the Texas Czechs who also published an article on the subject in the *Southwestern Historical Quarterly*.[57] *Pioneers*, like *Naše dějiny*, was well received by the Texas Czech public and may be taken to represent typical Czech ethnic attitudes. In spite of the Great Depression, the theme of constant economic and general material improvement is perhaps the most dominant one in the book. Chapter 1

[55] *Naše dějiny*, (Granger, Tex., 1939). Inspirational poems include *"Naše Dějiny"* by Rev. Alois J. Mořkovský, *"K prvním krokům našich dějin v Texase"* by Rev. Karel J. Dvořák, and *"K našim dějinam"* by Marie Nováková (6-8). Nováková, whose poetry is discussed in Chapter 6 of this study, also has an untitled poem on p. 654.

[56] See *Naše dějiny*, 666-74.

[57] Henry R. Maresh, "The Czechs in Texas," *The Southwestern Historical Quarterly*, vol. 50 (October 1946), 236-40.

is entitled "A Century of Progress." It quotes figures illustrating the growth of cotton production over the past century and compares the old, unsafe port of Galveston with the modern, $12,000,000 Houston ship channel. The third chapter, entitled simply "Texas," gives figures for total state assets and celebrates the glories of Texas history. Sandwiched in between these is Chapter 2, "Looking Backward — Czechoslovakia." The paradigm is set before the first "Czech pioneers" are discussed in Chapter 3. Passages such as the following illustrate the synthesis of ethnic pride and Americanism (Texanism): "That desire to attain the finer things in life, refinement, culture, knowledge of life in all its fullness, will not die in Texas any more than it will die in Czechoslovakia."[58] This double idealism informs an extravagant style:

> And one may look down the long vista of futurity to see an "empire" in extent, unequalled in advantages, a valuable part of the continent. And this extended empire, inhabited by the sons and daughters of Czech pioneers, inheriting the will and the purpose of the pioneer ancestors to maintain and carry them on. Owners of the soil on which they live, and with interests in institutions which they have labored to establish and uphold. The waters of an ocean lapping the shores of the great State, bearing on its bosom the commerce which the labors of the Texas-Czech citizens have helped to develop.[59]

This kind of inflated diction was more or less conventional in the thirties, but the point should be obvious: *Pioneers* conveys a great enthusiasm for a kind of marriage of ethnic and American values. At the time, the Czech language had been successfully introduced into the curriculum at the University of Texas, and dozens of Texas Czechs had followed in the footsteps of Judge Haidušek by "making it" in the professions; doctors were especially numerous. Men like Judge C. H. Chernosky of Houston, State Senator Gus Russek of Schulenburg, State Representative Charles D. Rutta of Columbus, and dozens of others (including Judge Haidušek's son, George) had clout in state politics. Czech farmers and businessmen were becoming more prosperous; more Czech students were receiving a higher education.[60] A

---

[58] Hudson and Maresh, 40.

[59] Hudson and Maresh, 372.

[60] For a more complete list of Texas Czechs in the professions, etc., see Hudson and Maresh, 311-37. Also see John M. Skrivanek, *The Education of the Czechs in Texas*, Masters Thesis at The University of Texas at Austin (1946), 93-131 and Joe Malik, Jr., "The Contributions and Life of the Czechs in Texas" in *The Czechs in Texas: A Symposium*, 16-17.

few, like Dr. Charles J. Hollub of Schulenburg, helped to reforge old links with the homeland by studying at Charles University in Prague.[61]

Texas Czechs in the thirties thought they were living in a special time, almost a golden age, and, in retrospect, they were correct in many ways. The revitalization of Czech ethnicity in the state as a result of the Czech national movement in Europe could not have lasted forever, in any case. And how could the "great genealogical tree of the Texas Czechs" celebrated in *Pioneers* be preserved indefinitely in a framework of progress and Americanization that would inevitably break up the isolated rural communities and bring intermarriage with other ethnic groups and continued decline of the Czech language? The Texas Czechs of that time could not fully realize, of course, that they were living in the context of delicately-balanced historical forces.

That World War II uprooted individuals and communities, accelerated the trends of urbanization and the growth of technology, fostered a revolution in mass communications, and so forth, is widely accepted. These factors explain the increased rate of assimilation among many American ethnic groups, not just the Texas Czechs. In their case, however, the loss of close contact with the Czech homeland was another important factor. Not only did current immigration decline to a relative trickle, as it did for many other nationalities, but the emotional impact and symbolic value of Czechoslovakia faded as that nation became more "foreign" to America and the West, a member of the "Eastern bloc."

[61] Hudson and Maresh, 290-91.

AFTERWORD

The forty years since the end of the time period covered by this study can be conveniently divided into two parts. The immediate post-war period saw a rapid decline in Texas Czech culture in Texas. While the idea of progress and American and Texan idealism remained strong among the Czechs, ethnic consciousness faded. Not only was the Czech language heard less frequently on the streets of Czech towns and in Czech homes, but it was phased out as the official language of Czech fraternal organizations, the language of the Brethren Church, and the language of some Texas Czech journals. Czech music suffered after the war before the old bands were able to regroup, and Czech ethnic festivals and celebrations were infrequent.

The trend toward the loss of ethnic consciousness was certainly reversed in the sixties and seventies, although the total number of fluent Czech speakers in Texas has continued to decline. It became increasingly rare for third- or fourth-generation Czechs to learn Czech in the home. Nevertheless, as part of a national trend, Czech ethnic festivals and celebrations began to flourish in the sixties, and continued to do so in the seventies and eighties. Anyone who has recently attended the annual celebration at Praha, the Ennis Polka Festival, Westfest, Czech Day at the State Fair, or any of a number of similar successful festivals throughout Texas will not doubt the popularity of Czech ethnicity today, although it might be argued that such awareness is increasingly superficial and that some of the ethnic events are highly "commercialized."

Meanwhile, the study of Czech in public schools and universities experienced a resurgence. Especially encouraging was the revitalization of the Czech program at Texas A&M University, the institution of a program at the University of Houston, and the strengthening of the program at the traditional stronghold, The University of Texas at Austin. It must be admitted, however, that in 1982, not a single Czech language program at a Texas school or university had better than a tenuous existence. One particularly encouraging development in the seventies was a special summer program at Prague's Charles University aimed in particular at Texas Czech students, but the future of that program, too, is uncertain.

Ethnoreligion may be making a modest comeback. During the seventies and early eighties, Czech-language masses were once again occasionally heard in some Catholic parishes, and the Catholic KJT-affiliated weekly journal, *Našinec,* printed entirely in Czech, still has a circulation of about 2,000. Members of a small Brethren congregation in College Station are considering the construction of a church closely modeled after the ancient Brethren edifice at Kunwald.

Czech-language journalism in Texas was enhanced when the monthly Omaha *Hospodář* moved to West, Texas, in 1961. *Hospodář* now has a circulation of about 6500, and the SPJST monthly *Věstník* continues to include a four-page Czech-language section. In 1982, a new English-language journal promised to be of special interest to Texas Czechs. Published in Hallettsville, it is entitled *Naše Dějiny: The Magazine of Czech Genealogy.*

Czech music is once again strongly established in the state, with traditionally favored bands such as Joe Patek's and Gil Baca's joined by other popular and successful family bands such as the Vrazels. But the incursion of American country music into the repertoire of these "polka bands" is increasingly noticeable.

The Texas Czech fraternal organizations, in particular the SPJST, have flourished during the past few decades. Total membership and total number of lodges have climbed steadily. But in this case, too, the implications for Czech culture in Texas are ambiguous. Some of the most recently-established lodges are not located in traditional Czech areas, and the ethnic factor seems to be playing a smaller part in these organizations.

Of course, such developments are not a conscious "betrayal" of the Czech heritage, but a product of social realities in current American life. In fact, the Texas Czechs have shown a remarkable cohesiveness as an ethnic group up to the present day. Perhaps their most striking characteristic in this regard is a quiet but persistent emotional attachment to the Czech language. Most Texas Czechs are no longer fluent in this language, and students do not flock to the Czech courses offered at Texas schools and universities. At the same time, however, the *idea* of the importance of speaking Czech — and of offering these courses — is strongly entrenched. The Czech-speaking *chalupníci* who settled Texas in the nineteenth century came from the heart of the Czech lands, and the Czech language was the chief symbol of their latent nation. English-speaking Czechs who argue for the maintenance of the Czech language today are reminiscent of the German-speaking intellectuals and artists in the Czech homeland who championed Czech language and literature in the late eighteenth and nineteenth centuries. These National Revivalists, of course, could turn to the Czech peasantry as the repository of the Czech language. In contrast, the descendents of the *chalupníci* who settled in Texas over a century ago have been largely assimilated into the fabric of American society.

Still, the culture of the Texas Czechs is far from dead. The prediction of journalist L. W. Dongres in 1924 that the Moravians in Texas would be the last Czechs in North America to become extinct has not lost its force.

Bibliographical Note

The standard works on the subject of Czechs in America are still Tomáš Čapek's 1926 *Naše Amerika* (Our America) and 1935 *Moje Amerika* (My America), both published in Prague, Czechoslovakia. Čapek's English-language version, *The Čechs (Bohemians) in America* (1920) is less complete and definitive but superior to any other English-language work. Obviously, a modern study is needed. Čapek had a comprehensive knowledge of Czech-American communities in the Midwest and Northeast; however, he was less familiar with Texas. Jan Habenicht's 1910 *Dějiny cechů amerických* (History of the Czechs in America) offers valuable information on the early history of the Czech settlements in Texas which is unavailable elsewhere. Unlike Čapek, who collected every conceivable United States and State Government statistic, not only on Czechs and Slovaks but on all Slavic groups, Habenicht relies more on personal observation and information from his informants. Both Habenicht and Čapek are interesting for their extensive personal contacts and their anecdotes, however.

In many ways, *Naše dějiny* (Our History), compiled by the National Council of Czech Catholics in Texas in 1939, is the most comprehensive work on the subject of Texas Czechs. Unfortunately, the important minority of non-Catholic Texas Czechs is slighted, although not entirely ignored. Estelle Hudson and Henry R. Maresh's 1934 *Czech Pioneers of the Southwest* provided a great deal of anecdotal information that attempted to cover the entire Texas Czech community but is uneven in its treatment and disorganized. William Phillip Hewitt's 1978 dissertation at the University of Texas, *The Czechs in Texas: A Study of the Immigration and the Development of Czech Ethnicity, 1850-1920* provides a good account of early immigration and settlement and is surely the best-documented study of the Texas Czechs up to the present time. *The Czechs in Texas: A Symposium* (1979), edited by Clinton Machann, provided new information on a variety of subjects related to Texas Czechs, but it, like other major sources, was not widely-known or readily available to the public.

Clearly, a major new work on the subject would have to take into account relatively obscure and unpublished sources, and especially the essential Czech-language sources — books, articles, and periodicals — that provide the bulk of the most useful information. Probably this necessity to fully take into account the Czech-language sources has been the most important impediment to the production of a full-scale study such as *Krásná Amerika* until now.

The most complete bibliography of publications about and by Czech-Americans is Esther Jerabek's *Czechs and Slovaks in North America: A Bibliography* (1976). This work, for the most part, supercedes Tomáš Čapek's

Padesát let českého tisku v Americe od vydání "Slowana amerikanského" v Racine, dne 1. ledna 1860, do 1. ledna 1910 (1911). The Čapek bibliography is still valuable for its extensive bibliographical essays and annotations, however. Starting with these two monumental works, the authors abstracted those entries which pertained to Texas Czechs in a special way or which were used in the preparation of this study. Decisions to include and exclude entries were often difficult and may occasionally seem arbitrary to the reader. For example, the bibliography lists several sermons by F. B. Zdrůbek, even though they were neither written nor published in Texas, because they might cast light on his religious opinions, which were so controversial during his tenure as Texas preacher. On the other hand, entries for Hugo Chotek include only those published stories that are set in Texas; others are excluded. The authors sought to keep the bibliography at a manageable length and at the same time make it as inclusive as possible in terms of the specific subject of the study. They attempted to locate and examine as many of the items as possible, but even Jerabek could not locate some of them; probably some of the more obscure items no longer exist. Thanks to the SPJST Library in Temple, Texas; the Barker Collection at The University of Texas-Austin Libraries; the assistance of Archivist Joseph Svoboda at the University of Nebraska-Lincoln; the Interlibrary Loan services of the Texas A&M Libraries; and the excellent cooperation from archives and libraries all over the nation, the authors were successful in locating and studying most of them. At any rate, entries gleaned from the great Czech-American bibliographies provided about half of the total listed below.

The other half comes from two sources. First, the authors added many items from bibliographies they had compiled over several years of interest and study. Many of these items are unpublished, published by the author, or published by small presses. An especially rich source that has been only partially mined by the national bibliographies is a series of masters theses in several disciplines written on various aspects of the Texas Czechs, beginning in the late thirties at The University of Texas at Austin. Second, the authors naturally included those general "background" and theoretical works, as well as government records, which were used in the study. The authors were able to list — and make use of — some Czechoslovak sources, but undoubtedly many more useful sources would have been located if they had had the opportunity to personally carry out reserach in Czechoslovak libraries and archives. (See Antonín Robek's *"K etnografické problematice českého vystěhovalectví do Ameriky,"* followed by its English translation, in *The Czechs in Texas: A Symposium,* pp. 19-43, for an overview of Czechoslovak sources.)

This bibliography strives to be comprehensive in only one respect, then (and no doubt falls short of its goal): in items that were written by or published by Texas Czechs and those others that pertain in a significant way to the Texas Czechs. Appendix D provides a list of every Czech-American periodical published by and for Czechs in Texas for which the authors could find a record.

BIBLIOGRAPHY

Books, Articles, and Documents

Abernethy, Francis Edward, ed. *The Folklore of Texan Cultures*. Austin: Encino Press, 1974.

Apperson, Henry M. *A History of West, Texas, 1836-1920: Conflict of Conservative Cultures*. Waco, Texas: Texian Press, 1969.

Arndt, Karl. "Charles Sealsfield, 'the Greatest American Author.'" American Antiquarian Society. Proceedings, 74 (1964), 249-59.

"Augustin Haidušek." *Věstník*. June 20, 1956.

"August Haidušek z La Grange, Okres Fayette." *Amerikán národní kalendář*, 1901.

Baca, Cleo. *Baca's Musical History 1860-1968*. La Grange, Texas: The La Grange Journal, 1968.

Baca, Marie. *Memorial Book and Recipes*. Taylor, Texas: Merchants Press, 1957.

Baker, T. Lindsay. *The First Polish Americans*. College Station, Texas: Texas A&M Press, 1979.

Balch, Emily. *Our Slavic Fellow Citizens*. New York: Charities Publication Committee, 1910.

"Barbara Tesařová." *Amerikán národní kalendář*. 1908.

Barton, Josef J. "Land, Labor, and Community in Nueces: Czech Farmers and Mexican Laborers in South Texas." In *Ethnicity on the Great Plains*, ed. Fredrick C. Luebke. Lincoln: The University of Nebraska Press, 1980, pp. 190-209.

Bartoš, F. *Česká čítanka*. Praha, 1912.

Beneš, Vojta. *České národní sdružení: vznik a historie revolučního hnutí osvobozenského mezi svobodomyslnými a evangelickými Čechy ve Spoj. Statech amerických*. Chicago, 1925.

Berger, Peter. "Religious Institutions" in *Sociology*, ed. Neil Smelser. New York: Wiley and Sons, 1967.

Bergman, Josef A. *Letopisy pamatných udalosti evang. křesťanské obce v Strauzným*. Brno: Biblické Jednoty, 1930.

Bicha, Karel D. "Researching the History of the Czechs in America: An Historian's View." A paper delivered at the 9th. World Congress of the Czechoslovak Society of Arts and Sciences in America. Cleveland, 1978. Unpublished manuscript.

____. "Settling Accounts with an Old Adversary: The Decatholization of Czech Immigrants in America." *Social History*, IV (November, 1972), 45-60.

____. Karel Jonáš of Racine: 'First Czech in America'," *Wisconsin Magazine of History,* 63 (Winter, 1979-80), 122-40.

Blaha, Albert and Dorothy Klumpp. *The Saga of Ernst Begmann.* Privately printed, 1981.

Blaha, Albert. *Czech Footprints Amongst Bluebonnet Fields of Texas.* Houston: Privately printed, 1981.

_____. comp. *Compilation of Baptismal Records of Rev. Jindřich Juren.* Unpublished manuscript.

Blum, Jerome. *The European Peasantry from the Fifteenth to the Nineteenth Century.* Washington: American Historical Service Center for Teachers of History, 1960.

_____. *Noble Landowners and Agriculture in Austria,* 1815-1848. Baltimore: Johns Hopkins Press, 1948.

Boethel, P. C. *History of Lavaca County.* San Antonio: The Naylor Company, 1936.

Borecký, Jan. *Kapitoly k dějepisu lidu českomoravského ve Spojených Statech.* Cedar Rapids, Iowa, 1896.

Borhek, J. T. "Ethnic-group Cohesion." *American Journal of Sociology,* 76, 33-46.

Bowmer, Martha. "Life as Loved By Our Unique Czech Texans." In *Bell County This Month.* Temple, Texas: Stillhouse Hollow Publishing Company, 1972; 2-5.

Bradley, J. F. N. *Czechoslovakia, A Short History.* Edinburgh: Edinburgh University Press, 1971.

Branecký, František. "František Branecký v Praze v Texasu." *Amerikán národní kalendář.* 1886.

Bruer, Hynek. *Rolník,* vi (1883), 117-27.

Brown, John Henry. *Indian Wars and Pioneers of Texas.* Austin: L. E. Daniell, 1904.

Bujarková, F. L. "Proti srdci-proti vůli; z utrpení texaských krajanů v době občanské valky." *Amerikán národní kalendář.* 1929.

_____. "Shledaní na pudě texasské." *Amerikán národní kalendář.* 1898.

_____. "Šlechetná pomsta; obrázek ze života Čechů texaských." *Amerikán národní kalendář.* 1899.

Buňata, Josef. *Pamatník Čechoslováků.* Rosenberg, Texas: Národní pokník, 1920.

_____. *Památník texasských Čechoslováků na práci vykonanou v letech 1914-1920 ve prospěch osvobození vlastí starých.* Ennis, Texas: Krajanský vybor ČNS pro Texas a Louisiany, 1921?

_____. "Putovaní českoamerického novináře" *Amerikán národní kalendář.* 1936.

_____. "Rozbor Socialismu." *Amerikán národní kalendář.* 1892.

_____. "Tomas Kraica." *Amerikán národní kalendář.* 1912.

_____. "Vlastní životopis. Kutnohorský Rozhled." *Kulturní měsíčník.* Part I in IV (June 1931), 83-88. Part II ("Můj pobyt v Americe.'") in IV (August-September 1931), 103-106.

_____. "Vzpomínky Buňaty, z počátku dělnického pracovníka." Psáno pro F. Cajthamla. ÚD KSČ, fond 49, č. jeden. 138, s. 4-5.

_____. "Z nejrannějších dob českého socialismu v Americe." *Americké dělnické listy.* Cleveland, 1934, XXVI, no. 6.

ČSPS, "Jednací pořádek pro schůze a obřady k uvádění údů i úředníků řádů ČSPS ve Spojených Statech amerických." Cleveland, *Dennice novověku,* 1898.

_____, *Konstituce a mimozakony Čecho-slovanského podporujícího spolku.* St. Louis, 1861.

Čada, Joseph. *Czech American Catholics, 1850-1920.* Lisle, Ill.: Center for Slav Culture, 1964.

_____. *Czech Church Pioneers in America.* Chicago: Czech Benedictine Abbey Press, 1964.

Čapek, Tomáš. *American Czechs in Public Office.* Omaha: Czech Historical Society of Nebraska, 1940.

_____. *Moje Amerika: Vzpominky a Uvahy. (1861-1934).* Praha: Fr. Borový, 1935.

_____. *Naše Amerika.* Praha: Národní Rada Česksoslovenská, 1926.

_____. *Návštěvníci z Čech a Moravy v Americe y letech 1848-1939. Příspěvek k dějinám amerických Čechů.* Chicago, 1940.

_____. *Padesát let Českého Tisku v Americe.* New York: "Bank of Europe," 1911.

_____. *Památky českých emigrantů v Americe, Příspěvek k dějinam česko-amerického vystěhovalectví.* Omaha, 1907.

_____. *The Čechs (Bohemians) in America.* Boston and New York: Houghton Mifflin, 1920.

_____. "Český Den ve Waco, Texas." *Amerikán národní kalendář.* 1912.

_____. "Český učitel Josef Mašik v Texasu." *Amerikán národní kalendář.* 1887.

_____. *Památky českých emigrantů v Americe.* Omaha: Pokrok Západu, 1889. Omaha: Národní Tiskarna, 1907.

Carrington, Ulrich S. *The Making of an American.* Dallas: Southern Methodist University Press, 1974.

Cat Spring Agricultural Society. *The Cat Spring Story.* San Antonio: Lone Star Printing Company, 1956.

_____. *Century of Agricultural Progress.* San Antonio: Lone Star Printing Company, 1956.

"Čechoslováci a tělesná vychova. Stručný přehled sokolských a jiných tělovychovných organisací československých ve Spoj. Statech v letech 1865-1933." *Denní hlasatel* (Chicago). August 20, 1933.

Čermak, Josef. "Dějiny občanské valky, s připojením skušeností českých vojínů." *Amerikán národní kalendář.* 1889.

Cervenka, R. W. *History of the J. H. Kohut Land Company.* Unpublished manuscript.

_____. *John Kohut and His Son Josef.* Waco, Texas: Texian Press, 1966.

Chmelar, John. "The Austrian Emigration, 1900-1914." Translated by

Thomas C. Childers. In *Perspectives in American History*, Volume III: *Dislocation and Emigration: The Social Background of American Emigration.* Cambridge, Mass.: Charles Warren Center for Studies in American History, 1973, pp 342-43.

Chervenka, Calvin C. and James W. Mendl, *The Czechs of Texas.* Unpublished manuscript written for the Southwest Educational Development Laboratory, Austin, Texas, 1975.

Chervenka, Calvin C. *Reference Information Concerning the Czechs of Texas.* Privately printed, 1977.

Chlumský, Adolf. *Historie česko-moravských bratři v Americe.* 1907. Also in English: *History of the Evangelic Union of Bohemian-Moravian Brethren in Texas.* Translated by Annie J. Juren. La Grange, Texas: Fayette County Record, n.d.

Chotek, Hugo. "Dějiny česko-slovanské bratrské podporující jednoty ve Spojených Statech, v Severní Americe." Dle spolkových zápisků zprac. Hugo Chotek, b. m. v. 1895, s. 118. Rkp. Dar krajanů u příl. Národopisné výstavy v Praze.

_____. "Metla západu; původní povídka ze života Cechů texaských." *Amerikán národní kalendář.* 1886.

_____, ed. *Památník 50 ti letého Č. S. P. S. 1854-1904.* Cleveland, 1904.

_____. "Pasák texaský." *Amerikán národní kalendář.* 1904.

_____. "Před dvaceti léty; původní povídka ze života Čechů texaských." *Amerikán národní kalendář.* 1885.

_____. "Z dob utrpení." *Amerikán národní kalendář.* 1900.

_____. "Záhuba města Galvestonu." *Amerikán národní kalendář.* 1906.

Christian Sisters Union Study Committee. *Unity of the Brethren in Texas, 1855-1966.* Taylor, Texas: Unity of the Brethren, 1970.

Chupik, J. F. *History of the Chupik Family.* Unpublished manuscript.

_____. *History of the Sebesta Family.* Unpublished manuscript.

Chval, Charles August. "John Machovsky." n.d., n.p.

_____. *Lví stopou; kytice basní. Ku dni svobody a Texasského bazaru.* Rosenberg, Texas: Narodní podník, 1918.

Cocke, William A. *The Bailey Controversy in Texas. I and II.* San Antonio: The Cocke Company, 1908.

Coleman, James S. "Social Cleavage and Religious Conflict." *Journal of Social Issues,* XXII, 44-56.

Comenius, John A. *The Bequest of the Unity of Brethren.* Translated by Matthew Spinka. Chicago: The National Union of Czechoslovak Protestants, 1940.

Conzen, Kathleen Neils. "Historical Approaches to the Study of Rural Ethnic Communities." In *Ethnicity on the Great Plains,* ed. Fredrick C. Luebke. Lincoln: The University of Nebraska Press, 1980, pp. 1-18.

Čtvrtníková, Karla. *Pod texasským sluncem.* Privately printed, 1945.

_____. *Stanovy spolku.* Austin: Texan Printery, 1929.

Czechoslovak National Council of America. *Panorama.* Cicero, Ill., 1970.

244   KRÁSNÁ AMERIKA

Davis, Brion. "Ten Gallon Hero." *American Quarterly*, VI (Summer 1954), 123-25.

Degh, Linda. "Folk Religion as Ideology for Ethnic Survival: The Hungarians of Kipling, Saskatchewan." In *Ethnicity on the Great Plains*, ed. Fredrick C. Luebke. Lincoln: The University of Nebraska Press, 1980, pp. 129-46.

Dějiny česko-slovanské bratrské podporující jednoty ve Spojených Státech. Od 16 března 1884-až do dubna 1895. Chicago, 1895.

De Schweinitz, Edmund. *The Unitas Fratrum*. Bethlehem, Pa.: The Moravian Publication Concern, 1901.

Dignowity, Anthony Michael. *Memorial of Anthony M. Dignowitz* (sic), *San Antonio, Texas. Praying for the military occupation of Texas, with a view of protecting loyal citizens.* Washington: Government Printing Office, 1861. 37th. Congress, 2nd. session, Senate misc. document no. 9, serial no. 1124.

_____. *Bohemia Under Austrian Despotism, Being an Autobiography.* New York: Privately printed, 1859.

_____. *Reconstruction!* Washington, 1865.

Dixon, S. H. and L. N. Kemp. *The Heroes of San Jacinto.* Houston, 1932.

Dongres, L. W. "Paměti starých českých osadníků v Americe." *Amerikán národní kalendář.* 1924.

Doubrava, Ferdinand F. "Experiences of a Bohemian Emigrant Family." *The Wisconsin Magazine of History*, VIII, 1925, 393-406.

Dusek (family tree), 1550-1966. n.a., n.d.

Dvorník, František., *Czech Contributions to the Growth of the United States.* Chicago: Benedictine Abbey Press, 1961.

Elsik, William C. and Mary Lynn Elsik. *Slovak Cemetery: Burleson County, Texas.* Houston: Privately printed, 1979.

Ellis County History Workshop, *History of Ellis County.* Waco, Texas, 1972.

Farmers Mutual Protective Association of Texas (RVOS). *Eightieth Anniversary.* Privately printed, 1981.

Faust, Albert Bernhardt. *Charles Sealsfield.* Baltimore: Friedenwald Company, 1891.

Fousek, Marianka S. "Perfectionism of the Early Unitas Fratrum." *Church History*, XXX. (1961), 396-413.

"František Boleslav Zdrůbek." *Amerikán národní kalendář.* 1913.

Gallia, I. J. "Jaký podil brali czechoslované (sic) na vybudovaní lepších poměru v státu Texas." *Věstník.* July 22, 1936.

Garver, Bruce. "Czech-American Freethinkers on the Great Plains, 1871-1914." In *Ethnicity on the Great Plains*, ed. Fredrick C. Luebke. Lincoln: The University of Nebraska Press, 1980, pp. 147-69.

Geary, Marjorie Crane. *Folk Dances of Czechoslovakia.* New York: A. S. Barnes Company, 1927.

Goldmark, Josephine. *Pilgrims of 1848.* New Haven: Yale University Press, 1930.

Gordon, Milton M. *Assimilation in American Life.* New York: Oxford University Press, 1964.

Habenicht, Jan. *Dějiny čechů amerických.* St. Louis: Hlas, 1904-1910.

Hanak, Miroslav. "Reformist Traditionalism and Courage to Synthesis: The Czech Experiment in Democratic Justice." In *The Czechs in Texas: A Symposium,* ed. Clinton Machann. College Station, Texas: Texas A&M University College of Liberal Arts, 1979, pp. 173-84.

Hand, Leonie and Houston Wade. *An Early Histsory of Fayette County.* La Grange, Texas; 1936.

Hasalová, Věra. *Folk Art of Czechoslovakia.* Translated by Ivo Dvořák. New York: Arno Publishing Company, 1974.

Hassell, Robert L. and T'Odon C. Leshikar. *Silar or Siller or Shiller or Schiller Family.* (Genealogical description). Unpublished computer printout, 1970.

Hegar, Joseph. "The Evangelical Unity of the Czecho-Moravian Brethren in North America." *The Moravian.* April 18, 1934.

_____. *Památník podpurně jednoty česko-moravských bratří.* (Memoirs of the Benevolent Society of the Czech-Moravian Brethren Church in Texas), n.d., n.p.

Hejl, Edward H. *Czech Footprints Across Bluebonnet Fields.* Fort Worth: Privately printed, 1979.

Hermann, A. H. *A History of the Czechs.* London: Allen Lane, 1975.

Hewitt, William Philip. "Czech Immigration and Community, 1850-1900." In *The Czechs in Texas: A Symposium,* College Station, Texas: Texas A&M University College of Liberal Arts, 1979, pp. 44-52.

_____. "The Czechs in Texas: A Study of the Immigration and the Development of Czech Ethnicity, 1850-1920." PhD. dissertation, The University of Texas at Austin, 1978.

Historical Society of the Dallas Czech Club. *Generation to Generation: Czech Customs, Foods, and Traditions Texas Style.* Privately printed, 1980.

Hodges, LeRoy. "The Bohemian Farmers of Texas." *The Texas Magazine,* IV (June, 1912), 87-96.

_____. "Slavs on the Southern Farms." *Senate Documents,* XXIX, No. 595, 13-14.

Holeček, Josef V. "Vystěhovalec v Americe." *Amerikán národní kalendář.* 1883.

Holick, Robert J. "A Comparison of Reading Vocabulary and Reading Comprehension Skills Between Bilingual and Monolingual Czech-American Students." In *The Czechs in Texas: A Symposium,* ed. Clinton Machann. College Station, Texas: Texas A&M University College of Liberal Arts, 1979, pp. 148-58.

_____. "A Comparison of Reading Vocabulary and Reading Comprehension Skills Between Bilingual and Monolingual Czech-American Students." PhD. dissertation, Texas A&M University, 1975.

Horecky, Paul L. "The Slavic and East European Resoutces and Facilities of the

Library of Congress." *Slavic Review.* XXIII. (1964), 310-27.

Hošek, L. C. "Začátky Sokola v Texas." *Věstník.* July 22, 1936.

Houšt, Antonin. *Kratké dějiny a seznam česko-katolických osad ve Spoj. Statech amerických.* St. Louis: Hlas, 1890.

Hranicky, Roy. "The History of the Czech Element in Texas." M.A. thesis, Texas College of Arts and Industries, 1954.

Hruška, Tom. "Z Dějin Našich Pionyrů." *Věstník.* April 17, 1933.

Hudson, Estelle and Henry R. Maresh. *Czech Pioneers of the Southwest.* Dallas: South-West Press, 1934.

"Hugo Chotek." *Amerikán národní kalendář.* 1912.

Huňáček, Václav. *Czechoslovakia: Information Minimum.* Austin: Texas Education Agency, 1970.

"Ignac Křenek." *Amerikán národní kalendář.* 1897.

Institute of Texan Cultures (ITC). *The Czech Texans.* Part of ITC series, "The Texians and the Texans." San Antonio, 1972.

_____. *Texané Českého Původu.* (Texans of Czech Descent). An audio-visual presentation. San Antonio, 1971.

Jandáček, Antonin J. *U dobrých lidí v zemi bavlny.* Unpublished manuscript.

_____. *U našinců v Texasu.* Granger, Texas: Našinec Publishing Company, 1955.

_____. *V zemi bavlny: cestopisná črta z přednášek v Texasu.* Privately printed, 1948?

Janak, Robert. *Czech Immigration to Texas.* Beaumont, Texas: Privately printed, 1975.

_____. The Demise of Czech in Texas." *Texas Foreign Language Association Bulletin.* December, 1975, 6-7.

_____. *Dubina, Hostyn, and Ammannsville: The Geographic Origin of Three Czech Communities in Fayette County, Texas.* Beaumont, Texas: Privately Printed. 1978.

_____. "Tombstone Inscriptions as a Source of Geographic Origins." in *The Czechs in Texas: A Symposium,* ed. Clinton Machann. College Station, Texas: Texas A&M University College of Liberal Arts, 1979, pp. 70-74.

Jenkins, John H. *Cracker Barrel Chronicles: A Bibliography of Texas Town and County Histories.* Austin: Pemberton Press, 1965.

Jerabek, Esther. *Czechs and Slovaks in North America: A Bibliography.* New York and Chicago: Czechoslovak Society of Arts and Sciences in America and Czechoslovak National Council of America, 1976.

Jochec, Jesse. "The Life and Career of Augustin Haidušek." M.A. thesis, The University of Texas at Austin, 1940.

Jordan, Terry G. "A Religious Geography of the Hill Country Germans in Texas." In *Ethnicity on the Great Plains,* ed Fredrick C. Luebke. Lincoln: The University of Nebraska Press, 1980, pp. 109-28.

Juránek, Tomáš. "Ze života Čechů amerických." *Amerikán národní kalendář.* 1880.

Katolická Jednota Texaská. *Short History of KJT.* La Grange, Texas, 1973.

Kallus, Bohdan. *Dějiny katolicko-jednoty texaské.* Taylor, Texas: Našinec Publishing Company, 1927.

Karas, John J. *ČESAT: Informative Brochure/Informační Příručka.* Czech Ex-Students Association of Texas, 1981.

Kleitsch, R. G. "Social Change: Ethnicity and the Religious System in a Rural Community." *American Catholic Sociological Review,* XXIV, 222-30.

Klima, Stanislav. *Čechove a slovaci za hranicemi.* Praha, 1925.

Knapik, Jane. *Schulenberg: 100 Years on the Road. 1873-1973.* Dallas: Nortex Offset Publications, 1973.

Knapton, Ernest and Thomas Derry. *Europe 1815-1914.* New York: Charles Scribner's Sons, 1965.

Kochis, Bruce. "Semiotics and Roots." In *The Czechs in Texas: A Symposium,* ed. Clinton Machann. College Station, Texas: Texas A&M University College of Liberal Arts, 1979, pp. 159-64.

Kolar, Roger "Early Czech Dance Halls in Texas." *Perspective,* VII; no. 1. Reprinted in *The Czechs in Texas: A Symposium,* ed. Clinton Machann. College Station, Texas: Texas A&M University College of Liberal Arts, 1979, pp. 122-27.

Kos, Josef. Památník župy jižní A.S.O. ze sletu v Corpus Christi dne 5. září 1948. Corpus Christi, Texas: Sokol Educational and Physical Culture Association, 1948.

Kroupa, Jan. *Kůň a jeho nemoce.* La Grange, Texas: Slovan, 188?.

Krušina, Jaromír. "Metla zapadů." *Amerikán národní kalendář.* 1886.

Kunc, Msgr. Josef C. [Untitled short biography.] Privately printed, n.d.

Kutac, Margaret. "English Loan Words in the Czech Literary Language of Texas. M.A. thesis, The University of Texas at Austin, 1967.

Kyncl, Karel. *Zpráva čestného občana Texasu.* Praha, 1969.

Laska, Vera. *The Czechs in America, 1633-1977: A Chronology and Fact Book.* Dobbs Ferry, New York: Oceana Publications, 1977.

Lešikar, Vincenc. "Vincenc Lešikar." *Amerikán národní kalendář.* 1912.

Leškovy, Anton, "Anton Leškovy." *Amerikán národní kalendář.* 1890.

Leslie, T. H. "The History of Lavaca County Schools." M.A. thesis, The University of Texas at Austin, 1935.

Lich, Glenn. "The Raba Question." In *The Czechs in Texas: A Symposium,* ed. Clinton Machann. College Station, Texas: Texas A&M University College of Liberal Arts, 1979, pp. 165-72.

Lotto, F. *Fayette County, Her History and Her People.* Schulenburg, Texas: Sticker Steam Press, 1902.

Lowenbach, Jan. *Czechoslovak Music. The Voice of A People.* New York: Czechoslovak Information Service, 1943.

Lynch, Russell Wilford. "Czech Farmers in Oklahoma." Oklahoma Agricultural and Mechanical College Bulletin, 39. (June, 1942).

Macha, Helen. "The Czechs in Texas from 1849 to 1900." *Věstník.* January 6 and 13, 1965.

Machalek, Richard. "The Ambivalence of Ethnoreligion." In *The Czechs in*

Texas: A Symposium, ed. Clinton Machann, College Station, Texas: Texas A&M University College of Liberal Arts, 1979, pp. 95-114.

_____. "Intra-Organizational Conflict and Schism in an Ethnic Minority Church: The Case of the Unity of the Brethren in Texas." M.A. thesis, The University of Texas at Austin, 1972.

Machann, Clinton. "Current State of the Czech Language in Texas," In *PISE VII: Southwest Areal Linguistics Then and Now,* ed. Bates Hoffer and Betty Lou Dubois. Trinity University, 1977.

_____. "Hugo Chotek and Czech-American Fiction." *MELUS, VI.* (1979), 32-40.

_____. ed. *The Czechs in Texas: A Symposium.* College Station, Texas: Texas A&M University College of Liberal Arts, 1979.

Malik, Joe, Jr. "The Contributions and Life of the Czechs in Texas." In *The Czechs in Texas: A Symposium,* ed. Clinton Machann. College Station, Texas: Texas A&M University College of Liberal Arts, 1979, pp. 11-18.

_____. "Efforts to Promote the Study of the Czech Language and Culture in Texas." M.A. thesis, The University of Texas at Austin, 1947.

Marák, Jindřich. "Texas." *Amerikán národní kalendář.* 1952.

Maresh, Henry R. "The Czechs in Texas." *The Southwestern Historical Quarterly,* L. (October, 1946), 236-40.

"Martin Ermis." *Amerikán národní kalendář.* 1897.

Marty, Martin E. "Ethnicity: The Skeleton of Religion in America." *Church History,* XXXXI (1972), 354-68.

Mašek, Matěj. "Mexický padre." *Amerikán národní kalendář.* 1907.

_____. "Nalezl matku i nevěstu." *Amerikán národní kalendář.* 1912.

Mastný, Vojtěch. Statistika Vystěhovalectví, českého proletariátu do Spojených Státu." *Demografia.* IV (1962), 204-11.

Matcek, Gabriel C. and William C. Elsik. *On the Occasion of the Frances Sebesta Mikeska Hejl Sumsal Reunion.* Privately printed, 1980.

Meining, Donald W. *Imperial Texas.* Austin: University of Texas Press, 1969.

Mendl, James. "Historical Czech and Moravian Dialects in the New World." M.A. thesis, The University of Texas at Austin, 1976.

_____. "Moravian Dialects in Texas." In *The Czechs in Texas: A Symposium,* ed. Clinton Machann. College Station, Texas: Texas A&M University College of Liberal Arts, 1979, pp. 128-41.

Míček, Eduard. *Česká čítanka: léto.* Austin, Texas: České literární sdružení, 1959.

_____. *Česká čítanka: podzim.* Austin, Texas: České literární sdružení, 1959.

_____. *Duch americké výchovy.* Praha, 1929.

_____. "How Czech Pioneers Helped To Make Texas History." *Central European Observer,* XIII. (1935), 341-42.

_____. *"Nová obrazková česká čítanka: jaro."* Austin, Texas: České literární sdružení, 1959.

_____. *Obrazková česká čítanka: zima.* Austin, Texas: České literární sdružení. 1959.

_____. *Amerika se učí.* Praha: Knihtiskarna Impressa, 1932.

Mikeska, Mrs. Jerry. *The John Valis Family.* Unpublished manuscript.

Miller, Kenneth D. "Bohemians in Texas." *Bohemian Review.* IV. (May 1917), 4-5.

_____. "Czech Patriots Make Good Citizens." *Austin Statesman.* May 23, 1917.

Miller, Olga K. *Genealogical Research for Czech and Slovak Americans.* Detroit: Gale Research Co., 1978.

_____. "Ways to a Successful Genealogical Research in Czechoslovakia." *The Genealogical Helper.* March-April, 1977, 155-57.

Mořkovský, Alois J. "The Church and the Czechs in Texas." In *The Czechs in Texas: A Symposium,* ed Clinton Machann. College Station, Texas: Texas A&M University College of Liberal Arts, 1979, pp. 88-94.

Moucka, F. "Čtyři desitek let podpůrné a národní prace." *Věstník.* July 22, 1936.

Národní svaz českých katolíků v Texas. Naše dějiny. Granger, Texas, 1939.

Národní zpěvník česko-americký. Omaha: Národní tiskarna, 1909.

Niebuhr, H. Richard. *The Social Sources of Denominationalism.* New York: The World Publishing Company, 1968.

Novák, Arne. *Czech Literature.* Translated by Peter Kussi. Ann Arbor: Michigan Slavic Publications, 1976.

Novaková, Marie. *Pod Texaským nebem.* East Bernard, Texas, 1934.

Novotný, Stanislav. "Ze státu 'Osamělé hvězdy'." *Amerikán národní kalendář.* 1948.

Osvald, Josef. "Výprava českého sokolstva v Americe." Příbram, 1909.

Otter, Jiří. *The Witness of Czech Protestantism.* Praha: Kalich, 1970.

Památní list tělocvičné jednoty Sokol. Milwaukee, 1918.

Památník národní jednoty sokolské ve Spojených Státech. New York, 1904.

Pazdral, Olga. "Czech Folklore in Texas." M.A. thesis, The University of Texas at Austin, 1942.

Pech, Stanley Z. *The Czech Revolution of 1848.* Chapel Hill: University of North Carolina Press, 1969.

Pečírka, Josef. *Domácí lékař.* Chicago: A. Geringer, 1890.

Perkowski, Jan. "Linguistic Change in Texas Czech." *Czechoslovak History.* II: 148-163, 1976.

_____. "On Teaching the Texas Czechs and Germans Their Ancestral Languages," *CESAT Newsletter,* 2 (December, 1981), 4-13.

_____. "Some Notes on a Literary Text in Texas Czech." In *The Czechs in Texas: A Symposium,* ed. Clinton Machann. College Station, Texas: Texas A&M University College of Liberal Arts, 1979, pp. 142-47.

_____. "A Survey of the West Slavic Immigrant Languages in Texas." In *Texas Studies in Bilingualism,* ed. Glenn G. Gilbert. Berlin: Walter de Gruyter, 1970, 163-169.

Petrus, Jan. "Pioneři v Texas." Racine, Wisconsin: Salie, 1875. (First published serially in *Slavie,* 1874.)

Petrželka, Václav. "Pod Šumavou." *Amerikán národní kalendář.* 1922.

_____. "Strašné dobrodružství; povídka z dob texaských rangerů." *Amerikán národní kalendář.* 1914.

Pierce, Richard. "Maticka Praha." *Texas Highways.* December, 1974, 8-13.

Pokorný, O. B. "Alespoň do Galvestonu." *Amerikán národní kalendář.* 1933.

_____. "Ve Francii to začlo-v Texasu to skončilo." *Amerikán národní kalendář.* 1936.

Polášek, Thadious. "Early Life in Moravia, Texas." In *The Czechs in Texas: A Symposium,* ed. Clinton Machann. College Station, Texas: Texas A&M University College of Liberal Arts, 1979, pp. 63-69.

Polišenský, Josef, ed. *Začiatky českej a slovenskej emigracie do USA.* Bratislava, 1970.

Preece, Harold. "Peoples Who Have Made Texas." *Progressive Farmer.* March, 1938.

"První Tajemník." *Věstník.* June 20, 1956.

"The Publications of the SPJST." *Věstník.* June 20, 1956.

Rechcigl, Miloslav, Jr., ed. *The Czechoslovak Contribution to World Culture.* New York: Czechoslovak Society of Arts and Sciences in America, 1964.

Reynolds, Joseph Jones. "Reconstruction of Texas a Failure!" Washington, 1868.

Robek, Antonín. "Ethnographic Questions of Czech Emigration to America." In *The Czech, in Texas: A Symposium,* ed. Clinton Machann. College Station, Texas: Texas A&M University College of Liberal Arts, 1979, pp. 19-43.

Rodnick, David. *The Strangled Democracy: Czechoslovakia 1948-1969.* Lubbock, Texas: The Caprock Press, 1970.

Roštinský, Josef. "Two Functional Aspects of Czech Journalism in Texas." In *The Czechs in Texas: A Symposium,* ed. Clinton Machann. College Station, Texas: Texas A&M University College of Liberal Arts, 1979, pp. 75-82.

Roucek, Joseph Slabey. "The Moravian Brethren in America." *Social Studies,* XXXXIII. (February, 1952), 58-61.

_____. "Passing of American Czecho-Slovaks." *American Journal of Sociology,* XXXIX (March 1954), 611-25.

Salaba-Vojan, J. E. *Česko-Americké Epištoly.* Chicago, 1911.

Salzmann, Zdenek and Vladimir Scheuffler. *Komorov: A Czech Farming Village.* New York: Holt, Rinehart and Winston, 1974.

Schovajsa, H. J. "August Haidusek and His Influence on Czech Culture in Texas." In *The Czechs in Texas: A Symposium,* ed. Clinton Machann. College Station, Texas: Texas A&M University College of Liberal Arts, 1979, pp. 83-87.

Schattschneider, Allen W. *Through Five Hundred Years: A Popular History of the Moravian Church.* Winston-Salem, North Carolina: Comenius Press, 1956.

Schmidt, Curt E. *Opa and Oma*. New Braunfels, Texas: Folkways Publishing Co., 1975.

Schnabel, G. N. *Statistik der landwirtschaftlichen Industrie Böhmens*. Prague, 1846.

Schnepp, G. J. "Nationality and Leakage." *American Catholic Sociological Review*, III (1942), 154-63.

Schweiker, W. F. "Religion as a Superordinate Meaning System and Socio-psychological Integration." *Journal for the Scientific Study of Religion*, VIII (1969), 300-307.

Sealsfield, Charles (Karel Postl). *America: Glorious and Chaotic Land*. Englewood Cliffs, New Jersey: Prentice-Hall, Inc., 1969.

_____. *Bílá Růže. Tokeah*. Translated by J. K. Mazáč and F. Fišera. Milwaukee: A. Novák, 1902.

_____. *The Cabin Book. Sketches of Life in Texas*. Translated by C. F. Mersch. New York: J. Winchester, 1844.

_____. *Frontier Life*. New York: Auburn, Miller, Orton and Mulligan, 1856.

Šiller, Vilém, Václav Proucha and R. M. De Castello, eds. *Památník českých evangelických církvi ve Spojených Státech*. Chicago: Křesťanského posla, 1900.

Skrabanek, Robert L. "Demographic Changes in a Texas Czech-American Rural Community." In *The Czechs in Texas: A Symposium*, ed. Clinton Machann. College Station, Texas: Texas A&M University College of Liberal Arts, 1979, pp. 115-21.

_____. "Forms of Cooperation and Mutual aid in a Czech-American Rural Community." *Southwestern Social Science Quarterly*, XXX. (December, 1949), 183-87.

_____. "The Influence of Cultural Backgrounds on Farming Practices in a Czech-American Community." *Southwestern Social Science Quarterly*, XXXI (1961), 258-66.

_____, and Vernon J. Parenton. "Social Life in a Czech-American Rural Community." *Rural Sociology*, XV (1950), 221-31.

_____. "Social Organization and Change in a Czech-American Rural Community." PhD. dissertation, Louisiana State University, 1950.

Skřivánek, J. "Český učitel Josef Mašik v Texasu." *Amerikán národní kalendář*. 1887.

Skřivánek, John M. "The Education of Czechs in Texas." M.A. thesis, The University of Texas at Austin, 1946.

Skřivánek, Rosalie, "Český učitel Josef Mašík." *Amerikán národní kalendář*. 1887.

Sládek, Josef Václav. "Z cesty do Texas." *Slavie*, VIII (May 19, 1869).

Slavonic Benevolent Order of the State of Texas (SPJST). *Constitution and By-laws*. 1902, 1916, 1920, 1924, 1928, 1932, 1936, 1940.

_____. "Věstník XII, sjezdu SPJST v East Bernard, Texas. "*Věstník*, XXIV, no. 37.

Slovacek, Marvin. "A Sixty Year Insurance History of the Slavonic Benevolent

Order of the State of Texas." M.A. thesis, The University of Texas at Austin, 1956.

Slovak League of America. "Soubor vzpomíñek na slavnou minulost Unie a Státu Texas." *Svoboda*, 1917.

Smetanka, Jaroslav F. "Čeština na amerických středních školach. *Naše zahraničí*, VII (1926), 117-20.

Sommer, J. G. *Das Königreich Böhmen, statistisch-topographisch dargestellt, Prague, 1833-1848.*

Southwest Educational Development Laboratory, Austin, Texas. *Texas Heritage Unit (Czechs, Poles and Germans).* Part of Ethnic Heritage Studies Program developed by Southwest Educational Development Laboratory in 1975. Unpublished.

Splawn, Vlasta Margaret. "Sociological Study of a Czech Community in Ellis County, Texas." M.A. thesis, Texas Tech University, 1972.

Stalmach, Hilda Schiller. *History of the Ministers and Churches of the Southwest Czech Presbytery.* Smithville, Texas: Synod of Texas, United Presbyterian Church, USA, 1962.

Stalmach, J. J. "Brief History of Josef Lidumil Lešikar." Minnesota Historical Society, 1965.

Stasney, Mollie Emma. "The Czechs in Texas." M.A. thesis, The University of Texas at Austin, 1938.

Statistical Report. Katolík Česko-Americký. Czech Benedictine Printing Office, n.d.

Stout, Harry S. "Ethnicity: The Vital Center of Religion in America." *Ethnicity*, II. 202-204.

"Strucná statistika osad, míst, měst a okresu ve Spojených Státech, Čechy obydlených." *Amerikán národní kalendář.* 1878. Updated in 1884.

Studičný, S. P. "Ze života krajanů Pavly a S. P. Studičný v Houston, Texas." *Amerikán národní kalendář.* 1952.

Štupl, Anton. "Anton Štupl." *Amerikán národní kalendář.* 1892.

Sturm, Rudolf. "America in the Life and Work of the Czech Poet Josef Sládek." *Harvard Slavic Studies*, II (1954), 287-96.

_____. "Czech Literature in America." In *Ethnic Literatures Since 1776: The Many Voices of America, Part I.* Proceedings of the Comparative Literature Symposium, Texas Tech University. Lubbock, Texas: Texas Tech University Press, 1978, pp. 161-72.

_____. "Sojourn of the Czech Poet Josef Sládek in the United States and the American Influences in His Writings." Ph.D. dissertation, Harvard University, 1956.

Styblo, Karel. V. "Václav F. Herold." *Amerikán národní kalendář.* 1921.

Svoboda, Joseph G. "Documentation of the Czech Ethnic Group in America: Problems of Identification and Location of Source Materials." Delivered at the 9th. World Congress of the Czechoslovak Society of Arts and Sciences in America. Cleveland, 1978. Unpublished manuscript.

Svrček, Rev. V. A., ed. *A History of the Czech-Moravian Catholic Communities of Texas.* Waco, Texas: Texian Press, 1974.

"Catechism of the Unity of the Brethren." Taylor, Texas: Synodical Committee, 1966.

Texas Department of Agriculture, *Texas in the Field of Agriculture.* Austin, 1939.

Texas Department of Education. Tentative Course of Study in Czech. Austin, Texas: State Curriculum Executive Committee, 1938.

Thurlings, J. M. G. "Functionalism, Social Change, and the Sociology of Religion." *Social Compass,* VIII (1961), 407-23.

Turner, Kay F. Program Notes for "Czech Music: Phyl and the Merry Musicians." Amon Carter Museum Theater, Fort Worth, Texas. November 12, 1978.

Uhlendorf, Bernhard Alexander. "Charles Sealsfield: Ethnic Elements and National Problems in his Works." Ph.D. dissertation, the University of Illinois, 1920.

United States Department of Commerce, Bureau of the Census, *Eighth Census of the United States: 1860.*

———. *Ninth Census of the United States: 1870.* Volume I, Statistics of the Population of the United States.

———. *Tenth Census of the United States: 1880.* Volume I, Population of the United States.

———. *Eleventh Census of the United States: 1890.* Population of the United States.

———. *Twelfth Census of the United States: 1900.* Population.

———. *Thirteenth Census of the United States: 1910.* Volume I, General Report and Analytical Tables.

———. *Fourteenth Census of the United States: 1920.* Volume II, General Report and Analytical Tables.

———. *Sixteenth Census of the United States: 1940.* Nativity and Parentage of the White Population.

Vivial, M. R. "Moravia—When Texas Was Young." *The Lavaca County Tribune-New Era Herald,* Hallettsville, Texas. April 16, 1946.

Wagner, Jan. "Čeští osadníci v severní Americe. Praha: Nakladatel Alois Hynek knihkupec, 1887.

Wallace, William V. *Czechoslovakia.* London: Ernest Benn, 1976.

Webb, Walter Prescott. *The Handbook of Texas.* Volume I. Chicago: Lakeside Press, 1952.

Weinlick, John Rudolf. "The Moravian Diaspora." *Moravian Historical Society,* XVII (1959), 1-217.

Western Bohemian Fraternal Association. "Zápisky třináctého sjezdu západní česko-bratrské jednoty." Dallas, 1955.

Weyand, Leonie. "History of Fayette County, 1822-1865." M.A. thesis, The University of Texas at Austin, 1932.

———, and Houston Wade. *An Early History of Fayette County.* La Grange, Texas: La Grange Journal Plant, 1936.

Wilcox, Walter F. and Imre Ferenczi. *International Migrations*. 2 volumes. New York, 1929-1931.

Williams, Robin. "Religion, Value-Orientations, and Inter-Group Conflict." *Journal of Social Issues*. XII (1956), 12-20.

Wolny, G. *Die Markgrafschaft Mähren*, 6 volumes. Brünn, 1835-1842.

Wurstialová-Janečková, Julie. *Za neodvislost Texasu*. Translated by T. Vonášek. Chicago: A. Geringer, 1902.

Wychopeň, L. C. "Vzpominky ze starych casu v Texasu." *Věstník*. January 20, 1937.

Young, Edgar E. *Czechoslovakia: Keystone of Peace and Democracy*. London: Victor Gollanez, 1938.

Zahradecký, J. B. "Ovoce poznání." *Amerikán národní kalendář*. 1911.

"Životopisy českých zákonodárců v Americe za rok 1879." *Amerikán národní kalendář*. 1880.

Zdrůbek. F. B. *Dějiny americké*. Omaha: Pokrok západu, n.d.

_____. *Disputace*. Chicago: Chicagský věstník, 1877.

_____. *Dvě veřejná náboženské hádání mezi F. B. Zdrůbkem, redaktorem "Svornosti" a p. V. Cokou, farářem u sv. Prokopa, odbývaná dne 17. a 19. dubna 1877*. Chicago: A. Geringer, 1877.

_____. *Jak povstal svět*. Omaha: Privately printed, 1874.

_____. *Ježíšovo mládí*. Omaha: Privately printed, 1874.

_____. *Kázání o svaté víře*. Chicago: A Geringer, 1879.

_____. *Křesťanství a vzdělanost*. Chicago: A. Geringer, n.d.

_____. *Náboženské lže*. Omaha?, 187?.

_____. *Rodopis Boha*. Omaha: Privately printed, 1873.

_____. Sobotní a nedělní školy české v Americe." *Amerikán národní kalendář*. 1888.

_____. *Svět a jeho povstaní*. Omaha: Privately printed, 1874.

_____. *Vyvoj práva*. Omaha: Privately printed, 1874.

_____. *Postavení žen v cirkvi*. Chicago: A. Geringer, 1885.

_____. "První český časopis v Americe 'Národní noviny'." *Amerikán národní kalendář*. 1878.

_____. *Ústava státu Texas*. Translation of Texas Constitution. Chicago: A. Geringer, 1875.

Zeman, Jarold Knox. "*Kolébka náboženské svobody na Moravě*. Chicago: Baptist Convention of North America, 1962.

"*Zpěvníček českoamerický*." Omaha: Národní tiskarna, 1903.

Correspondence and Personal Interviews

Correspondence with Gil Baca, August, 1978.

Correspondence with Vladimir G. Bílý, April 1, 1981.

Interview with Henry Haisler, March 9, 1975.

Interview with Mary Haisler, March 9, 1975.

Interview with Marvin Hegar, November 14, 1975.

Interview with Betty Beran Marek, March 21, 1975.

Interview with Frances Mendl, August 20, 1971.

Interview with Lee Pavlas, Sr., May 22, 1975.

Interview with Andrew Prikryl, September 15, 1975.

Interview with Al Vrana, March 20, 1980.

APPENDIX A

GUIDE TO CZECH PRONUNCIATION

A	a	as in father but shorter *
Á	á	same as a but longer *
B	b	as in bank
C	c	as ts in hats
Č	č	as ch in church
D	d	as in dime
Ď	ď	as in duel (British pronunciation: "dyuel")
E	e	as in net
É	é	same as e but longer
F	f	as in fame
G	g	as in glory
H	h	as in hand; unlike English h — the vocal cords vibrate as it is pronounced.
Ch	ch	as in Bach
I	i	as in it
Í	í	as in it but longer
J	j	as in yes
K	k	as in Karla
L	l	as in let
M	m	as in man
N	n	as in no
Ň	ň	as in onion
O	o	as in yodel
Ó	ó	same as o but longer
P	p	as in pear
R	r	rolled r
Ř	ř	no English equivalent; say ž and at the same time pronounce a rolled r; a rare and difficult sound.
S	s	as in sang
Š	š	as in shoot
T	t	as in tame
Ť	ť	as in tune (British pronunciation: "tyune")
U	u	as in do
Ů ú	ů	as in room
V	v	as in vain

Y	y	same as i
Ý	ý	same as í
Z	z	as in zenith
Ž	ž	as s in measure

* ´ in Czech (čárka) is an indication of length, not accent.

The diphthong "ou" is found in Bohemian dialects but not in Moravian. it is a combination of the sounds "o" and "u."

APPENDIX B

A CHRONOLOGY OF CZECH SETTLEMENTS IN TEXAS, BY REGION AND COUNTY

Information about villages and towns settled, dates of settlement, names of early settlers, and establishment of selected churches and ethnically-related organizations is given in order to suggest the relative strength of the Texas Czech community at a particular time. No claim is made for completeness. Some Czech communities have been much better documented than others, and much work remains to be done in this area. The following principal sources have been used: *The Czechs in Texas: A Study of the Immigration and the Development of Czech Ethnicity, 1850-1920; Czech Pioneers of the Southwest; Dějiny čechů amerických; Naše dějiny; Památník českých evangelických církví;* and *Unity of the Brethren in Texas, 1855-1966.*

CENTRAL TEXAS

AUSTIN COUNTY — Rev. Josef Bergman arrives in Cat Spring, March, 1850. Josef Šilar group arrives in late 1851, followed by Josef Lešikar and other groups of families. Industry settled in 1856; early family names: Macháček, Polčak, Fiala, Pšenčík, Wurtz, Zimmerhanzel, Hajek. Rev. Josef Chromčík begins to visit Industry Catholics in 1872; Rev. Martin Krč begins to serve in 1876. Brethren minister Josef Opočenský comes to Industry in 1860. Sealy settled in 1883; Brethren begin meeting in 1890; Rev. Jan Šiller serves as pastor in 1897. In 1890, Catholics build a church, served by Rev. Vilém Skoček. Wallis settled in in 1890; school established in 1892, year of first recorded deaths: Marie Litvík, Václav Černý, Anna Boháčík. KJT lodge established 1892. By 1899, 25-30 Czech families in the area. By 1938, nearly 300 Czech families belong to Catholic church. Brethren first organized in 1906 by Rev. Jindřich Juren. First known settler at Frýdek is Josef Železník from Jankovice, Moravia. August Mlčák and family come in 1871; by 1883, settlers include Peter Ležák and Jan Bardoděj from Fayetteville, Matěj and Frank Kutra (with Frank's family and a grandmother), Vincenc Vašina and family. By 1896, there are about 60 Czech families living near Frýdek.

FAYETTE COUNTY — Tomáš Hruška arrives in 1855 with parents; already present: Wychopeň, Laštovica, Kozel, Dančák, Kotrla families near Fayetteville; Hřibek, Matus, Rubač families at Biegel; Bubela, Kocurek, Stasny, Martinek families at Rabbs Creek; Joe Rypl at Ellinger; Terezie Elšík at Cistern. Valentin Haidušek and Josef Petr, Sr. first Czechs to settle west of Colorado River. Other early county settlers (all from Moravia): Konstantin Chovanec (Trojanovice u Frenštatu), Josef Mikula and Jan Kocurek (Darební u Hovězího), Jan Bečka (Vsetín), Jan Hruška (Jablunky), Jan Odloželík (Pacetluk u Holešova), Josef Laštovica (Hovězí), Josef Ječmenek (Johanova), Pavel Ječmenek (Vsetín), Ignác Křenek (Bordovice), František Zapalač (Vsetín), František Piskaček (Holešova), František Destěnský (Vyzovice), Vilém Wiesner (Frenštat). Many of these come as early as 1856; most settle around Ross Prairie ("Rossprerie"). Rev. Josef Chromčík, first important Czech Catholic priest in Texas, arrives in Fayetteville in 1872. By 1900, there are 220 Moravians in Catholic church and church school enrolls 150 children. Brethren church erected in 1874; by 1900, about 60 families in church. Czech-dominated Presbyterian church erected in 1894; Rev. Václav Pazdral pastor. By 1900, Czechs outnumber Germans in Ellinger. In 1856, Matěj Novák arrives in Mulberry; followed by Ondřej Gallia, František and Václav Matula, Josef Vyvala, František Branecký, Josef Horák in 1860s. 20 Brethren families live near Mulberry by 1864; town's name changed to Praha. First Czechs to arrive in Bluff (1856): Josef Janda, Alois Klimiček, Benjamin Klimiček, Valentin Kolibal, František Koza, František Marak, all from Trojanovice, Moravia; in same year, Catholic church made of logs; name of town officially changed to Hostýn, after the Moravian village, in 1925. In 1856 Czechs begin to move to Navidad. Valentin Haidušek changes name of town to Dubina. Log house of Josef Petr serves as church. Czechs move to Cistern in late 1870s. Among first families: Antonin Ferdinand, František and Jan Pšenčík, Matěj and Josef Ziegelbauer, František Holub, Jan Macháček, Sr., Jan Macháček, Jr., František Hanzelka, Adolf Kreml, Vincent and Josef Mareš, Antonin Hybner, Jan Valek. Pšenčík School built in 1888, a Catholic church in 1890. Czechs settle in Ammansville in about 1870; early settlers' family names: Smajstrla, Kosa, Sobotík, Barta, Horák, Filip, Bartoš. Plum established in 1890 by Pavel Kořenek, Jan Matocha, Josef Vacula; by 1896 there are 24 Czech families, mostly from Hovězí. Flatonia, Schulenburg, Warrenton, High Hill, West Point, Cedar, Warda, Ruthersville, Engle, Rožnov, St. John, Oldenburg, Nechanice all founded or settled by Czechs in 1870s or 1880s. By 1900 about 12 Czech families live in La Grange. About 1,000 Czech families live in the county in 1900.

LAVACA COUNTY — First Moravian Alois Klimiček from Frenštat. Arrives in county 1858, followed by Josef Kutač, Jan Satský, Josef Kahánek, Jan Morris, Václav Michan, Václav Kuboš, Martin Chaloupka, Ondřej Matula, Jan Matušek, František Bosak, and František Bjalek, all in 1860. First Czechs in Shiner are Josef A. Kopecký and Jan and Josef Hybneř, 1888. Soon followed by Jan Wagner, Jan Vališ, Jakub Straus, František Simper, Joseph Pecháček, Jan Dušek, Antonin Jakš, Antonín Horký, George Koliba, František Kašpárek, August Hošek, Josef and František Ermis, Hynek Sisa, Hynek Šulak, František Janda, Jan Havel, Jakub Pátek, Martin Vackář, František Krejčí, Jakub Řebeček, Vojtěch Pelech, František Jílek, Alfons Grill and Alfons Janota. In 1891 Cyril and Methodius Church built and in 1892 Rev. K. J. Beneš sent to serve Shiner and Moulton. First Brethren service in Shiner 1888; congregation organized by Rev. Jindřich Juren in 1891. Moulton founded by first Czech settler Edward Boehm. Czechs, including Jan Mastuštík, also settle around Sweet Home. By 1900 CSPS and SPJST lodges established in Hackberry. About 1880 Alois Rohan, Jan Raška, Leopold Valenta, Jan Možišek and Václav Juren arrive in Koerth. Wied is originally a German community, but after Josef Liverda comes in 1873 followed by Jan and František Janak, Matouš Pustka, František Opela and the Kikulas family, among others, the Germans gradually move away, selling their farms to Czechs. Even local German shooting hall is sold to Czechs, who turn it into a church. Breslau, also originally German, becomes Czech after the Najvar, Světlík, Hanzlík, Janáček, Konečný, Klekar, Olšovský, Restler, Horký and Greš families arrive about 1900. First Czech, Jan Svoboda, in Yoakum arrives in 1883, followed by František Jakubik, who establishes newspaper *Nový domov*. Other early Yoakum families are Skřehot, Šindler, Orsák, Peter, Muška, Eicher, Nietschman, Brosman. Williamsburg has 30 Czech families by 1900 and Hope 25. First Czech to settle in Moravia is Václav Matula in 1870 followed by brother František in 1872; then Martin Kažmiř and Martin Kopecký, both from Hrozenkov, Moravia. Jan Hrnčíř, son of Josef from Europe, becomes translator for whole community in court cases involving Czechs. By 1900 four Czech lodges: two CSPS and two SPJST. Novohrad is established in 1876 by Czechs. Bílá Hora and Vsetín established by Brethren, served by Rev. Jindřich Juren and Adolf Chlumský. In 1895, Jan Trlica donates land and church is erected.

WASHINGTON COUNTY — In 1864 Rev. Josef Opočenský moves to Wesley (Veselý) and organizes a Brethren church with these families: Pavel Šebesta, Petr Mikeska, Josef Skřivánek, Karel Josef Rypl, Jan Zabčík, Jan Baletka, Jiří Chupík, Arnošt Schuerer, Josef Ježek, František Šebesta and Jiří Pšenčík. Latium and Greenvine receive Czechs about 1860. By 1900 about 100 Czech families in vicinity. In 1868, Brenham receives Czechs.

OTHER IMPORTANT CENTRAL TEXAS COUNTIES

COLORADO COUNTY — By 1883, Josef Trojan owns a restaurant and later Václav Stančík owns a blacksmith shop. Frelsburg receives first Czech in 1848: Jan Walla, from Moravia. In 1850 Jakub Břenek and J. Košárek arrive, followed by Jan Martinák and the Vavra, Pecháček and Miňák families. Nada established in 1882 by Josef Labaj and family. With them come Florian Frnka, Josef Blinka, Martin Heja and Martin Holčák. Weimar, Oakland, Voxpopuli and Garwood also attract Czechs.

BURLESON COUNTY — Alois, Martin, and František Knězek first to settle in Frenštat, 1884. About one year later Jan, Adolf and Robert Polanský and Antonín Bordovský arrive from Fayetteville. These four originally from Frenštat pod Radhoštěm, Moravia. 1886 Adolf Polanský donates 20 acres for school to be named Frenštat. In 1886, the Švejda, Hlavatý, Beran, Pavlas, and Nosek families arrive. In 1895, Czech Catholic church erected. Brethren organize congregation with Rev. Frank Horák in 1924. Other communities to receive Czechs: Caldwell, Deanville, Somerville, Lyons, New Tabor, Snook (Šebesta), and Cooks Point, which organizes Brethren church in 1915. Rev. Joseph Hegar serves as pastor. Snook Brethren have first service in 1886 and Rev. Adolf Chlumský organizes congregation in 1891.

BASTROP COUNTY — Czechs settle around Smithville, Rosanky, Elgin and Kovář, named for early settler who arrives in 1870. 1894 Rev. Juren and about 30 Brethren organize church in Kovář. Includes both Czech Presbyterians and Brethren. 1895 Josef Pšenčík moves to Smithville and in 1912 helps build Catholic church. About 200 Czech families are in county by 1900.

LEE COUNTY — By 1900 over 50 Czech families are in county, including Jan and Tomáš Kocurek, Jan and Josef Hejtmančík, Václav Baklin, Matouš Kral, two families of Kostelíks and the Kuběna, Kučera, Valigura, Šupak, Kroupa, Pinter and Šrubář families. In 1904 first Czech Catholic church erected. Brethren hold first service in 1893 and organize congregation in 1904 with Rev. Chlumský.

BRAZOS COUNTY — First Czechs arrive in Millican in 1871, directly from Europe. In 1879 several Moravian families move to area around Kurten and establish Tabor. Around 1900 some, including the Wathuber, Luža, Babek, Výmola, Brandejský, Horák, Košárek families, move to Bryan. By 1904 about 200 Czech families in county.

MILAM COUNTY — Marák established by Jiří, Štěpan and Tomáš Marák from Dubina in about 1881. Cyril and Methodius church erected 1903. Czechs come to Cameron in 1887; families were: Parma, Rusek, Matula, Kašpar, Kubečka, Matocha, Stoklas, Valek, Mondřík. Brethren congregations established in Buckholts (1907), Cameron (1910). By 1904 about 300 Czech families in county.

WILLIAMSON COUNTY — First Czech is in Taylor, 1870. By 1905 German priest sent to serve Germans decides he must learn Czech, also recommends a Czech priest be sent. Josef Šťastný and Frank Holub first Czechs; soon others are Šafařík, Kašpar, Urbanek, Zycha, Čuba, Zelinka. Taylor Brethren organized by Rev. Motyčka in 1895. First Czechs to move to Granger in 1881 are Jan Najzr, O. R. Bartoš, Valentin Bartoš, Ludvík Červenka, Josef Pecka, Ondřej Přikryl, Jan Tobolka, Valentín Krkoška, Pavel Kopecký, Ferdinand Kaděrka, Jan Martinka, Jiří Jurečka, Jan David, Jan Janak, Josef Kaděrka, Jan Kalinec, Antonín Zrůbek, Martin Kopecký, Vincent Struhal, Josef Červenka, Jan Mazáč, František Červenka, Václav Němec, J. Rychlík and Ondřej Janak. Rev. Chlumský organizes a Brethren congregation there in 1895 and a Catholic church is erected in the same year. Corn Hill established about 1880 by immigrants from Moravská Ostrava.

BELL COUNTY — Czechs arrive in 1876, mostly Brethren. By 1893, Ocker has about 78 Czech families; 30 belong to Brethren congregation built in 1892. In 1906 Seaton organizes Brethren church; Cyclone erects Czech-German Catholic church in 1901, with about 36 Czech families in parish. Czechs in Holland organize Brethren church in 1910.

FALLS COUNTY — Lott and Rosebud attract a few Czech families around 1900. About 10 Czech families are in Rosebud by 1938.

McLENNAN COUNTY — First Czechs arrive in West, 1874, including Václav Mašek. Soon come František Soukup, František Urbanovský, and the Bezděk, Pustějovský, Hromadka, Grossman, Marák, Čoček, Kramoliš, Karlík and Stanislav families. The Brethren hold their first service in 1888 and organize a congregation in 1892. The Mašek, Urbanovský, Mynář, Kramoliš, Stanislav, Pustějovsky, Smajstrla, Dulak, Vrba, Hanzelík, Macik and Marák families settle around Tours. The Kuvica, Pecháček, Beralek, Farek, Polk families come to Elk in the late 1880s.

HILL COUNTY — First Czechs are Jan Urbiš, Jan Čoček, Karel Šňapek, František Koláček, Edward Šňapek, František Čoček, František Černošek, Antonín Černošek, František Macháč, František Novák, Jan Mikulik, Karel Horák, Vincenc Marák and Jan Šrubář, settling in Penelope in 1890s. In 1908 Catholic church erected there. In 1912 Mt. Calm Brethren organize church. Later, Czechs move to Hillsboro, Abbot.

ELLIS COUNTY — First to arrive is Jan Jakub Šebesta in 1873 from Netolice, Bohemia. In 1875 from Ždanice, Moravia, comes Bartoloměj Laniček. By 1887 about 40 Czech families live around Ennis. Later, many more arrive, especially from Provdova, Moravia. In 1901 Catholics build own Czech parish, Rev. Bohumil Kramoliš serves as priest. Brethren congregation organized by Rev. Chlumský in 1905.

DALLAS COUNTY — Czechs start arriving in city of Dallas about 1910. By 1915 about 15 families live there. Brethren organize church in 1929; Rev. Frank Kostohryz is minister.

KAUFMAN COUNTY — First Czechs: František Pechal, František Bedřich, Emil Drožd, Louise and František Barta, and the Šimiček family. They arrive in 1910 and soon after.

TARRANT COUNTY — First Czech, Pavel Valigura, later moves to Voxpopuli to farm. Later come August Lebeda, Anton Koldin (1902). Some attracted to high paying jobs in Fort Worth factories, especially Armour and Swift slaughter houses built in 1902. Koldin is sent from St. Louis as foreman of one.

ERATH and PALO PINTO COUNTIES — Thurber and Lyra draw Czech miners to coal mines around 1900. They soon establish SPJST lodge and church.

IMPORTANT NORTH TEXAS COUNTIES

WICHITA COUNTY — First Czechs arrive in 1880: Krajča, Kovařík, Plašek, Matouška, Žaludek, Nekuža families. By 1938, 35 Czech, mostly Catholic, families are there. In addition, several families from Burkburnett.

WILBARGER COUNTY — In 1890 František Minařík settles in Vernon, followed by brother Josef and sister Marie. In 1905 František Mičola and Josef Kalinec arrive, followed by František Vaňek and František Tomšů the next year. By 1938 about 19 Czech families live in the area.

BAYLOR COUNTY — First Czech, Antonín Mocek, arrives in Seymour in 1907. Others follow and by 1910 about 30 families are there. In 1906 Jan Horký, Sr., Jan Horký, Jr., and Josef Kulhanek, Jan Hanzelka, Rudolf Horký, and František Trojčák arrive, followed by Jan Sykora and Josef Kulhanek in Seaborn. By 1900 about 500 Czech families live in the county.

ARCHER COUNTY — Matěj Brom, Vincent Dařilek, Antonín Březina and Kristian Šembera from Praha, Texas arrive in Megargel in 1907.

OTHER COUNTIES IN NORTH AND NORTHWEST TEXAS

RUNNELS COUNTY — In early 1890s Czechs and Germans arrive and buy land from land companies after cattlemen go broke. Many Czechs settle around Rowena and Ballinger. Among the first are Jan Žák, Josef Kabela, P. J. Baron, Pavel Kořenek, Josef Kohutek, P. Hořelica, Vincenc Hořelica, Josef Tomášek, Jan Svrček, Ludvík Teplíček and Eman. Chýlek.

SCURRY COUNTY — Hermleigh established by 5 Czech and 5 German families mainly from Fayette and Lavaca counties in 1907. By 1938 there are about 40 Czech and German families.

HOCKLEY & LAMB COUNTIES — Czechs arrive in Anton (Littlefield) and Pep in 1920s. Czech priest, Karel J. Dvořák, serves Catholics from Littlefield. Rev. Joseph Hegar organizes Brethren congregation in Anton in 1929.

COUNTIES IN SOUTH AND EAST TEXAS

FORT BEND COUNTY — In 1901 the Horák, Bartoš, Barta, Hubeňák, Štefek, and Menšík families move from Ammansville, Hostýn, Ellinger and Weimar to Needville. In 1911 they build Catholic church. In 1926 Rev. Innocence Raška becomes permanent priest. By 1938, 150 Czech families are in parish. In 1910 Czech farmers begin to buy unbroken prairie around Rosenberg. By 1915 the Catholic community gets Czech priest, Rev. Eduard Hajek. By 1938 most of 100 families in parish are Czech.

WHARTON COUNTY — In 1896 František and Jan Buček from Fayette County and Alois Matušek, Filip Chumchal, Jan Dušek and a Mr. Chaloupka from Lavaca Co. establish a Czech settlement around Hungerford. In 1916 they build a Catholic church; by 1938 Czech parish has 80 members. East Bernard is settled by Czechs from Fayette and Lavaca counties in late 1890s. In 1901 Rev. Vilém Skoček visits parish irregularly. Later, church named *Povýšení Sv. Kříže* built after Josef Pražák requests contributions in pages of Czech newspapers *Hlas* (St. Louis), *Katolík* (Chicago) and *Nový domov* (Hallettsville, Tex.). By 1898 Pavel Dorňák, Martin Heja, Josef Vašiček, Ignác Kocurek, Jan Holčák and Ludvík Wychopen are members of growing Czech community in El Campo. In 1930s State Senator L. J. Sulak buys famous Czech newspaper *Svoboda* and moves it to El Campo. From 1894 to 1899 the Dorotik, Bačák, Pratka, Slíva, Holub, Mazoch, Šumbera, Valigura, Kruppa, Dluhoš, Naizer, Merta, Burecký, Draštáta, Kahánek, Macek, Stavinoha, Jurašek and Lichnovský families follow František Buzek and Antonín Hajovský to Taiton. A school is built in 1897. Czechs also settle around Hillje and Wharton. By 1938, 59 Czech Catholic families live in Wharton.

WALLER COUNTY — First Czech is František Divin in 1902, followed by Ludvík Mikulenka. Either break prairie land or work in salt bed operations in Waller. By 1938, 30 Czech Catholic families served by mission station Virgin Mary built by Czech pioneers.

MATAGORDA COUNTY — Blessing and Bay City attract Czechs beginning in 1920s. By 1938 over 150 Czech families in county. Both Catholic and Brethren congregations present.

BRAZORIA COUNTY — First Czechs to arrive in Damon are Michail Volek, Pavel Orsak, Vincenc Pekář, Václav Plachý, Ludvík Jakubec, Fred Koenig, Karel Kofron, Al Kocurek, and Josef Matula. A Catholic church is erected in 1925, dedicated to Sts. Cyril and Methodius. Danbury attracts both Catholics and Brethren by 1920. In 1927 Jan and Josef Chupik take possession of several thousand acres of abandoned land and offer to sell it to Czech farmers. Some of the earliest buyers are Jan Valušek and Emil and Louis Macik. By 1938, 20 Czech families are there.

GALVESTON COUNTY — City of Galveston used as port of entry by most Czech immigrants to Texas. Some Czechs worked on docks as early as 1900. Earliest Czech organization a KJZT lodge begun in 1936.

HARRIS COUNTY — In 1912, I. P. Křenek moves to Crosby and finds Josef Volčík, F. J. Morávek, Josef Širočka, Karel Machala, Josef Franta, Jan Kristiník, and a certain Šťastný. In 1914, Czechs in Catholic parish number 15 or 16. Rev. Barton organizes Brethren church in 1914. By 1938 about 350 Czechs live in Houston. Jakub Bujnoch is one of first.

LIBERTY COUNTY — In 1911 the Janáček family arrives, followed by the Hajovský, Buchta, and Jarma families to East Gate. In 1918 a Catholic church built. By 1938, 40 Czech families are in parish.

HOUSTON COUNTY — In 1907 a group of Czechs from Petrovice u Čermna, Bohemia arrive in Lovelady and Crockett. Work in mines and farm.

SOUTH TEXAS COUNTIES

CALHOUN COUNTY — By 1938 only about 10 Czech families live in Port Lavaca and all of the county.

JACKSON COUNTY — In 1912 Ben Fridřich; Jan Matocha; Jan Kašpar; Petr, Jan and Václav Šulak; and August Špalek arrive in county and buy land around Ganado. Later, more arrive and create a mostly Czech Catholic parish there.

VICTORIA COUNTY — In 1890 Pavel Merečka, Jan Polášek, Jan Frydrich, Valentín and Alois Štubář and Tom Charbula establish Inez. Later, 30 Czech families settle in Benview (today La Salle). Czechs also establish Holub.

DeWITT COUNTY — 6 Czechs establish community of Svatá anna při Yoakum in 1886. In 1906, 16 Czech Catholic families build church. By 1938 Cuero has about 85 Czech families and Yorktown has the Boháč, Wagner, Konecký, Strakoš, Volný, Kubala, Krč, Lobojacký, Pustka, Matějek and Rohan families, some as early as 1889.

GOLIAD COUNTY — Attracts only a few Czechs. One, Matěj Novák, settles in Goliad and a few settle in Charco.

BEE COUNTY — First come Štěpan and Valentin Kubala in 1889, followed by Jan Barton, August Gallia, František Hrček, Petr Blaží and others. Soon about 30 Czech families live around Beeville. In 1889 Josef Barton moves to Olmus Ranch; he is followed by František Šugarek and four other families. Some move to Oklahoma and other Czechs arrive: among them Josef Boháč, Petr Nedbálek, František Vavruša, Karel Šugarek and Karel Dudek. By 1935 30 Czech families live near Olmus. Some also settle around Skidmore, including Jan Mičulka and Vincent Doubrava. Brethren church organized in 1925.

LIVE OAK COUNTY — Czechs move to George M. West ranch between George West and Three Rivers in early 1900s.

SAN PATRICIO COUNTY — By 1928 there are 16 Czech Catholic families in Taft.

JIM WELLS COUNTY — In 1913 J. C. Mrázek moves to Agua Dulce and is followed by the Zapalač, Žurovec, Procházka, Špičák, Šablatura, Ermis, Levek and Podest families. Very active Czech community in 1920s, includes own theatre group, "Rozkvět Agua Dulce." In 1913 Klement Petr and Jan Jurek move to Scott Ranch. Soon the Rohan, Šefčík, Janča, Hájek, Jareš, Kalinec, Olšovský, Ondrušek, Schodec and Kulčák families follow.

NUECES COUNTY — In 1904 Stanley L. Kostohryz buys 7,000 acres of land and begins Bohemia Colony Settlement. By 1900 over 100 foreign-born Czechs live there. In 1905 Josef Oujezdský and Jan Brandejský, from Bryan, buy land near Corpus Christi and settle Czechs there. In 1915 Leo Netek, Fabian Havelka, Vincenc Březina, and Frank Slezinger of Corn Hill follow Rudolf Polášek to Corpus Christi. In 1920 Lamar and Songin Folda buy Kostohryz settlement and renewed Czech settlement begins in the area. Robstown also attracts Czechs in early 1900s. By 1938, 35 Czech Catholic families are in Robstown. The Brethren establish a church in 1913. By 1920 over 360 Czechs are in county.

KLEBERG COUNTY — Kingsville attracts about 14 Czech Catholic families by 1938. By 1909 Matěj Novák owns 160 acres near Kingsville and his brother Jan owns a hotel in town. Rev. Joseph Barton establishes Brethren Church in 1920.

CAMERON COUNTY — In 1915 a few Czechs move to Rio Hondo. By 1938 some 16 Czech families are in Catholic parish there, including the Petrášek, Vick, Čálek, Hanušek, Bednář, and Kastík.

HIDALGO COUNTY — By 1938, 10 Czech families live in Edinburg. In Mercedes, the Jakub Jindra and Jan Pavlice families. A land company succeeds in settling several Czechs in McCook.

KARNES COUNTY — Bishop Forest opens up settlement around Hobson and Karnes City. Among the Czechs are Vilém Kutač, Josef Ondřej and Josef Honč. By 1938 about 200 Czech families live in the area. By 1938 about 27 Czech families live in Runge. Family names are Slavík, Smykal, Vyvlecký, Liška, Matula, Pivetz, Petrů.

WILSON COUNTY — By 1908 the Jan Raška, Jakub Zahn, Josef Jánský, Bohuslav Pavlíska, Tomáš and František Chupík, Lambert Chylek, Jan Marečka, and Lukáš Srala live in Floresville. By 1938, 50 Czech Catholic families are in the parish. The first Czechs in Poth are August, Jan and Pavel Hošek, C. Stavinoha, Štěpán Švertlich, and Vinc Košárek.

GONZALES COUNTY — By 1938 there are about 25 Czech families in Gonzales.

BEXAR COUNTY — The first Czech is Anthony Dignowity, followed by a family named Kříž, František Kahánek, Leopold Kliš, Lidvík Štefek and Ferdinand Malý. San Antonio is extremely important for Czechs because many Czech priests attend St. John's Seminary. Brethren establish preaching station in 1936.

COMAL & GUADALUPE COUNTIES — A few Czechs. Seven families in Seguin parish in 1938.

ATASCOSA COUNTY — In 1917 Cyril Netardus and his sons Josef and Tomáš along with Edmund Špaček, Jan Dorňák, František Malátek, Pavel Orsák, František Jalůfka, Antonín Krpec and Josef Tomáš settle in and near Jourdanton. Loire attracts the four Jakšik brothers, Vincenc, František, Michal and Josef, in 1900.

ZAVALA COUNTY — František Hanák, a land agent, persuades a group of Czechs to move to Crystal City. Among them are Josef Solanský, Václav Šramek, Josef Slavík, Eduard Marek and Josef Gold. Many are unhappy there and soon move.

FRIO COUNTY — In 1920s Jan Hruška, Jan Chupík, Valentin Sladeček, František Kuběna, Josef Valíček, Josef Urban, and Jan Merečka move to Dilley. Some become unhappy with the dry climate and leave.

VAL VERDE COUNTY — Del Rio founded by Anthony Dignowity's son, František. Very few Czechs live there, however.

APPENDIX C

CZECH FOLKLORE IN TEXAS COLLECTED BY OLGA PAZDRAL

Olga Pazdral's Masters Thesis *Czech Folklore in Texas* (The University of Texas at Austin, 1940) is one of the very few sources, and, by far, the most complete source for Czech folklore in Texas. As a high school teacher in West, Pazdral collected hundreds of songs, proverbs, rhymes, games, tales, customs, and beliefs familiar to her Texas Czech students, their families, and other residents in this predominantly Czech community. (See the discussion of West in Chapter 7.) As she notes, the majority of her informants were of Moravian descent (p. 6), and they were probably representative of Texas Czechs as a whole. The folklore items from Pazdral listed or summarized below seem especially representative and typical, based on the experience of the authors. Pazdral documents her informants for most items, and this information can be found on the pages cited in parentheses here. Additional material from Pazdral has been incorporated into Chapter 5 of this book.

SUPERSTITIONS AND CUSTOMS

A crowing hen means impending disaster. Chicken feathers should not be used in feather beds because anyone that dies on them has a much harder death than one who dies on goose feathers. If a person wants more roosters than hens, he should set the hen on the eggs in the evening; if he wants more hens than roosters, he should set the hen in the afternoon. If a person carries away and abandons cats that have been raised at home, his children will run away from home. If a rabbit runs across the road, a traveller had better return home in order to avoid misfortune. (Rabbits are generally considered unlucky.) Spiders should not be killed, as they bring money.

Many superstitions are associated with celestial bodies. Homemade soap cooked during the days of a full moon will be good. If a person clips his hair during a new moon, his hair will grow much faster. Looking at the moon through the branches of a tree brings blindness or some other bad luck. (To avoid this bad luck, a person can get the left foot of a hoot owl and bury it.) Looking at the moon from under a roof is the sign of a quarrel. A falling star signifies the death of someone. If a girl counts nine stars for six nights (or three stars for seven nights), she will dream of her future husband. Other astrological beliefs will be discussed in terms of "customs" below.

Probably the most common category of superstition is that dealing with "good luck" and "bad luck." The Czechs had a number of these that may or may not be familiar to other Americans. Friday is an unlucky day. No project should be begun on a Friday, and nothing should be chosen or bought on that day. One should not move into a house nor begin a long journey on Friday. Bad luck can result from sitting on a threshold, returning home for something forgotten, ringing bells inside the house, sweeping under people's feet, having more than one clock in the house, carrying a hoe through the house, and various other actions. If a person breaks a dish or anything made of glass, he will break three pieces of glassware within the next few days. A pin should never be given as a present, nor should it ever be pinned by one person on another, because pins "stab love to death." Anyone who looks into a mirror very much will become ugly. If a child points his finger at a rainbow, his finger may come off. One should remember to use the same door in leaving that he used in entering: otherwise bad luck will overtake him. A button that is found and put into one's shoe will bring good luck. The more a child cries, the prettier it will become. A wish will come true if the person making the wish will turn a ring on his finger. If a girl who puts on a dress wrong-side-out makes a wish before changing it, her wish will come true. Anyone born in March will live ten years longer than the other members of his family.

The following are a few of many superstitions concerning dreams: a dream about a wedding predicts a funeral, and vice versa; a dream about a dead person foretells rain the next day; a dream about a white cat or a black horse brings good luck for two years; a dream about a white horse or the loss of a tooth foretells death; a dream about drowning predicts illness. The first dream that a person has upon moving to a new home should come true within a year, but if a person looks out a window immediately upon awaking from a dream, his dream will not come true.

Various customs associated with superstitions could be listed. One that is probably peculiar to the Czech ethnic group in Texas is the writing of the letters K, M, and B, the initials of the three wise men of the Christmas story, above doors (with blessed chalk). Usually the letters were joined by crosses: "K + M + B." This symbol was supposed to bring good luck and happiness. Interestingly, Pazdral recorded some customs and superstitions that were remembered in Texas long after they could be practiced. For example, one could procure good luck by touching the button of a chimneysweep before he passed one on the street.

To remove warts for a friend, a person could tie as many knots in a string as the other had warts and then bury the string without telling the other what he had done. The warts would not disappear until the string had rotted; after that, they would not reappear even if the secret were revealed. When a child lost a tooth, it was customary for him to throw it behind the stove and ask a mouse to bring him a new one. (Pazdral, 143--66.)

SUPERNATURAL CREATURES

The *Vodník* or *Hastrman* is discussed in Chapter 5. Less common, but also present in Texas, were the *rusalka* (nymph), the *bludička* or *světlonoh* (will-o-the-wisp), and the *vodní víly* (water fairies). Among this group, the *bludička* was the best known, and anecdotes about mysterious, wandering lights, sometimes hovering around cemeteries, sometimes seeking to scare the traveller or lead him astray, are numerous.

Various other ghosts, witches, and supernatural characters well-known in traditional Czech folklore were known in fragmentary or distorted versions in Texas. The *rarášek* and *šotek* are both evil spirits, although the *rarášek* is more dangerous. In Texas, it was said that a man might produce a *rarášek* by keeping the egg of a black hen under his armpit for nine days, during which time he must not eat or drink. (In Europe this is the method for producing the *šotek*.) A man who is becoming wealthy is said to have a *rarášek*. Having a *rarášek* is similar to "selling one's soul to the devil," and the owner often pays the consequences. The *rarášek* is also the evil spirit inside the whirlwind. In Texas the *šotek* is generally considered to be a kind of mischievous imp who is always tricking someone, but the *šotek* is sometimes confused with the *rarášek*, with the *Vodník*, or with a *šašek* (clown). The *trpaslíci* (dwarfs) live in the forests and punish disobedient children. *Čarodějnice* (witches) can cast evil spells, especially on cows in Texas. The witch can appear not only as an old hag but as a beautiful young woman or some form of animal as well. A certain kind of witch called *Ježibab, Jedubaba*, or *Ježinka* was also known in Texas. She is less evil than the *čarodějnice*; sometimes she can give good advice or gifts, but she also eats human flesh and dead souls. Occasional references to the *Bílá Paní* or *Bílá Žena* (White Lady), the *Bezhlavý Kapucín* (Headless Capuchin [monk]), the *Ohnivý Muž* (Fiery Man), the *Divé Ženy* (Wild Women) *Polednice* (a Wild Woman who steals children), and Meluzína (Melusina) were heard in Texas, but in each case the traditional legend had been transformed or almost completely lost.

The vampire superstition was also well known among Texas Czechs. (It may have been reinforced by the Anglo fascination with the Dracula legend.) Some Czechs believed that if the friends of a person who has died do not sit up with the corpse during the night before its burial, his spirit will come out of the grave and suck their blood. Actually, two vampire figures appear in Texas Czech superstitions. The *upír* is the vampire known to most American readers: he comes out of the grave to suck people's blood. The *můra*, on the other hand, is a live man or woman whose soul comes out at night, leaving the body looking dead. The *můra* sometimes affects sleepers by sitting heavily on their chests, causing bad dreams and preventing them from waking up. He may also suck a person's blood. The *můra* was evidently much better known in Texas than was the *upír*. Cases were reported in which the *můra* was supposed to have caused aberrations of behavior or death. (Pazdral, 46-71.)

FOLK LITERATURE

Children's rhymes were often used in games with feet and hands. While tapping a child's heel lightly, one recites a poem which begins

Kovej, kovej, kovářičku,	Shoe, shoe, little blacksmith,
okovej my mou nožičku,	Shoe my little foot.
okovej my obě,	Shoe them both,
zaplatím já tobě.	And I'll pay you well.

Many counting-out rhymes makes use of nonsense words that are untranslatable:

Angle, pangle, verkum pek,
štaple, makle, šlaka, flek.

Others have the familiar opening *Jeden, dva, tři, my jsme bratři.* (One, two, three, we are brothers.) Jeering rhymes were also very popular, especially among boys. An example is

Adámku náš, co pak děláš	Our little Adam, what are you doing
že ty koně v zitě máš?	That you have the horses in the wheat?

Other taunts do not use popular names:

Hloupý, hloupý,	Silly one, silly one,
vezl kroupy	He hauled barley
od chalupy	From cottage
do chalupy	To cottage
jako osel hloupý.	Like a silly jackass.

Pazdral records dozens of other examples of children's rhymes. Many of them deal with animals or with details of a rural way of life. Some, like some of the English Mother Goose rhymes, are slightly sadistic. Some rhymes were associated with holidays, especially Christmas.

Tongue-twisters and riddles were both very popular, also. Perhaps the most famous tongue-twister, known to Texas Czechs and to Czech speakers throughout the world is

Tři sta třiatřicet stříbrných křepelek přeletelo přes tři sta třiatřicet stříbrných střech. (Three hundred thirty-three silver quails flew over three hundred thirty-three silver roofs.)

A typical riddle is

Čím vic ubereš,	The more you take away,
tím je to větši.	the bigger it becomes.
(Dira.)	(A hole.)

Linguistic play of these types were enjoyed by children and adults alike. A related form of play is the "silly answer" (to an ordinary question):

Kolik je hodin?	What time is it?
Jako včera této doby.	The same as yesterday at this time.

The Czech *pohadky* (fairy tales) include versions of many "international" tales, such as Cinderella, often with unique variations. In one version of Cinderella (called Popelka) recorded by Pazdral, Popelka has a dream in which her dead mother tells her to go to a certain place where she will find three nuts, each containing a beautiful evening dress. These she wears to the prince's ball (which was held on three successive nights). The story continues with the loss of one golden slipper on the third night and ends much as does the version better known to American readers. Another tale, concerning the experiences of three brothers, includes a linguistic misunderstanding in which a German word is misunderstood for Czech.

Pazdral records several fables, such as the story about Brains and Luck, that have morals ("Some people have more luck than brains, but you must have brains before you have luck") and a variety of beast fables. Some of the stories explain the origin of certain animals or natural phenomena. A turtle was once a woman who hid under a tub when a storm was approaching, for example, and a group of cruel, heartless people were turned into frogs. The change of seasons is explained in a story about a *kouzelník* (necromancer). The *kouzelník*, who lived in an ice castle, decided to go out and see the world, but the sun became cold before him and his breath froze the flowers. Disappointed and angry, he cut off his head. Then flowers sprang from his body and birds sang in the meadows.

Some of the characters in the Czech tales are culturally specific and some are the supernatural creatures discussed earlier in this chapter. Krakonoš, for example, is the ghost of the Krkonoše Mountains. In one of several tales associated with him, Krakonoš gives a whistle to a poor boy who is starting out in the world. When the boy plays it, every hearer begins to laugh and dance. After a series of misadventures, the boy is able to cheer up a princess who has been pining away and makes his fortune. In one of the most common stories involving the *Vodník*, a poor carpenter accidentally drops his ax into a river. A *Vodník* appears and promises to help. He first brings a silver, and then a gold, ax to the carpenter, but each time the man says it is not his. The third time, the carpenter receives his ax, thanks the *Vodník*, and goes home. A neighbor who hears the story drops his own ax into the water and subsequently claims the gold one which the *Vodník* offers him. Because of his greed, however, the man ultimately receives no ax at all.

Cycles of tales are associated with other figures as well. Paleček is a kind of "wise fool" figure, of "Tom Thumb" size. He is sometimes described as a little boy who was able to walk on the day of his birth. Kacafírek is also thought of as a man of very small stature although not so small as Paleček. Also like Paleček, he is able to outwit conceited and stupid rich men, but he is even more a prankster figure in his tales. Among the Czechs, a mischievous or jolly person is sometimes referred to as a "Kacafírek."

Some popular proverbs are listed below.

Bez práce nejsou koláče.
Without work there are no *koláče* (tarts).

Čiň čertu dobře, peklem se ti odslouží.
Treat the devil well, and he gives you hell.

Člověk míní a Panbůh mění.
Man proposes and God alters.

Co na srdci, to na jazyku.
What is on the heart is on the tongue.

Dej krávě do škopa, ona ti dá do kopka.
Give to the cow in a tub and she will give to you in a pail.

Dostaneš-li velikého věna, bude ti proručet žena.
If you get a big dower, you'll feel your wife's power.

Každý sobě štěstí kuje.
Everyone forges his own happiness.

Kde česká hospodyňka vaří, tam se dobře daří.
Where a Czech housekeeper cooks, everything fares well.

Kdo dbá, ten má.
He who cares, has.

Kdo dva zajíce honí, žádného nechytí.
He who chases two rabbits will catch neither one.

Kdyby nebylo oráče, nebylo by boháče.
If there were no plowman, there would be no rich man.

Kdo sám cti nemá, jinému jí nedá.
He who has no honor cannot give it to another.

Kdo se sám chválí, není chvály hoden.
He who praises himself is not worthy of praise.

Když jest nejmilejší hra, tehdy přestaň.
When the game is most enjoyable, stop.

Kolik hlav tolik smyslův.
There are as many opinions as there are heads.

Mladost, radost.
Youth, joy.

Mladý lhář — starý zloděj.
A young liar — an old thief.

Mráz kopřivu nespálí.
Frost will not burn up the nettle.

Nechval dne před večerem.
Do not praise the day before evening comes.

Ohlídej se na zadní kola.
Look back at the rear wheels.

Tichá voda břehy myje.
Still water undermines the banks.

V pátek, zlý začátek.
On Friday, a bad beginning.

Všecko má konec ale jitrnice má dva.
Everything has an end, but a sausage has two.

U sedláka černé ruce a chlebíček bílý.
At the farmer's are black hands and white bread.

(Pazdral, 88-106; 114-31; 73-83. A few apparent errors or inconsistencies in her text have been quietly edited.)

APPENDIX D

A LIST OF TEXAS CZECH PERIODICALS AND NEWSPAPERS

Americký Čech. Houston, Texas monthly. v. 1, no. 1-5; Oct. 1932-Feb. 1933.
Bratrské listy. Austin, Brenham, La Grange and Hallettsville, Texas (Evangelical Unity of Czech-Moravian Brethren in North America), monthly Jan. 1902- Also called *Brethren Journal.*
Buditel. Georgetown, Texas monthly Jan. 1908-1910?
Čechoslovák. Rosenberg, Texas weekly 1918-1920.
Čechoslovák a Westské noviny. West, Texas weekly Jan. 1, 1920-1961. Merged with *Westské noviny.*
Cesko-slovanský rolník v Texasu. Bryan, Texas weekly? (Farmers Alliance). Mar. 1885-Jan. 10, 1889.
Hospodář-Čechoslovák. West, Texas semi-monthly v. 71, no. 15, Aug. 1, 1961- Continued numbering of *Hospodář* (Omaha, Nebraska).
Husita. Rosenberg, Texas semi-monthly 1918?-1952?
Kalendář Slovan. La Grange, Texas v. 1, 1894. No more pub.
Kalendář Svoboda. La Grange, Texas annual 1908-1910?
Katolický Sokol. St. Louis and Halletsville, Texas monthly and bimonthly (Katolická jednota Sokol). 1912-1940?
Listy poučné a vzdělávajíci. Nelsonville, Texas 1897.
Náš cíl. West, Texas weekly (National Non-Partisan League). 1920?-1924.
Našinec. Taylor, Houston and Granger, Texas weekly (Římsko-katolická jednota texaská). 1914-
Nový domov. Hallettsville, Texas weekly and semi-weekly. (Czech Catholic Women's Union of Texas). Mar. 7, 1895-196-?
Obzor; týdenník politický, hospodářský a zábavný. Hallettsville and La Grange, Texas weekly and biweekly (Slovanská podpůrna jednota). July 16, 1891-Aug. 1912. Suspended Feb. 14, 1895-Nov. 1897. Dec. 15, 1897-Sept. 1899 called *Obzor hospodářský.*
Ohlas. Dallas, Texas (Jižní župa, Am. Sokol Organization). 1968?
Pokrok jihu. Fayetteville, Texas weekly 1932.

Posel světla. Rosenberg, Texas monthly 1925. Absorbed by *Zenské listy* (Chicago).

Rolník Texaský. Bryan and La Grange, Texas weekly (Státní farmerská jednota v Texas). Mar. 26, 1887-Mar. 7? 1888. Called *Rolník* from v. 2, no. 32, 1888.

Sealské Noviny. Sealy, Texas 19--?

Slovan. La Grange and Bryan, Texas weekly Sept. 7, 1879-May 1890. Succeeded *Texan.*

Slovanská jednota. La Grange, Texas semi-monthly (Slavonic Benevolent Order of the State of Texas). Sept. 1897-1898?

Svoboda. La Grange and El Campo, Texas weekly and semi-weekly Dec. 1885-1966.

Taylor journal. Taylor, Texas weekly Czech section. Feb. 1906-1909.

Texan. La Grange, Texas weekly Feb. 6-July 1879.

Texan (2). Galveston, Granger and Houston, Texas weekly and semi-weekly Dec. 1908-1943?

Texaský rolník (Texas farmer) Taylor and Temple, Texas monthly (Farmers Mutual Protective Association of Texas). 1914?-

Věstník. Fayetteville, Temple and West, Texas weekly (Slavonic Benevolent Order of Texas). Sept. 1, 1912-

Volná myšlenka. Houston, Texas monthly and weekly. (Svaz svobodomyslných v státu Texas). June 1919-1932?

Vůdce osadní. Rosenberg, Texas monthly (Church of Mary of the Rosary). 1931-?

Westské noviny. West, Texas weekly 1909-1911.

Sokol Žižka notes. Dallas, Texas bi-monthly 1968.

APPENDIX E

A LIST OF TEXAS SLOVAK PERIODICALS AND NEWSPAPERS

Kazateľna. Rosenberg, Texas 1891?-1897?

Literárne listy. Rosenberg, Texas v. 1-7, no. 3; 1891-1897. Suppl. to *Kazateľna.*

Svet; časopis pre poučenie a zábavu. Rosenberg, Texas bi-weekly v. 1, no. 1-3; July 15-Aug. 15, 1890.

Index